THE HERMITAGE JOURNALS

John Howard Griffin

A Diary Kept While Working on
the Biography of Thomas Merton

Edited by Conger Beasley, Jr.

IMAGE BOOKS

A Division of Doubleday & Company, Inc.
Garden City, New York
1983

Image Book edition published March 1983 by special arrangement with Andrews and McMeel, Inc.

Library of Congress Cataloging in Publication Data

Griffin, John Howard, 1920-80
The hermitage journals.

1. Griffin, John Howard, 1920-80 . 2. Merton, Thomas, 1915-1968. 3. Abbey of Our Lady of Gethsemani (Trappist, Ky.) 4. Catholics — United States — Biography. I. Beasley, Conger. II. Title.
BX4705.G62244A33 1983   282'.092'4 [B]   82-45833
ISBN 0-385-18470-0 (pbk.)

Introduction

John Howard Griffin was that rare combination—a remarkable writer and an appealing man. He wrote with a fluency and ease that seemed a natural outpouring from the vast reservoirs of love and faith that buoyed and sustained him during his life. His sense of moral fitness—how people should behave in order to make the world a better place—was acute, honed to an edge that he himself, by his own actions, continually sharpened and refined. In his writing, he sought to discover and reveal as much of himself as he could translate into words. In his novels, his journals, his essays and first-person accounts, he defined and articulated the important experiences of his life—family, friends, his faith, his hopes for a better world. It was out of these experiences that he attempted to arrive at an understanding of both himself and the world he inhabited.

For Griffin, experience was not something to be observed at a distance or treated intellectually, a construct attracting the powers of his mind, to be chewed and shredded by the teeth of rational analysis. Experience was to be lived, physically and emotionally; it was a phenomenon into which the writer plunged body and soul, in a conscientious effort to define the meaning of other selves and other realities.

Such immersion is not practiced solely by candidates for sainthood; immolation is not the desideratum here, but rather clarity—fidelity to specific events and emotions. Such immersion has a specific objective: truth; the truth of a particular experience, compassionately described and precisely rendered; a truth uncluttered as much as humanly possible by the sensibility of the participant. Such immersion, then, provides the means by which an honest writer can recast himself in the focus of an alien perspective, and emerge with a faithful account of that perspective, as well as information regarding the limitations of his own point of view.

In *Black Like Me*, his best-selling book of the 1960s, Griffin entered literally into the milieu of a people scorned and despised by white America. The story is well known. After a series of treatments in New Orleans which resulted in the darkening of his skin, Griffin, in the fall of 1959, took a journey through the Deep South, experiencing firsthand the prejudice and oppression which millions of black people experienced every day. The book was a masterpiece of empathetic revelation. To get into someone else's skin is, of course, one of the aims of the narrative artist — to bring that person to life through incident and detail so the reader can see and feel the reality of that person; to act as a lens, focusing intently on the object, till the object becomes paramount and the lens is forgotten.

These skills Griffin had developed long before the publication of *Black Like Me*. In two early novels, *The Devil Rides Outside* and *Nuni*, Griffin evoked two disparate realities — life in a French Benedictine monastery, and tribal life among a group of South Pacific aborigines. These experiences, though occurring at antipodal poles of the globe, share a common denominator: the effort of the narrator to discover his true humanity in the face of corrosive pressures that seek to deny him that discovery; the effort to integrate the objective values of honesty and compassion into the fabric of his personality so that living by their promptings becomes reflexive and forthright.

In 1969, Griffin was appointed by the Merton Legacy Trust to be the official biographer of Thomas Merton. The choice was a good one. Griffin, a Catholic convert, was a great admirer of Merton and a close personal friend. At first, Griffin did not want the job; he would be required to read Merton's voluminous personal journals, which he was reluctant to do out of respect for such an intensely private man. Finally he accepted, and in August 1969 began a series of visits to Gethsemani Abbey, where Merton lived from 1941 till his death in 1968.

Periodically during the next three years, Griffin traveled from his home in Fort Worth, Texas, to the monastery, where he remained for a week or ten days at a stretch. The purpose of the visits was twofold: first, to avail himself of the mass of unprinted material left by Merton, including the extraordinary diaries; and second, to live and work in Merton's hermitage — the modest cinderblock dwelling located deep inside the monastery grounds where Merton, by his own admission, spent his happiest and most productive years. By following Merton's routine—up at 3:00 a.m., observance of the morning offices, work, lunch, more work, celebration of the evening offices, then to bed by 8:00 or 9:00 p.m.—Griffin hoped to enrich his understanding of not only Merton the author, but Merton the Trappist monk.

Only by such immersion could the subject of Griffin's endeavors be reproduced with any degree of authenticity. As Merton's biographer, Griffin aimed not to interpret, but as much as possible to remove himself from the process; to function rather as a conduit through which the character of the man he so much admired could emerge. "I pray to the Holy Spirit to direct me in making it purely the life of Tom and not the life of Tom *as seen by* anyone, or as analyzed by anyone," he says at one point. " ... It means that I give up what I am ... in order to feed into myself, into my actions and reactions, so much of what he was that for the time I am writing this biography, I will in effect be writing a kind of autobiography of him, hoping to select those highlights that he might very well have selected, to see as important what he saw as important."

Griffin was an inveterate journal-keeper, and so it was natural while at the hermitage that he keep one there. Almost every day he made entries — typed, single-spaced, on plain sheets of paper. He was very good about this, and would scold himself when he missed a day. The purpose of the journal was to maintain a record of the mechanics of the undertaking (the books to read, the people to interview, the research materials to consult) as well as to maintain a kind of interior ledger regarding the development of his own awareness of the hardships and consolations of the solitary experience.

It is on this level that *The Hermitage Journals* proves most noteworthy. Adjusting to the isolation proved easier than Griffin expected. His first day back after a spell in Fort Worth or traveling around the country was usually a lost day, a period of transition during which his mind and body settled into a state of repose. Once the normal energy on which he operated had been replaced by a natural energy fostered by the stillness of his surroundings, Griffin experienced a kind of illumination. It was at these moments that he recorded his profoundest observations, passages of ravishing beauty and elation that fed back into his ongoing exploration of the life of Thomas Merton.

As the visits progressed, Griffin's eye sharpened; details of everyday life inside and outside the hermitage appear in the pages. The antics of birds and squirrels, the color and texture of the countryside, the subtle alterations in the weather preoccupied his attention. Domestic activities—elevated to the status of "rituals" by the absence of a conventional time-frame — became more important: the morning ablutions, sweeping and dusting, building a fire, washing clothes, preparing food. Griffin's years in France before World War II had given him a taste for *haute cuisine*, and with only a two-burner hot plate he managed to concoct a variety of delights.

This attention to detail strikes a familiar chord. Facts — natural and domestic—offer a way for the writer, the American writer especially, to subsume the cravings and yearnings of the self into a more meaningful pattern. Posited on empirical evidence, facts provide a means by which the self can escape the limitations of its own urges. Recognition of other realities (the search of birds for food, for example) is the first step in an expanding awareness of the multiple significance of all living things. The endeavors of a single (albeit gifted) man in a cinderblock retreat in the heart of the Kentucky landscape become but one of many manifestations of creativity in the world.

These pages resonate with what readers familiar with American literature have heard before. The journals of Emerson and Thoreau, the cetology of the white whale, the incantations of *Leaves of Grass*, Hemingway's meticulous recording of sights and tastes, the attempt by James Agee in *Let Us Now Praise Famous Men* to elevate ordinary objects into lexical rapture. They are part of our heritage, a fundamental urge to discover mystery and meaning in the thing observed ... an impulse first instilled in our literature by early Puritans like Edward Taylor and Jonathan Edwards, who sought to wrest from the forbidding landscape of the New World paradigmatic evidence of the presence of God. *The Hermitage Journals* reflects this passion; with a keen, selective eye, Griffin observes the life around him, and reports those observations in a supple, luminous prose that paradoxically exalts at the same time that it remains faithful to what it sees.

Both the entries in this journal and the more demanding efforts on behalf of the Merton biography were accomplished in spite of a variety of physical problems that plagued Griffin all his life. He was diabetic; he suffered kidney trouble, lung congestion, and a weak heart. When he died in September 1980, he died, as his wife said, of "everything." Several of these ailments are alluded to, but never explicitly, and never in sorrow or anger. Caring for them—like the other activities that made up life in the hermitage—was integrated into the overall process of edifying ritual that made his visits to the place so rewarding.

The housekeeping chores that Griffin was unable to perform were done by a trio of monks whose names appear frequently in these pages. Brother Patrick Hart was Thomas Merton's secretary, and he supplied Griffin with the bulk of the resource materials; he also contributed many personal anecdotes about Merton. Brother Maurice Flood looked after the hermitage and grounds; he was responsible for the clean interior and well-stocked larder which Griffin always found upon returning. Because of his work schedule and physical condition, Griffin was unable to go down to the monastery to celebrate the offices. Instead, Father Tarcisius Conner came frequently in the evening to offer Mass in the little hermitage chapel.

In the spring of 1980, Griffin sent the manuscript of *The Hermitage Journals* to Jim Andrews, editor-in-chief of Andrews and McMeel. Jim had known Griffin for many years, and once when Griffin was staying at the hermitage, Jim had interviewed him for the *National Catholic Reporter*. About the manuscript Jim was tremendously enthusiastic, and he was looking forward to editing it himself; his unfortunate death in October 1980 prevented him from doing so. It is to him that the foresight for publishing this remarkable document must be credited.

When necessary, I have inserted within brackets the identities of individuals mentioned in the text. John Howard Griffin was a famous man who attracted his share of well-wishers and curiosity-seekers; he also enjoyed numerous personal friendships. Despite the isolation he cherished, many people found their way to the hermitage to celebrate with him the spirit of the amazing man who almost singlehandedly revived interest among Western thinkers in the eremitical life.

For if there is one thing this book makes clear — one message that rings loud — it is that the solitary life cannot be equated with escapism, that there is nothing remotely analogous between the two. The violence of the external world intrudes frequently into the sanctity of Griffin's sojourns at the hermitage. Friends and relatives die, and Griffin reacts with acute anguish. The late 1960s and early 1970s form the backdrop to these pages, and there are innumerable references to Vietnam, the civil rights movement, and activists like the Berrigan brothers and Clyde Kennard. The intrusion of these events provides a dramatic and at times wrenching counterpoint to the profound repose of Griffin's life there.

The experience of solitude is unlike any other. There are depths to plumb and truths to perceive from a steadfast contemplation of the creative wellsprings of the universe. Griffin's own experience at the hermitage vividly documents this fact. It enabled him to continue his exploration into his own spirit; it provided the context in which he could probe deeper into the mysteries of the solitary life ... a different life, to be sure, rigorous and unconventional, questing and energetic, resistant to petty gratifications, acutely perceptive to the interrelationship of all creatures in the great chain of being. Unlike other experiences he had known, including activism, Griffin finds this one the most nourishing; upon it he feeds with the hunger of his total self. Within it, contradictions are resolved, and a true and lasting and meaningful sense of self emerges. Inherent to the experience is an unmistakable feeling of solidity, of reality. "There is no hint of any escape from reality," Griffin concludes, "no need even for such a hint. The dissonances between reality of the things of the earth and the body, and those of the spirit and nerves, simply are resolved and cease to exist."

Conger Beasley, Jr.
Kansas City, Missouri
May 1981

Preface

In 1969 I was asked by the Merton Legacy Trust to write the biography of Thomas Merton, the famed Trappist monk and writer. Father Louis, as he was known in religion, had lived twenty-seven years at the Monastery in Gethsemani, Kentucky. While attending a meeting of Asian and European religious leaders near Bangkok, Thailand, he was accidentally electrocuted on December 10, 1968.

Since we had long worked together in the area of social justice and had become close friends, I accepted the invitation to prepare his biography. This meant spending a great deal of time at the monastery studying his journals, notebooks, and correspondence. At first the monks gave me work space in the guest house, but I quickly got permission to spend the night in the pine forest in the hermitage where Father Merton had lived his last years in relative solitude.

After spending one night there in that profound isolation, I sought and got permission from Abbot Flavian Burns to live in the hermitage during my work sessions at Gethsemani.

Brothers Patrick Hart and Maurice Flood and Father Tarcisius Conner came each day to bring supplies and say Mass in the small hermitage chapel. Otherwise I led a solitary life, following Father Merton's own routine as much as possible. I was there usually two weeks each month for the next several years, and kept these journals.

Father Merton was probably the first modern Trappist to follow a hermit vocation. When he went to live in the cabin in the forest, he explained that he went there not to find Christ but because he believed that was where Christ wanted to find him. He also believed that no one can live fully without the experience of solitude. I had known certain types of solitude, having been blind for a prolonged period, having lived on islands in the South Pacific, having studied with the Dominicans and Benedictines in France, but this was something entirely different. Here one was alone without the slightest sense of loneliness, and the longer it lasted the more profound grew the felicity, the sense of freedom, the faith, the loving.

Father Merton was, of course, a priest. I was a married man with a wife and four children. When he spoke of what solitude teaches, he was not referring specifically to priests or other professed religious, but to all of us.

And yet I wondered how could one find such solitude in the world for a sufficiently long period to learn what it had to teach, and how many of us spend our entire lives without ever experiencing it, or even a hint of it. Solitude in this sense differs vastly from merely being alone or simply passing the hours. The creator and all of creation are one's constant companions, day and night, in all one's occupations. Living in that solitude, I often thought of Cassian's "We pray best when we are no longer aware we are praying."

John Howard Griffin
January 3, 1980
Fort Worth, Texas

First Visit

AUGUST 5, 1969 . . .

AUGUST 5, 1969

Gethsemani. Two long and uneventful days of driving brought me here. Arrived this evening around 7:00 p.m. Brother Patrick brought me up to the hermitage where Brother Maurice fixed some supper of rye bread, pineapple, and cheese. We visited briefly before they left to return to the Abbey.

Now, for a couple of hours, I have been alone. I fight away the fatigue and sleepiness only long enough to make these notes before going to bed. It is surprisingly cool here tonight. I have bathed, taken my medication, listened to the night sounds, and am now ready for sleep.

AUGUST 6, 1969

5:45 a.m. Before dawn. Even this quiet typewriter motor sounds an ungodly racket in the silence that possesses the countryside. I have coffee heating on the hot plate. Slept well and profoundly.

Bells from the monastery drift up through the trees. With the beginnings of predawn light, some of the birds come to life—not with singing yet, but with a kind of murmuring. I carried my coffee out on the concrete porch and drank it walking back and forth. The air is cool, almost cold, and fresh. Light came slowly. I watched the trees assume black shapes through the fog. I thought of Tom who saw the sounds, smelled the same predawn freshness, allowed the same silences to do their work in him.

8:30 a.m. Father Tarcisius came at 7:00 to celebrate Mass in the little chapel. Brother Maurice arrived moments later.

Today is the Feast of the Transfiguration, the liturgy especially appropriate to Gregory's [Griffin's youngest son] twelfth birthday. We made his birthday the intention of the Mass.

Afterward, Father Tarcisius and Brother Maurice cooked breakfast: eggs (scrambled), buttered toast, honey, milk. Brother Pat joined us in time to share the breakfast. He puffed up the hill, loaded with materials for my work—Tom's correspondence, the Asian journal [later to be published as *The Asian Journal of Thomas Merton* by New Directions], and the manuscript "The Inner Experience."

Now they have gone. The sun is full up and the hills take form through the mists. The hermitage continues to smell strong of the fragrance of beeswax candles snuffed after Mass— that peculiar ageless odor has already permeated the walls of that tiny chapel.

Begin to read the Asian journal, sitting out on the porch. Fascinating. It warms up quickly. Sense of the hermitage, of the isolation. But part of that sense is destroyed by the sight of the car parked at the side—a way of leaving, of making quick contact with the world. It is a line that keeps things open and isolation less perfect to the senses. I cannot walk—so on foot, if I depended on that, I could not go anywhere—thus the isolation is total. So, finally, irritated at myself for being so irritated by the sight of a car here at the hermitage, I drove it around the back, out of sight. And now the illusion of being alone, of being *cut off* from contact, is restored and the irritation gone. A great need to sense the isolation to the fullest.

Nearly noon—Getting hot outside. I sit on the porch in the rocking chair, in pajama pants and tee shirt, sweating as I read Tom's descriptions of the heats and stenches of India and his own comments about "sweating and eating curry." The heat, the lazy rasping of locusts, the absolute stillness (not the slightest breeze) overwhelm me with drowsiness. I come in, drink a glass of cold water. I don't want to nap before Brother Pat comes. He will bring me some meat patty for lunch ("I want you to have meat at least once a day," he insisted). After that I will nap. Then take a cold shower. (The tiny bathroom and chapel were added shortly before Tom left for India. The shower is one of those cheap metal kinds that reverberates like a great gong every time you strike the sides with your elbows or drop a bar of soap on the floor.)

Tom's notes from the Asian journal are vivid and strong, full of freshness, full of a vitality that seems all the more extraordinary in that he was constantly on the move, constantly looking for quiet in the midst of great (and undoubtedly tiring) activity, physically harassed by the heat and the bouts of diarrhea.

Bees appear on the porch, loud, exploring, around my foot, up my leg, landing on my pajama fly. Breathless moment. I dare not move. One black bee went inside, disappearing behind the blue cloth, turned and reappeared, flew off.

3:45 p.m. Slept deeply for thirty minutes and rested thirty more—after a good and heavy lunch with Brother Pat. He brought up two plates for us—two large meat patties with onions and a huge serving of macaroni and red beans; we had rye bread and butter and milk with this. He also brought up some marvelous pictures of Tom as a youngster, recently sent here by Tom's elderly aunt in New Zealand. I will make copies of them this afternoon. Some wonderful things, including the menu (designed by Tom's artist parents) for Tom's first birthday dinner, featuring "Rooster *Rôti*." What a marvelous-looking youngster he was—quite recognizable, too. He did not change all that much.

Then I read the excellent account in French by Dom Jean Leclercq. In describing Tom's last days there, he mentions that after his death, Tom was returned to the U.S. in a jet carrying the bodies of dead soldiers from Vietnam. ". . . le paradoxe de son retour à son pays dans un 'jet' qui ramenait les corps de jeunes soldats tues en cette guerre du Vietnam dont il avait lui-même tant souffert." [". . . the paradox of his return to his country in a jet which was bringing back the bodies of young soldiers killed in this Vietnamese war from which he himself had suffered so much."]

From the same article, entitled "Derniers Souvenirs":

"Le 12 décembre 1968, un quotidien de Thaïlande, *The Bangkok Post*, donnait un entrefilet sous ce titre, écrit lui-même en abrégé: 'Un moine catholique meurt, *R. C. Monk Dies*,' annonçant que le Père Thomas Merton avait été victime d'une crise cardiaque. Ce fait divers occupait quelques lignes en cinquième page . . . .

"Les derniers mots de sa causerie devait avoir une résonance qu'il ne soupçonnait pas: 'Et maintenant, puisque les conférences de ce matin feront l'objet de la discussion de ce soir, je vais disparaître, *I will disappear*.'

"Le moment venu, selon son dernier mot, il 'disparaît.' Mais en même temps, et pour toujours, il *reste*."

["On December 12, 1968, a daily newspaper of Thailand, *The Bangkok Post*, gave a brief item under this title, itself written in summary: 'A Catholic Monk Dies,' announcing that Father Thomas Merton had been the victim of a heart attack. This news item took up a few lines on the fifth page. . . .

"The last words of his talk had to have a resonance that he didn't suspect: 'And now, since the conferences of this morning will be the object of this evening's discussion, I am going to disappear, *I will disappear*.'

"The moment having come, according to his last word, he disappeared. But at the same time, and forever, he remains."]

8:00 p.m. Brother Pat brought supper—some potato salad and lunch meat. We ate together here and talked about the Merton material. I had a lot of questions that I had simply recorded on tape today as I read; and of course Brother Pat either knew the answers right away or knew where he could find them. He left early, after helping me clean up the dishes. Now it is still dusk-light outside.

I go frequently into the chapel where the fragrance lingers. Some of it, I believe, comes from the altar which appears to be made from some fragrant wood—probably cedar of a particularly sweet scent.

What a glorious illusion of time in which to get things done, of calm and peace in this solitude, so that with a great deal of work to get done, there is no sense of rush. I take the time to keep things in order—the papers, the studies. I have the luxury of that extra time in which to do things right and thoroughly. This was one of the things Tom apparently cherished about the hermit life.

"Actually I find the solitary life very happy because it seems to be that for which I was intended. Not that I am a rigorous hermit type: or that I fly from the face of human beings. But it just seems that even when I am alone I cannot find time to fit in all that I want to get done in a day. Twenty-four hours are not enough. I do know that the best way to really waste time is to get with a lot of other people: then it will be killed for certain." (Letter to Sister Anne Saword, OCSO— *Cistercian Studies*, Vol. III, 1968, 4, p. 271.)

A fly irritates the air around my head. I spray with *Slug a Bug* and stay out of the room a moment. As soon as I sit back down, the beast rises laboriously up across my chest and then disappears into the curtains.

Am tired now at the end of a long day. I should write a couple of letters but I put them off until morning, early morning, mainly because I want to use my remaining forces tonight to continue reading in the Asian journal. I wonder how Tom arranged his workday. I know correspondence was a chore, but he got it done. Probably living this way, he did the same thing— did the fascinating things (reading, studying) at night when he was tired, did the "chores" quickly in the morning (the letter writing, etc.). I doubt if that is a good system, since one should do the creative work while fresh. I expect he did that and answered the mail during the afternoon whenever he could.

Things that happen here are too precious to spill out in letters—or at least there is not the strength to do that and keep this journal, too. I decide to write everything in the journals and scant the correspondence.

All day, in the midst of all this work, I have thought about Greg's birthday. I must write him at least a note before I go to sleep.

AUGUST 7, 1969

Finally I worked until 1:30 a.m., finishing up the Asian journal. Slept until 6:00, got up and shaved, cleaned the hermitage, and was ready for Mass at 7:00. Father Tarcisius and Brother Maurice celebrated a beautiful Mass of the Holy Spirit for the intention of this book, that I may be guided (and all artists, as Brother Maurice prayed) by the Holy Spirit in my work, particularly in this biography. Beautiful, simple, and strong Mass. Then Father Tarcisius made French toast for us. He brought some dietetic syrup for me. It was a good solid breakfast. Brother Maurice thinks of everything and does everything to fulfill my needs even before I have them. They washed dishes while I arranged the table here to resume work, and then quickly left so I could return to the work without any further intrusion.

The Asian journal fascinated me, though Tom only jotted down notes and reactions in the hastiest form, and therefore much of it, particularly the Asian terms, escaped me. But I was nevertheless deeply interested and could not stop reading. I want to make extensive notes from the unedited version, particularly his remarks about his photography and his references to things he photographed.

9:30 a.m. I have taken care of the wash; it hangs in the sun to dry. The sun is pale, there is a haze over the mountains, but the heat begins to penetrate the stones of this house. The sounds of heat in the rasping of locusts and droning of insects, with one sweet bird call above, drift from the trees and fields. The idea of napping in midmorning is suddenly appealing.

11:45. What insanity to have stayed up so late last night! It has shot this morning, for I have felt half-sick trying to stay awake, and finally slept deeply until just this moment—and still feel dragged out and worthless. Father Eudes [Father John Eudes Bamberger, now Abbot of the Genesee Monastery, Piffard, New York] told me Tom was a man of iron discipline (what a strange-sounding term in connection with Tom), insofar as his organization of work and life. I think he went to bed when he was supposed to and got up when he was supposed to and prayed when he was supposed to, and meditated when he planned to—in general, at least. I know that in the Asian journal he speaks with high irritation about being tired of the invitations, the activities, and expresses his determination to get to bed that night at 8:00 p.m. . . . the hour the day ends here with the Trappists. Even on special occasions here, as when we came with Jacques [Maritain], he stayed up and talked but still left us by 9:30 p.m. I must, in order to know something of his life, attempt at least to do this, though I will make my schedule a 10:00 p.m. retirement and a 5:00 a.m. arising, with a short siesta in early afternoon.

I have hot coffee and am dressed now, slacks and tee shirt, waiting for Brother Patrick to come and bring some lunch and some more work materials.

I have put off reading the correspondence, preferring to do the other things first—but really because I have not yet adjusted myself to reading anyone else's mail. Even though he saved these things, intending them for the biographer and others, it is still difficult to break my habit of never sticking my nose into anyone else's private affairs. I did read last night the correspondence between Tom and Jacques. It is easy to give myself over to his life, but not easy to intrude myself into his life.

2:30 p.m. Brother Patrick brought me some lunch—two large pieces of very delicious beefsteak (I could eat only one and we put back the other one for supper) with white beans, a green salad. We ate together and then talked at great length about some of the mail that came in from various people who were with Tom at the end—including a splendid letter from Father Francois de Grunne, OSB. I am going to go through these this afternoon.

The transcript of the police investigation came also this morning. How strange to read the reports . . . cold, methodical (mercifully so, really), and detailed, made by men who knew nothing of the victim, who were dealing with a corpse and a cause of death. For us who knew him in all his liveliness, we are reading about him as though he were a piece of cardboard, a debris that had to be processed by men who had no idea who he was, what he was a few hours before they took over. The report, for example, says cold that the body lay in a "pool of urine" (whereas the Sister M.D. said the liquid was uric acid that had sweated out from the dead body).

Very hot now. I went out, after Brother Pat's departure, to walk a bit around the hermitage and to make some color photographs of the exterior. After awhile I couldn't see the viewfinder, my glasses were so streaked with sweat.

Now I must get into the materials Patrick brought up—the letters to the Abbot.

Letters from Dom Jean Leclercq, written from Bangkok, December 11, 1969, to Father Flavian about Tom's death. He had been away during the afternoon of the tenth "visiting pagodas and monasteries in the city. When I came back at 6:00 p.m., Fr. de Floris was expecting me, to tell me with caution, knowing my friendship with him, the 'sad news.' I immediately said: 'C'est magnifique!' Such a great man did not deserve a usual, ordinary death. He fell in full work, after delivering his last message, his *ultima verba*."

10:30 p.m. I have not exactly kept my resolve to retire at 10:00. I could not tonight. I have been going through, as in a trance of fascination, the "official reports": inventory of Tom's effects, medical report, death report, reports made by the witnesses. This makes for a kind of "found poetry" in Tom's sense of the term. Only here it is "found narrative" that chills all the more because most of it tells the story, even down to minute details, in forms, printed forms. I must say that the officials at the American Embassy were extraordinary in their completeness, and also thoughtful. They even wrote personally to express their regrets to the Father Abbot. Katherine Berry had charge (she is Vice Consul), and although everything is meticulous and businesslike (it is that, really, that gives these things the quality of extraordinary narrative), they are totally unfurbished. The whole thing ends up being tremendously moving precisely because it is handled in this way.

The ironies come in: at the end Tom was subjected to all the things he loathed (and this fact probably would have amused him). He who so loathed things like the body count . . . death officially recorded (No. 388/2511) December 11, 1968, at Office of Civil Registrar (Nel Amphur) Muang District, Samuprakarn Province, Thailand . . . became a body count number; and he who so loathed the cataloguing of men (the machine destroying the individual) has had all his official death information, effects, etc., filed under PS-9 "in the correspondence of this office."

The language of the reports would have won his admiration, I think. "The toes of both feet seemed to be cramped.

"At the point where the switch touched the shorts and the body a wound, a hand-breadth in width, gaped open. The raw flesh was visible and the base of the wound was blood-shot.

"The face was deep blue. The eyes were half open. So was the mouth." (Consecutive excerpts from the immediate report made for the police by "Odo Haas, OSB, Abbot of Waegevan.")

Must mention, too, the list of effects from the embassy with a value in dollars for each effect. At the very end, signed by three embassy officials, is this statement: "The above-mentioned articles have been examined by us, and we hereby certify that the value placed after each article listed is a fair and just appraisal."

But they list under "Miscellaneous Effects" the Canon FX 1.8 lens at $40; and the accompanying 100 mm lens at $5; but turn around and list his Timex watch at $10. That lens is certainly valued at a dozen times what the Timex should be, but they did not think so.

Strange items, eloquent in this inventory:

1 pair dark glasses in tortoise frames . . . . nil
2 pairs bifocal eyeglasses in plastic frames . . . . nil
2 Cistercian leather-bound breviaries . . . . nil
1 Rosary (broken) . . . . nil
1 small icon on wood of Virgin and Child . . . . nil

AUGUST 8, 1969

9:00 a.m. Up at 5:30 after retiring finally last night at 11:00 p.m. Father Tarcisius and Brother Maurice came at 7:00 and we celebrated the Mass for the Feast of St. John Vianney. A beautiful Mass—*Justus ut palma*. . . . Then breakfast prepared by Father Tarcisius: fried eggs, sweet bread, milk, and coffee. We washed the dishes and they were gone by 8:00. Since the morning is overcast, they drove the car on down. The road is impassable to an automobile if it rains—and I am pleased to have it gone. I needed really only to go out for one thing—to get a haircut; and the moment I mentioned it, they said the barber here would be glad to do the job. So he will come up here and cut my hair tomorrow.

Dunstan Coleman, Jacques Maritain's godson, a novice here, will come and bring lunch today. I look forward to seeing him again. We met only briefly the day following Tom's funeral here.

A great emptiness and weakness this morning, coupled with peace and profound contentment . . . and also growing fascination. I asked yesterday about Tom's schedule, work habits, etc. This morning at dawn I went out on the porch to read the Psalms by the first light. As I sat there, paging through, a small slip of paper fell out of the pages; on it in the dimmest pencil and in Tom's hand, this:

> Schedule
> 3:15 Rise
>   Vigils
>   —eat
> 5:15 Lauds
>   go to Mass or wait for priest
>   Thanksgiving
> 8:00 *Climate of Monastic Prayer*
> 9:00 Short walk or work
> 10:30 *Wisdom*—Baker
> 3:30 Work
> 5:00 Private prayer
> 5:30–6—Vespers
>   Eat
> Compline 7:30 Prayer
>   Sleep
>   Amen

Here begins the exact copy of Sister Edeltrud Weist's statement. (Made in English and in her handwriting.)

Report on the first impressions after Rev. F. Thomas Merton's tragic death given by an eyewitness, Sr. M. Edeltrud Weist, OSB, Dr. Med., Specialist of Internal Medicine, Prioress of the Missionary Benedictine Sisters in Tacgu, South Korea.

December 10, 1968, just after 4:00 p.m., I suddenly heard someone saying: "Father Thomas Merton is lying dead in his room." Hoping that there was still something to be done, I hurried immediately to his room.

Father Merton was lying on the terrazzo floor, his eyes half-open, no breathing, no pulse, no heartsounds, no light reactions of the pupils. The face was deep bluish-red, and the lower arms and hands showed spots of the same colour. The arms were lying stretched beside the body. The feet were somewhat turned inside like in convulsion. F. Merton was only in shorts. An electric fan of about 150 cm height was lying across his body. The electric cord was pulled out of the plug lying on the floor. A smell of burned flesh was in the air.

As I turned the fan somewhat aside, I realized that there was a third degree burn, just in the right upper abdominal region, the place where the middle part of the fan with the switchboard had touched the skin. The burnt area of about one hand's breadth was extended to the whole right lower abdomen, including the right genital region. The cloth of the shorts covering the burnt area showed no sign of burning itself. The fan itself had lain direct on the skin above the upper part of the shorts. On the lower region of the right upper arm (or on the upper part of the lower arm) were also signs of stripe-like burns.

I only could give the declaration of death. I was convinced it was due to an electric shock by the fan.

However, I could not decide if this was the first reason, or if F. Merton first fell down (by fainting, dizziness, or heart attack?), pulling the fan over himself, or if he first got a shock from the electric fan, and then falling down, had dragged it along. That he had fallen down was obvious by a bleeding wound on the back of his head.

As I was told later, Abbot Odo Haas, OSB, of Waekwan (sic), South Korea, and Prior Celestine Say, OSB, of Manila, P.I., were the first ones who had found F. Merton about 4 p.m. lying on the floor. Abbot Odo, who had tried to remove the fan, had got also a slight electric shock. So Prior Say had pulled the electric cord out of the plug.

When the police arrived at 6:00 p.m., the body of F. Merton showed already rigor mortis.

F. Grunne, OSB, who had his room on the floor above F. Merton's room, heard a shout about 3:00 p.m. He went down to look for the source of the shouting. Because after the one shout all remained quiet, F. Grunne again went up to his room. However, this could have been just the time when F. Merton fell and died.

M. Edeltrud Weist, OSB
Bangkok, Dec. 11, 1968

It has rained a little—enough to create a good sound and to freshen the air; but now—at four—the sun is back out and the humidity drags the sweat from every pore of the body. Have worked well since Brother Pat left. Dunstan Coleman is coming this evening for supper. I must take another shower before continuing the work.

Brother Pat brought the photos—some of them extraordinary—of Tom in the last days and on his bed in death during the vigil.

Questions: Why, when the flesh burns were so severe and the very air smelled of roasted flesh, did the cloth of Tom's shorts remain undamaged? Must ask about this.

Why did rigor mortis set in so fast, within about three hours? Is this normal?

Why the contradictions about the liquid on the floor? Haas says only that it was not water. One of the other witnesses says that Dr. Nun from Korea called it uric acid. The police report calls it a "puddle of urine." (Yet it was up under Tom's arm.)

Why, with the burns so severe, did this not have a cauterizing effect? Odo states specifically that there were great open wounds along the path of the area where the fan had lain on Tom and burned the flesh, but that these wounds were open and bloodshot at the bottom.

Later. Nearly 6:00, and I have showered and shaved and await the arrival of Dunstan Coleman for a little visit. We are compadres in the sense that Jacques Maritain is his godfather as well as Amanda's [Griffin's youngest daughter].

AUGUST 9, 1969

Saturday. Finally, my body worked its way around to the monastic schedule kept by Tom here in the hermitage. After the visit and supper last evening with Dunstan Coleman, I retired and fell asleep immediately around 8:30 p.m. and awakened at 3:15 a.m. With strong coffee and the silence and darkness before dawn, I have worked well—getting the inquiries off to Japan and Belgium in order to finish out the written testimony of witnesses. It is now 4:45 a.m.

These are marvelous hours before dawn. It is warm, the bugs slap against the window, trying to get to the light here at the desk (which is the only light on). Odors of humid greenery . . . the trees and the grasses invisible in the darkness . . . surround me through the open windows. The bells ring 5:00 a.m. from the Abbey below, soft, almost imperceptible, as though coming from a much greater distance.

Something strange is going on here. I am really feeling my way, absorbing everything I can, not only from the written materials, but from living on Tom's schedule, even saying the same office at the hours he said it, and the walls of this place fill in a thousand details. He wrote me often of the heat and humidity. This morning the air is still and the humidity high. I sit here in a sweat (though before it has got chilly by this hour of the morning and I have had to put covers on my bed). I have to keep a towel here to wipe the sweat from my neck and forehead.

But that is not really it, of course. From all this there comes that deeper experience of the silence and the solitude from which Tom drew so much of his preoccupation. The sense of loneliness is gone. In its place there is a growing reliance on the solitude and the silence (of natural sounds), and these things serve merely as the background for the intimate preoccupation of the Christ that Tom sought in the silence, of the Christ that surrounded as the silence surrounds: and out of that a tremendous enthusiasm and vitality that fills the hours, even the hours of contemplation, with a flow and rhythm that stimulates everything and reconciles superbly the realities of the body's needs with the needs of the spirit, the mind. This is one of the things that made Tom unshockable in the face of any reality.

What I am trying to say, without quite knowing how, is that there is really no sense of need now to do a lot of interviews with Tom's friends. I will, of course, because that is part of it, but where before I thought it important, and felt that from such interviews I would learn indispensable truths about Tom, I become aware that I am learning them from Tom and Tom's surroundings . . . almost intuitively . . . far more authentically and truthfully. I am more and more convinced that though his friends knew a lot *about* Tom (and he did not consciously hold things back from those with whom he was intimate), there was neither the time nor the prolonged physical presence necessary for his friends to know in detail the hidden parts of this life: those parts that he was too busy experiencing and contemplating and speculating about to share with others, even through his books. All of us knew, and perhaps intimately, parts of Tom, aspects of Tom.

What I am learning here is that in his own discoveries, in his own lived experience, the greatest part remained unexpressed, the greatest and most valuable part was hidden, secret. I cannot become him, God knows; and such an idea would utterly repel Tom himself; but I can become enough of him to perceive that the hidden part was the essential and the revealed part was infinitely less important, given only in hints (which is one of the things that gave an illusion of ambivalence and contradiction to much of what he revealed). He was simply not interested, despite his vocation as a writer, in revealing. His most vital writing is private, what he did for himself, because he made constant notes to help clarify things for himself. He thought and sought to express experience on paper; but as a self-guide more than in order to reveal anything. He sought to get rid of the role—to flee the "role" of the monk in order to *become* the monk; to be and not merely to appear to be. (There are great and profound differences which few perceive, even in the religious life.) He was insisting on this to the very end of his life, and made such a statement only an hour before he died. In essence, he was saying: stop yakking Christ and become simply the mirror of Christ, and the rest will take care of itself.

His deepest discomfort came when people, by the force of their admiration and enthusiasm for him, pressured him into the role-playing bit. He understood it, was as gracious as possible about it, and fled from it whenever he could. Men otherwise highly advanced, even connoisseurs of the spiritual life (at least world-renowned as connoisseurs), often fell into the trap of urging him to play the "role." I think of Jean Leclercq countering Tom's authentic reticence about being the "star" at Bangkok, where Tom tried to efface himself and remain in the background, by reminding Tom that he was Thomas Merton: "N'oubliez pas que vous êtes Thomas Merton." ["Do not forget that you are Thomas Merton."] The pressure on Tom to "edify" in a way that was, for Tom, completely unedifying.

I believe one of the marks of the authentic contemplative is a growing need to hide himself, to draw ever more deeply into secrecy, to efface himself, become invisible. As this part of his life grows into the great preoccupation, the other more visible and tangible realities fade until they become only the annoying clutter (the fame, the honors—all that). Sister Marie de la Croix, in her magnificent frankness, remarked that reports of the conference in Bangkok indicating they were all "deeply moved" by the presence of the [Buddhist] Patriarch [Somdet Phra Ariawong Sankarat] and the ceremonies surrounding his appearance were "exaggerated." In fact, she said, they found it more or less *cocasse* [comical], and she photographed Tom, looking utterly bored, and remarked that the TV people from Holland were trying to find him and could not: he remained hidden, immovable except for giving her and Mother Christina private, knowing winks of great eloquence. All of us who knew Tom knew those winks . . . half-grimaces in which he screwed up one corner of his mouth and shut one eye tightly in the drollest kind of expression; pointing out secretly the absurdity of many an edifying "solemnity."

Stopped long enough to drink a glass of milk and wash up the dishes from last night, dried them, put them away.

Monastery bells remind me that it is 6:15 (though no hint of daylight yet), so I stop here and go brush my teeth and get into some clothes for 7:00 a.m. Mass. There are special techniques for these things. To brush teeth, I have to draw a glass of pure water from the metal container in the kitchen, take my pills (diabetes) with the first swig, then dip my toothbrush in the glass, brush teeth, and rinse the mouth with the remaining water after pouring some over the toothbrush to get the toothpaste off of it.

Some first light now, full of mists. The birds come awake.

8:45 a.m. Mass at 7:00, and then breakfast. A still, hot moment, unlike the other mornings here. After Mass, Father Tarcisius prepared our breakfast—pancakes that were delicious, with butter and dietetic syrup, and a big glass of milk. Then we washed up the dishes while Brother Maurice put things where

15

they belong; and they have just left. The air now is bated, still, a deep overcast so menacing (in its stillness) that I have to have the lights on inside. A moment ago the stillness was broken by a large swoosh of wind in the trees, the sound approaching from a great distance, almost a roar, and I thought surely the rain would come; but within moments it is still again. I believe it will pour before long. The air is much cooler now than it was a few hours ago. Thank God it is a little cooler because I can turn off the fan, which makes a real racket.

An absolutely scorching and humid afternoon—impossible to stay dry. Brother Pius is due at 5:00, in a few moments, so I have dressed now. He is to give me a haircut and have supper with me, but my hair is so soggy from the sweating (even though it is clean), I don't know how he will manage to cut it. I wanted to reproduce some of the photos sent to Dom Flavian from Bangkok, but I cannot do it in this heat—every time I bend over to focus the close-up lens on the picture, sweat drops down on the picture—and it would quickly ruin them. Perhaps it will get chilly here before morning, and I can do them early before the heat gets severe tomorrow.

8:00 p.m. A storm is brewing. Thunder rumbles through the woods and the wind is gusting with rain. Good. Busy afternoon. Brother Pius came at 5:00 and cut my hair, explaining carefully that he was not a barber and that this was the first time he had ever tried using thinning shears. He did a fine job. We fixed supper—soup, a tuna sandwich, milk. Then Brothers Pat and Thomas and Maurice came in bringing things—a fan, some groceries. They had some supper and left immediately afterward. I am ready to go get in bed and sleep—though it is not yet dark. Wonderful to retire at this hour, good and tired.

AUGUST 10, 1969

Sunday. Heavy rains last night, and the night turned cold. I had to get up and put a blanket on my bed. Now, at dawn, it is still and clear. My window looks out to a soaked green countryside. Took another antibiotic this morning and have been cleaning up the hermitage because the two Abbots (visiting here) will be coming up during my absence to take a look.

Brother Maurice is coming to pick me up in the jeep at 9:15 for a session with Father Flavian before Mass, lunch, and a session with Dom James [Fox, former Abbot of Gethsemani] after lunch.

9:00 a.m. The sun is out—but soft on the land, and the air remains wonderfully cool. I have cleaned the hermitage and made it as neat as I can. Now I am dressed and waiting for Brother Maurice to come and drive me down the hill to the Abbey for Mass. In the meantime, I listen to Lili Kraus playing the Beethoven Concerto no. 4 (on one of the tape cassettes I brought). This music fits the morning and seems to spring directly from the trees and mountains that surround me.

4:30 p.m. Only now back. I went down for the Mass, which was one of the most beautiful in all memory. Dom Laurence, the Definitor, was here on visitation. He agreed with me afterward that Father Chrysogonus has composed a new kind of Gregorian that is breathtakingly apt for the spirit of the Trappist liturgy. It is not Gregorian, of course. It is another musical language, but it has the same capabilities as Gregorian. A nice, short visit with Father Flavian and a very good session with Dom James, the former Abbot. He took me up to his hermitage, hidden away through miles of woods on a small peninsula high in the mountains—a place of magnificent vistas and total isolation. Dom James was in the pink, we understood one another perfectly, and I am glad for the encounter. I photographed him with the other Abbots, and also in his "natural habitat," and think I got some very good ones. Now, though, I am extremely tired. I will spend the rest of the afternoon reading and resting. The antibiotics take their toll.

This evening, I took more antibiotics and lay on the bed reading the letters Tom wrote to Father Flavian, which Father Flavian generously turned over to me today. In them, Tom talks mostly about the "secret mission" to find a truly isolated spot for a hermitage or for a small group of monk-contemplatives from Gethsemani. There are only a few letters. Obviously, Tom was always here and had no need to write to Flavian.

Then I read through the material Dom James confided to me: some very good clarifications. Must ask him to write more of his memories.

I should clear with Father Flavian about the "secret mission," which obviously has no reason for secrecy now; but to make sure it is all right to mention this. Tom was moving more and more toward not only solitude but isolation. There is much here that I need to understand better. He told Father James that if he had to move over further into the mountains (where Father James has his hermitage), he would end up in a mental hospital. And yet, he was seeking for a place in Alaska where the solitude and isolation would be much greater than what he had here. This has to be handled well. Many thought he was simply going . . . out, out beyond the walls. He says himself that he would always return here, keep this place as a base, and remain within the family, of course; but that he would need to find deeper isolation.

Yet, in the Asian journal, in one of the entries where he was in solitude facing the towering Himalayas, an overwhelming view, he remarked that it was, after all, no better than Gethsemani or the Redwoods. Of all the few places he investigated, the Trappistines at the Redwoods seemed to have stirred his greatest enthusiasm.

Dom James hammered at two things: Tom's profound, almost childlike faith and his *ultimate humility*. If he had ever left, it would only be to go more deeply into solitude and isolation in his search for contemplative union with God. That is certain. He felt that Western monks were not yet profoundly enough skilled in contemplation and was trying to learn—that was the real reason for the trip: the Bangkok Conference and the visit to Indonesia were only the "legal reasons."

How often I am reminded of Pierre Reverdy [French poet] in reading through these materials on Tom. Dom James said that writing was a compulsion for Tom, and that Tom had told him that if he could not write, he would break down mentally. I remember Reverdy telling me: "Si je n'avais pas écrit, je serais devenu fou." ["If I had not written, I would have gone mad."]

18

AUGUST 12, 1969

Dawn. **Feast of St. Clare.** We prepare to celebrate the Mass on this feast day of our daughter Amanda Clare. God love her. She is present in all things this morning, as though she were the sunlight breaking through the mists of this cold early dawn, shedding a soft light over the countryside at least as it is reflected in my sight and in my other senses. I talked with her a moment last night when I got the chance to telephone Piedy [Griffin's wife]. In the near background, I heard her ask: "Who is that on the phone?"

A heavy schedule of work to get done today. I went to bed last night at 8:30 but could not stop reading before 1:00 this a.m. so I slept on till 6:00. Remarkable materials.

9:00 a.m. Beautiful Mass for Amanda Clare, then breakfast with Brother Maurice and Father Tarcisius. I forgot to mention the Masses yesterday and today were in Latin.

Father Tarcisius started to prepare breakfast, coddling nine eggs and some canned milk in a bowl. When we asked him what he was fixing, he said, "An omelette."

"Ah, good," I said, wondering how in God's scheme he would ever cook a nine-egg omelette in a small (perhaps six-inch, maybe eight-inch) skillet.

Brother Maurice, thinking along the same lines, suggested that a nine-egg omelette would end up overflowing and reaching to the ceiling.

"Maybe you could have a soufflé," I suggested.

"Oh . . . well, maybe we could cook it in smaller batches," Tarcisius said. We agreed that would be the best.

He melted some grease and poured in about a third of the mixture. I suggested he shake the pan a bit, and finally showed him how, and finally ended up cooking and showing him how to turn omelettes, but of course made a bigger mess than he could have. In the meantime we were cooking toast on a little piece of wire set over the other burner of the hot plate, but the omelettes became so dramatic that we consistently burned the toast. Anyway, we had a good, nourishing breakfast even if we did commit a kind of culinary blasphemy all along the line.

Much work to do now. Magnificent materials to handle before I send them back to the archives.

All the private archival papers indicate one overwhelming fact: Tom was driven almost from the beginning to total abandonment to God: absolute and perfect. And in his struggles, the chief difficulty lay always in seeking to find ways to become more solitary, more united—seeking to remove the imperfections, the intrusions, the sounds, the other things: he died really looking ardently for that place where there would be nothing but him and God in uninterrupted silence and solitude, far from the proximity of men, though united to mankind, but absent mankind. This must be understood. It was thought that when he was allowed to live as a hermit here, the problem of solitude was solved. His solitude was guarded and respected, certainly, but he lived constantly with the *potentiality* of its being unexpectedly interrupted. Though his solitude was guarded by the Abbot and his fellow monks, there were the potential intrusions—the sound of a tractor or bulldozer suddenly nearby, people finding reasons to drop up, Tom even inviting them up in a moment of generosity and affection. In other words, he did not have here the *long stretches of time ahead of him in which there was no possibility that his solitude would be broken*, either by himself or by others. This fact made for an imperfect interior repose in the realization that even if he were not "got to," there was the potentiality that he could be got to, and that it might happen unexpectedly at any moment.

This thirst for total solitary union with God was the driving restlessness. It is too easy to say merely, as some have, that he was a genius, unlike ordinary men, and lacked stability. It was more than that. The search was relentless and constant and could only come to rest with his finding the means of quenching it in an authentic solitude (and he included in this what he termed the monastic vanities—the perfect bow, the images— all of the externals). He did not seek self-fulfillment, but self-abandonment; not to become something, but to become nothing. His great anguish was not with the monastic life, but with those aspects of it that might cause him, at least, to fail to become a true monk—which is the purpose of the monastic life.

How to say this? One goes through certain forms in order to form oneself in the contemplative life. The goal is union with

God, utter submission to God's will, utter deafness to all that is not God; but then there comes a point with some men where those things that guided them that far become the impediments to their going on and have to be done away with; when the need for progress *after* formation is a stripping away of all things, even the forms that led up to that development.

With others, there is no need for this; with Tom there was need for absolute bareness. In fact, even to the very end of his life, he would make little notes from the books he had read. On the India trip, he noted on a piece of paper an admonition about total nakedness before God. This and the innocence—through experience, back to innocence—preoccupied him, if one can judge by his notes, at the end of his life.

How strange that the very things I mentioned earlier—the *potentiality* for intrusions—have been fulfilled this morning. There have been two wholly unexpected visits; one in particular from a young poet, Bill Davis, here on a visit, I suppose, who just appeared and very humbly asked if he could see inside. Who could say no? I understood perfectly the importance to him. Of course I said yes, and above his constant protestations that he did not want to disturb me, shushed the idea. He wanted to take some pictures. How could I turn him away? How could Tom have turned him away? He could not, of course.

The young man had asked if he might just come up and take a peek, and had been told they were sure I would not mind. I did not, of course, but also I had every minute of the day set aside for work, and for an hour of it the work was muted by the knowledge of his presence in the house, his deeply reverent presence. Then timidly, as he left with overwhelming thanks, he asked would it be at all possible for him to bring his friend up this afternoon, just to sit and talk a little bit about Thomas Merton. What could I say? My heart sank. I explained that I had such a heavy work schedule, I would be happy to see his friend, but we would have to keep the visit short—no longer than fifteen minutes. I love such visits, wish I had time to bull with them as long as they want.

But again this is one of the answers to Tom's problems. Charity demands the yesses that nevertheless end up altering and distorting solitude, and so he felt the need simply to get

21

further away, to become less approachable, more hidden. These things that have somehow puzzled me in a sense (his constant quest for a place of even greater solitude), now come clear through my own problems with the solitude necessary to work. If I say one word to the monks, they will of course stop the leakage and absolutely forbid anyone to come near. And then young men like Bill Davis—to whom this is obviously a profoundly reverberant experience and one that will mark him forever, perhaps—will be denied that experience; and I cannot do that. So I remain silent. It is not terribly important, in any event, but it teaches me how it could be tremendously important as a problem for Tom.

Then a visit, wanted by me and requested by me, of Father Matthew Kelty here, who wrote so magnificently about Tom shortly after the death; but, of course, it was nothing because neither of us wanted to speak in the presence of the young man who was in photographing Tom's chapel. So we kept making face signs to be careful and talking about matters that could safely be overheard. Not that there is any great secret that we wanted to discuss, but simply because of a sense of discretion for Tom: we did not want to say anything that might, no matter how innocently, be repeated outside, expanded upon, become rumor.

3:00 p.m. And I realize that I am suddenly overwhelmed with fatigue. This has been a lengthy and concentrated and magnificent work session. I have been carried by the energies of my enthusiasm, and now, on my last day here, with still a great deal to get done before my departure tomorrow morning, I am suddenly emptied of energy. Everything seems difficult. I have some documents to photograph, and I cannot quite find the energy to do them, but I will. I need to shave, but I keep putting it off as though suddenly it were a great task. I know that my companions here—Brother Patrick, Father Tarcisius, and Brother Maurice—plan to come up for a little celebration this evening: a kind of thanksgiving party that things have gone so well this worktrip. We pray for the book at Mass each morning and during the intentions. When it comes to my turn, I always make an intention of Thanksgiving for the profound privilege of working on this book, but also for being able to work on it here in the hermitage in the solitude and silence.

Since the days of my old and horrible nightmares following the *Black Like Me* experience, I have never had any dreams vivid enough to recall. But last night, after reading far too late, questing, questioning, meditating, seeking to grasp these things about Tom, I finally went into a deep sleep and had the most startling and vivid dream about St. John of the Cross all mixed up with Tom's presence. I saw them both in a silent kaleidoscope changing set of patterns, like a cubist painting of great brilliance. Neither of them seemed aware of the other's presence; but they were combined: St. John of the Cross would have Tom's legs, or a hand with the scar, or Tom would have St. John's profile staring out of the side of Tom's head, where his ear ought to have been. It was, or seemed to be, prolonged. My reaction was neither fear nor joy, but tremendous astonishment and a fascination that glued all my concentration on them and made me really unaware of myself. It was a mounting thing until it finally woke me up, and I remember staring into the darkness of that room and telling myself out loud with a groan: "You're concentrating too much on it. You're working too relentlessly on it."

There was nothing of the "vision" in this, God knows, and not even the slightest implication of that should be allowed to creep into it. It was, I am sure, due to the fact that, in so much of what I read about Tom's quest for the ultimate, I am reading echoes of St. John of the Cross. I am at the level now of sufficient depth in uncovering the hidden Tom (through his own notes and those sudden luminous passages that abound in his notes) to perceive the similarity of spirit between the two—a similarity that was never obvious, or at least never as striking as in the surface Tom. It is one of those growing realizations that simply climaxed in the dream.

Fatigue and weakness nearly paralyze me. I am too tired, and yet there is the need to go on. There is no question of my stopping now and going to the cool sheets of that cot. I will get up, slug coffee, take the quick icy shower.

Now I am torn between continuing the work and going to

take another quick shower, covered as I am with sweat, and shave for the little festivity tonight. I must photograph that. Yes, if they are going to all that trouble, I must certainly clean up for it. Perhaps I will have time to make a few more notes before they arrive, after cleaning up, if I hurry. I hurry.

I have left the door open and now the room is full of flies. The little black snake is around here again. It is the same one or perhaps a grandson to the one that Tom used to find in the outhouse when he would stand outside the door before entering and say: "Are you in there, you black bastard?"

Now, everything has been done, and I am glad. I have shaved, cleaned up the bathroom, polished the fixtures, made the copies of the materials I need to send back down to the archives, drunk a glass of apple juice (and now prepare coffee—am groggy).

I am preoccupied about these work journals. I need to put in a great deal of material and speculation that I as the biographer alone am authorized to see. (At least for many years, and some things forever. Since the materials are so vast, I must have them, the excerpted portions at least, here to draw upon, and to document—without actually revealing them—later if the need be. And yet they must not be seen by others, probably ever. I must perhaps get a small safe in which to keep them. People are too indiscreet. The very word *confidential* marked on the documents or journals is an open invitation to some spirits to go immediately and directly *there*.)

8:30 p.m. They have just left, Brother Patrick, Brother Maurice, and Father Tarcisius. A marvelous final evening together. They arrived with provisions around 6:30, we cleared off this work table and had a leisurely supper together. Nothing very ambitious—lunch meat sandwiches, fresh tomatoes, hard-boiled eggs, potato chips; but for us it was festive. We talked, talked, talked, and thoroughly enjoyed ourselves. Brother Patrick is very cultivated and very funny and tells good stories. It was easy, a lovely time. Since I insisted on paying for the provisions, they embarrassed me by washing my car and filling it up with gas. Of course they would have done this anyway, and in

24

fact I am sure they had already done it before I even insisted on buying the groceries. Now, really, I am sleepy and relaxed, and though there is a tiny bit left to do, I am not going to run the risk of getting caught up in something and not getting to sleep. They will come for 7:00 a.m. Mass here, and then after breakfast, they will help me pack my car and I will get away around 9:00, I imagine. So now to go to bed while the sleep is on me and I am relaxed.

Note: must reproduce some of the photos when I return—photos that were taken of Tom on his bed during the vigil before his body was claimed. He died apparently in some agony (the feet were cramped and drawn in); but in his habit, lying on the bed, there are no traces of any agony. Sister Marie de la Croix spoke of his expression as one of profound peace and sleep. I do not find this exactly in what I see. The eyes are closed, but not as though in sleep, for the lower lid comes up halfway and the upper lid comes down to meet it in a slit. The face is indeed serene, but as though he were in deep and contented meditation—or at least in thought or with the eyes closed the way one does when trying to remember something.

The thing that strikes overwhelmingly is that he looks like a child—there is a haunting resemblance between his face in death and the photos of him as a young child (four and six years of age). I thought of his preoccupation with the cycle innocence-experience-innocence again; and what other word is there to describe that expression on his face. It is the expression of innocence that is so haunting, the return to his face of childhood, not smiling, no . . . no gruesome mortuary grin (because he had only been toweled down and put into his monastic robes), but with an expression of full contentment; somewhat like the face of any child who has been told to go to sleep and who closes his eyes and pretends to sleep when his parent comes in to check on him.

AUGUST 13, 1969

Wednesday. Dawn, and I prepare to finish up the last notes in this and pack for the departure. Night of terrible nightmares, each one awaking me to trembling and prayers for mercy; but all is calm this morning. I read *Emblems of a Season of Fury* just before sleeping and was very impressed with the poems of Ernesto Cardenal and Alfonso Cortes.

Magnificent week here. I look forward to my return next month. Now, I look forward with the deepest joy to getting home to Piedy and the children. How I wished for her last night during that long stretch of nightmares!

SEPTEMBER 15, 1969

Monday. Returned to Gethsemani this morning. Brother Pat brought me directly up to the hermitage where I am settled once more, unpacked. We have had lunch and a talk, and now I am going to fall into the bed for a good nap before doing any work. Brother Maurice has cleaned everything, mowed around the perimeter, and stocked the refrigerator with supplies, as well as bringing up a new can of drinking water. He thinks of everything.

How happy I am to be here.

Later. Slept deeply for an hour and a half. The silence and the peace here slugs you, assaults you at the outset. I am only beginning to get into it, to let my nerves match the serenity here. It is a marvelous, still afternoon, not too hot. The assault is a happy one, a blessed one to all the senses. But I know why Tom was irritated in what seemed an exaggerated manner by the intrusions of sound here. Even the sounds that have grown to be a part of our system and no longer noticeable come as a deep intrusion. A plane just flew over. I have never noticed such things elsewhere, but here it seems magnified and outrageous precisely because the calm is so much deeper than that of other places.

Later: past 8:00 p.m. Supper with Brothers Maurice and Patrick. I fixed a kind of *ronde de saumon*, but no *ronde*, and just a mixture of salmon (not good) and rice with mayonnaise on top—served lukewarm yet. We did not have time to let it chill through as it should have. Ah, well, it was nourishing. Now they have gone. Night is full on us, and very dark, and I should retire right now, but cannot. Too much material that is too exciting. So, I will work a little.

It is so late I dare not look at the clock. Have read the journals without taking notes almost all the way through. Will go back and make the notes. Stopped now for a moment to make some drink—milk with a raw egg beaten into it (very badly with a fork). Tom talks a great deal about his first days and nights of discovery here at the hermitage—remarkable pages, and remarkable experience to read them sitting in that same hermitage, facing many of the same problems of physical living.

I regret staying up late only because it will cheat me out of those marvelous hours of work before dawn.

12:14. Finished a first reading of the journal and went to check the time. Surprised. Thought it would be about 3:00 a.m. So I can get sleep and still get up early. The woods are alive with sounds—dogs barking in the distance. A bull roaring somewhere far away.

SEPTEMBER 16, 1969

Feast of Saints Cornelius and Cyprian. Up at 5:00 a.m. Read *Silence dans le ciel* after going to bed last night. (Arthaud, 1956. A beautiful book with Tom's text and some great photos taken in various cloisters.) The alarm went off at 3:00 a.m. I reset it for 5:00 and slept well. Got up a moment ago. Chilly. Put on a sweater and boiled water for the coffee, which I made strong and which I have here beside me on the worktable.

Difficult to wake up. I keep dozing as I sit here. It is dark, starless outside. Nothing is visible.

The bells from the Abbey call monks to 6:00 a.m. conventual Mass.

Now, 6:30, and I have finished the body's things—shaved, brushed teeth, combed hair, carefully treated the wounds. The air seems warmer, probably because I have stirred about and am now wide awake. I have stepped outside. The stars are brilliant, the air fragrant with damp odors of pine and cedar. Predawn quiet. Soon Father Tarcisius and Brother Maurice will arrive for Mass here, and then breakfast. I have had nothing but two cups of coffee. I will eat too much breakfast, and then be sleepy again. Well, no problem. The first day here is always filled with dozing, to get on schedule, to let the body calm to a new rhythm, a more profoundly natural one, one without the stimulation of talk, noise, people to chop things up.

The bells ring 6:45. Time to put on clothes for the Mass.

Later. The sun streams in long slants through the front window here where I work. Beautiful Mass. Then a breakfast of eggs and toast, prepared by Father Tarcisius, who left a few moments ago. We will celebrate Mass henceforth at 6:30 to give them more time to get to their work.

To be here is a kind of total emptying. Mass was so absorbing I forgot to take the paten at communion, forgot to give Brother Maurice the embrace. Feel the need and the desire to sleep. The belly, the senses, the spirit, the nerves . . . all feel emptied of accumulated dross. A great but simple and natural beauty possesses the whole man—seeps into the emptied places, physical and spiritual . . . you let it happen, glad it is happening, but in reality you do not call it. You simply submit to what happens: you "allow it to be done to you." A cool, fresh, sunlit morning, a soft chill in the breeze. It is too beautiful. I go to lie on the sheets and let it happen.

Later. Slept deeply for forty-five minutes, awakened, obsessed with all thoughts centered on God, adoring the Christ of these silences, slept again, aware of the cold sheets, the cold walls . . . the porous, unfinished texture close to my eye, grey cement blocks seamed together with grey mortar. Empty, desire to sleep, but am up now, with more coffee, trying to come alive and get to work.

I see many spindly spiders, with tiny brown bodies and long threadlike legs of unbelievable fragility (in appearance at least).

Suddenly it becomes noisy. Jets, their roar bounding about the hills; and down below somewhere, out of sight, large machines start up with a clatter. The silence is shattered though the sight remains uncluttered; no wonder Tom found problems with retaining the illusion of solitude here. These things are a terrible intrusion.

SEPTEMBER 17, 1969

4:00 a.m. To bed at 8:30 last night, right after supper with Brother Patrick and Brother Richard, and up at 3:30, medicated and coffeed (or coffeeing). Chilly, but less so than yesterday morning.

Finished up all the letters of condolences (three large volumes of them). Very moving, this outpouring from hundreds of people bewildered and shocked by the death, mostly people who had never met or corresponded with Tom, but who had been deeply affected by his books.

Here is an exact copy of the telegram that brought the first news of the death. (Printed in ink at the top: "The first announcement Dec. 10. 10:00 a.m.")

ABBOTT BURNS
TRAPIST POST OFC GETHSEMENI KY
DEPARTMENT REGRETS INFORM YOU FOLLOWING MES-
SAGE RECEIVED FOR YOU FROM AMERICAN EMBASSY
BANGKOK THAILAND: "INFORMED BY ABBOTT WEAK-
LAND THAT THOMAS MERTON HAS DIED. MR. HOBART
LUPPI DIR. SPECIAL CONSULAR SERVICES DEPT OF STATE

Must ask Brother Patrick who actually received the message and the events surrounding that. Which Brother was on the switchboard. Also, should photograph this telegram. Need all the events surrounding this incident: the weather, the full sequence.

4:45. I watch the time (listening to the Abbey clock bells), because we are going to celebrate Mass at 6:30 this morning, and then Brother Patrick and I will go to Lexington to visit some of Tom's friends there at the home of Mrs. Hammer [Carolyn, wife of the Austrian artist, Victor Hammer]. So I must bathe and shave and do all that before Mass. Such outings are necessary for the book, but how I dread to leave this place even for a moment.

Also, and I am not going to get into this, I am terribly preoccupied by the news Father Dan Walsh [Merton's teacher at Columbia] sent me yesterday through Brother Pat. I am apparently to receive the letter here today from Monsignor Horrigan [then president of Bellarmine College in Louisville, Kentucky] about receiving the doctorate in a big ceremony in November, along with Ethel Kennedy. When this came up before, I begged Brother Patrick to discourage it. I am deeply embarrassed by such things. They are not for me and should be for others who deserve them and who would be edified and uplifted (encouraged) by them. But it is difficult, perhaps impossible, to refuse. Already Ethel Kennedy has accepted. My refusal would make her look a bit upstaged. Tom accepted one, so did Father Stan [Murphy, Canadian Basilian]. I cannot find a good way to get out of it.

Today is the Mass for the Stigmata of St. Francis. That was a glorious sign, a glorious stigmata. I suppose I accept this as a stigmata in the other sense. I will keep my mouth shut and accept, because not to do so would offend a great many people and embarrass people I would never embarrass. It is to launch the Merton-Loftus library—I am all for that, all for Bellarmine. How can I refuse without seeming to refuse support of these things that I do support with all my heart?

What I do not support is this kind of honor accorded to me (though such honors should be accorded to others). It is profoundly against my grain. I will ride it a bit, see if I can gracefully find a way out; if not, then just accept it with as good grace as possible. I am trying desperately to think of someone else, so I could suggest an alternative. But it is not really my business to tell the officials at Bellarmine who should receive their doctorates. For me, I am ashamed to say, it seems only more clutter in my life. (I keep hearing myself mutter obscenities under my breath: well, I know it is not the first time these holy walls have heard such. I imagine that Tom must have uttered the very same ones when he was so honored, though I do not know for sure.)

I am not going to go on writing about this, not going to make a big thing of it or let it become a depressing preoccupation. Brother Patrick said: "You'll be in good company." I said nothing but thought: "I know that, but I'm not damned sure *they* will be in such good company with me." I leave it in God's hands. Maybe there is some mistake. I have not been notified. Maybe they will have some good illumination before mailing the letter.

I offer it up, but not with as much good grace as I feel I would like to.

SEPTEMBER 18, 1969

Thursday. 6:00 a.m. Rough this morning. Brother Patrick and I went to Lexington yesterday, stopping by Shakertown (Pleasant Hill) on the way, seeing a few things, then going on to Lexington to the home of Carolyn Hammer for lunch. There we met Wendell Berry [poet and author] and Bob Shepherd [old Merton friend]. Carolyn had a great wealth of material about Tom and her husband, Victor Hammer. Beautiful lunch and then a great deal of talk and discussion. Rain came and then cleared. We could not get away. She gave me a copy of the Merton-Hammer *Hagia Sophia*, a priceless gift. Then around 5:00, we went to the Shepherds' for a light supper, intending to get away by 7:00. We talked and stayed on until 8:30 and drove back, arriving here after 10:00.

I felt terribly guilty about keeping Brother Pat out so late, and I was almost dead from fatigue and pain myself. He dropped me here at the hermitage. I went to bed immediately and read through a couple of books on the Shakers I had picked up at Shakertown—one on furniture and crafts, and the other on Shaker cooking. Enough to fascinate me and keep me awake until after midnight. Then sleep, and did not awaken until 5:30 this morning. Feeling exhausted and shot, but glad for yesterday and everything about it. Much, much to get done here today. I will go at it steadily (I hope), but easily. Now time to put on some pants for Mass.

Later. Beautiful Mass, in Latin, this morning; long recollection in the dark chapel afterward; then breakfast with Father Tarcisius and Brother Maurice. Father cooked waffles, and they were very good. The morning is grey, heavily overcast, as though rain could begin to fall any moment—the kindest kind of light over the countryside. The air is cool, damp, and still. Must now go out and photograph some documents that must be returned at noon (out on the porch, I mean, where the light is right).

Monsignor Horrigan just called, and wants me to speak at

the function (briefly) on November 9. I told him I would if I could, but that I didn't know my schedule; he is to write me, then call me on Monday, September 29, after I get a chance to study the proposal. No mention, thank God, of any honors. Maybe they will spare me that. Great Lord, why did they *ever* put a phone in the hermitage? For emergency use, okay—but just to receive calls, what a mess.

Almost 9:00 p.m., and am ready to go to bed. Strange, the sense of joy I have in going to bed here, after a good long day's work. It is a new feeling for me, one I have never had anywhere else. An anticipation that is full of contentment to get into that bed, get the lights off, get between the sheets, listen briefly to all the night sounds, and drift easily into sleep. Perhaps it is because there is a particular joy in getting up and beginning my day at 3:00 a.m. (and that can't be done without the early bedtime). Tremendous happiness in those hours of solitary work before dawn. I remember long ago reading somewhere where Tom remarked to the effect that getting to bed, and those first moments after retiring and before sleep, were akin to paradise.

SEPTEMBER 19, 1969

4:30 and cold. A first rooster crows somewhere far away. Have been slugging coffee, huddling in my sweater, studying the Hammer exposition booklet, with pieces by Tom, Jacques, Lexi [Alexander de Grunelius], etc.

Deep and good sleep last night. The thirst for this solitude grows. The week here comes to an end too soon, but thank God for this week each month.

Now, I have to get up and do the things of morning— bathe and dress the wounds, which get worse and not better, brush my teeth, take the medication, make up the bed.

Now it is done, and I hear the jeep coming up the hillside and see the lights in the darkness. They are here for Mass.

Later. Mass is over, and breakfast (French toast *à la* Tarcisius), and they have cleaned up and left. Daylight has come, grey and overcast and still quite uncomfortably cool. Beautiful . . . the hills and trees vague in white haze.

Later: and I have added to that haze. I decided to build a small fire in the fireplace, so I put on shoes (the grass is wet with dew) and went to the woodshed in back. I opened it and looked in. I hesitated—on the roof beam I saw three nests of large black wasps (hornets??). But they did not seem disturbed, so I went in. Logs and kindling are neatly stacked inside, plus work tools (shovels, forks, etc.), a gallon of kerosene. As I reached for a small log, I stopped in fright. The long white sheath of a snake's discarded skin spread downward over the top logs—the biggest damned snakeskin (though probably not as big as it appeared). Was he in there somewhere? Or had he just come in to shed his skin? I carefully took a log as far from that skin as I could, grabbed a few pieces of kindling and a handful of straw (to start the fire), and got my ass gone.

Now the fire is going, very gently, and from the front window I see whitish smoke from the chimney drifting down toward the ground, settling among the trees. Great contentment to have the fire, more for the crackling and the companionship than for the little warmth it gives. And, of course, Tom had to build his fires, and I need the experience, too, of building the fire, sweeping the hearth. Now I go to sit in front of it to warm my feet and perhaps read.

Later: Brother Patrick came up, sat by the fire and had a cup of coffee with me. The sky looked so threatening we decided to go on and do the shopping (pick my suit up at cleaner) now, because the hill road can become impassable after rain.

Early afternoon, still dark, but up around seventy and very calm outside. It could rain any moment—the air damp. The fire has gone out, but I will have another one this evening when the chill begins.

Brother Pat found some wide gauze, which reminds me that the other day, when I began bleeding again, I asked if they could find wide gauze to bring up. Brother Richard brought up a few rolls of narrow (one-inch) gauze and some tape, handed it to me and asked: "Will that be large enough, John?" I looked at that tape, and looked at him and then back at the tape, and he began to turn absolutely crimson as he realized all the implications. I set the gauze on the table, turning my back to him and muttering, "Hell, that wouldn't have been big enough when I was two years old." But he didn't get that as he was saying in that soft and gentle voice: "It was the largest they had."

I gently assured him that I could certainly manage fine. I was wanting to burst out laughing, but knew that would only add to his confusion. I guess he said something about this to Brother Pat, because Brother Pat later came up with two gauzes a little more realistic in size, said that was all they had. This morning, we just went and bought some at the store, and also a pan for me to take the baths in, because I cannot manage what needs to be done here with the shower and all the good progress in healing has been undone by my messing around and trying to make do without taking the soakings every couple of hours.

Later. Brother Patrick has realized that I need more time absolutely to myself. They have tried to break the solitude up a little, by brief visits. The Mass in the morning (which I want above all to continue), then Brother Pat bringing me something to eat and the mail at noon, and answering all my questions, and carrying back research material with which I have finished; then he returns briefly for supper and sometimes brings a Father or Brother who knew Tom and who could help me with the questions. But that was really because they thought the solitude too hard for me, and did not know how much I thrive on it. So we have decided on the future trips to keep the Masses each morning; and to keep the noon visits (because we get a great deal of work done—I save all my questions about the research for them); but to have no evening visitors, not even Pat. I eat too much. Out of their scruple to see that I get properly nourished, they bring me too much. So I told Pat I would really prefer to heat up a can of soup for supper, and I can do that without any help.

I am very happy indeed. This will be an ideal arrangement. I can work right on through, take my soup alone, get right back to work and still get to bed by 8:30 in order to awaken at 3:15. The only imperfection this week has been simply the imperfection of the solitude. I have got a great deal done, had very few interruptions actually (and they were benign and pleasant ones); but I have a great need and a great longing for the total solitude, without even those interruptions. (I mean the afternoon and evening ones: the Mass and breakfast with Father

Tarcisius and Brother Maurice is no interruption—it is as necessary as the food and the silence; the same with Brother Pat's noon visits. They keep me supplied with the materials necessary to work.)

My fear has been that they would refuse to allow people to come up who wanted only to see Tom's hermitage. I have got that clear. They must let them come. Such a visit to the hermitage means too much to those who want to visit or just see it. There are very few such visits (only two or three this week), and they last only a couple of minutes because the people don't come to see me, just to see the place. That is fine. No one should be denied that blessing at this time, and I insist that they be allowed to come up briefly; only asking them to give me warning from the gatehouse so I have time to get ready.

The wind stirs now. At a little after 1:00 p.m. it has got darker, like dusk. What the hell, I will go ahead and start up the fire again. Marvelous afternoon. Must finish up the new articles on Tom, then the Hammer episodes concerning his friendship with Tom, then finish up the notes from the 1964–65 journals by bedtime. Only this afternoon, tomorrow and part of Sunday remain. How I wish I had not accepted that Canada thing [speaking invitation] so I could stay on at least a few more days.

Must remember to send Brother Maurice my future times here. Poor thing, he holds open a couple of weeks for me (otherwise the monks here come up individually for a week at a time). I told Maurice this morning that as soon as I got back and had my schedule, I would write him a list of the exact dates when I would be here throughout the year, so he would know how to schedule the place for the others without always having to wait to see when I would need it.

I sit here looking at that pitiful little roll of gauze Brother Richard left for me, and burst out laughing every time I see it.

Later: 4:10, still, cool, dark. A day of the purest serenity, I can almost perceive the leaves turn scarlet out front. I work, with no sense of rush, steadily, easily, full of contentment and attuned now to the natural rhythms of solitude. An all-pervasive awareness of God, an awareness even beyond thought, distills the atmosphere. "I am here," Tom wrote once, "not because I come here seeking God, but because God wants to find me here" (inexact quote, from memory). That's the sense of it anyway, and the sense of my feelings here. I work, go about my business, aware of the chapel next to the kitchen with its lingering fragrance from this morning's Mass as a place of light; but all of this is done, even concentratedly, without ever for an instant losing a sense of receptivity. "I am here where Christ wants to find me." That is enough. No seeking, because there in the surrounding silence all that would otherwise be loneliness is filled with Christ, filled with that ravishment.

No, I do not even play music, though I have tapes and records here. No music could add anything to this kind of silence, and no music could ever equal it. Music is necessary elsewhere as a substitute for it. Here, I choose the better of the two—the silence that is filled with Christ. I know that I am living a tremendous privilege here—I am awe-stricken with gratitude: that is all, everything within me goes out and fuses with that Christ-filled silence; every action, everything I do. I listen to it, let it tell me what to do, what to write: I am fused with it when I fix coffee or drink water or read or write or bathe or nap or fix the fire, so that all those things are fused with it in a kind of bareness and simplicity that hides nothing from Christ, that separates no action from Christ of the silences.

Whereas in places where there is never silence or solitude for any extended period, these actions distract one from thoughts of God, here they simply fuse into that tremendous awareness. Such an awareness does not destroy the solitude as any human presence might (though not all human presences do); no, it simply fills solitude which, without it, would be only void, only hollowness. I live in the silence where Christ can find me and do with me or not whatever he wishes; and as a result the solitude has no hollow, no void, no loneliness—only felicity. I do not ask for or seek the felicity, because I know that is Christ's choice, and I simply revel in it knowing that for the moment it is a tremendous gift. But I must be ready to accept, whenever and in whatever way God wills it, the Cross—and to accept that with the same gratitude as I accept this.

Brother Patrick brought up the September, 1969, issue of *The Cord*, which has just come, with an article, "Thomas Merton: Who Was He?" by Sister Mary Seraphim (a contemplative nun at the Poor Clare Monastery of Santa Clara, Canton, Ohio). It has some fine insights—extraordinary ones, really, for someone who never met or corresponded with Thomas Merton. She knew someone who had known him.

I read it wondering what Tom would think of it. I think he would have liked it, but would have been embarrassed that she was quite so positive in her statements: "He attained the seemingly impossible integration of unlimited apostolic drive with undivided devotion to contemplation." There is truth in it, of course, but not truth really in her speculation that this would create tensions in most but not in Tom. It created profound tensions in him: no, the tensions were finally created by his need to go deeper, deeper; to find a way to go deeper into silence and solitude, to be completely alone with God and completely naked before God . . . "*dans le vrai.*" He copied such passages in his final journal, near the end: "naked before God"; and "innocence-experience-innocence" (from innocence through experience to innocence, or the innocence that is not maintained through *ignorance* from knowledge and experience of sin, but the innocence that passes through those, and is restored). He was moving, after the experience, into and toward that nakedness (innocence) before God. He was not seeking to leave the order or the place—no, he was seeking single-mindedly to become more truly *monk*. He was not leaving anything, but rather going *toward*.

Third Visit

OCTOBER 11, 1969 . . .

OCTOBER 11, 1969

Saturday. As ravishing a morning as I can ever remember. I arrived here at 6:30, in the darkness before dawn, driving from Elizabethtown. Brother Patrick and Father Tarcisius were waiting for me, and emerged into the beam of my headlights. We drove up to the hermitage where Brother Maurice had spent the night and had everything clean and ready for my arrival. He had had the old phonograph repaired, and as we entered the hermitage he turned it on full blast to that part of the *William Tell* Overture that has the Lone Ranger theme. The blatant music blared out. It was so funny that I almost rolled on the floor laughing, and of course Brother Maurice was overjoyed to see that his "welcome" was appreciated by the "Texan."

Marvelous moments of seeing one another again, but we quickly got ready for Mass and afterward breakfast. They told me I would have more perfect seclusion, that Father Abbot had prohibited all visits up here, not only for me, but because it is a place of retreat for the monks and the visits disturbed them, too.

After clearing the table and cleaning up the dishes, they left me here alone. I have to ease into this new thing every time. So I put on a recording of the Mozart C Major Quintet and began to unpack and get myself ready for work. A calm, serene morning. A moment ago the rain began to fall . . . quietly, gently, straight down. I turned off that sublime music for the sublimer silence. And now I listen to rain, which is so extraordinary here. The day remains warm, full of freshness. Odors of wet rain on the dried autumnal grasses and woods surround me, and I experience a time of the rarest and purest joy, with communion still dazzling within me.

Later—5:00 p.m. The most perfect solitude. There is now, with Father Abbot's new ruling that no one can come near this place, a whole new spareness in the atmosphere, the illusion that nothing is going to disturb it—no presence, no sound; where before I had the solitude, but always the illusion that it could be destroyed. One has to sink into it, and it has to be total before the real work begins. How to express this.

Today has been a day of that kind of saturation . . . ease, saturation, emptying, cleansing. It happens more quickly as I return here at more frequent intervals. At first it took a couple of days. Now it is accomplished after only a few hours. I have not slept a full night in several days, but here I do not even feel fatigued—enormous enthusiasm to work, read, study, and be. I know that I will retire early and sleep like an infant.

I have done immediately all the things that needed doing: writing the necessary business and other letters, sending off the checks and expense accounts. That has to be done early, because very quickly that kind of connection with the "outside" becomes too barbarous an intrusion, and if you wait, you just go on waiting, because what happens here is just overwhelmingly more important than even these necessary things.

I am aware that in addition to doing the very best work here that can be done on this book—the most concentrated and sustained—I am also privileged to live some of the highest moments of my life, of my interior life. This hermit-existence, which in no way nullifies or reduces my family existence, is d∽eply and profoundly tasted in all its rarity. Where in the world today can men simply have the prolonged experience of true solitude, as hermits? Surely it is almost impossible in the world, and indeed almost impossible even in monasteries and convents: there the starkness, purity, simplicity are softened by contacts or at least by a knowledge, an awareness of the proximity of others.

Now the quiet, the stillness of an early, overcast evening. A soft green countryside with an occasional splash of vermilion where a tree is turning red early. In fact, the trees on the hills across the valley are filled with such touches. Now I stop typing to let the stillness saturate.

OCTOBER 12, 1969

Sunday. 4:15 a.m. Up since 3:15 of an almost warm and still October morning. I stepped out on the porch to see the sky clear, the stars brilliant—no moon. Did a lot of washing and cleaning—shirt, socks, underwear, preparing for tonight's appearance at Nazareth College near here. Then I prepared the batter for the *crepes* we will have for breakfast up here this morning after our 7:15 Mass. Have been promising this to Brother Maurice and Father Tarcisius for some time. So the clothes are hanging up to dry in the bathroom, and the *crepes* are ready to cook, and I have done all the things I needed to do . . . all these things to the accompaniment of this silence, this solitude, this stillness. I was asleep by 8:00 last night, retiring at 7:45.

No music this morning. There was the temptation for a moment, but the silence is too perfect to disturb. Cannot get the poems of Dan Berrigan out of my mind—those in *Continuum* about Tom's death. I dreamt about them last night.

How I dread going out for that lecture this evening—not because of the lecture, but because it means leaving this hermitage.

I realize that I am missing, in these journal notes, the ability to express what it really means to be here, to be here as a hermit, to be here surrounded by the extraordinary graces of the Christ of silence and solitude . . . the intense internal joy that is there to fill body, mind, and spirit, with no effort, nothing but receptivity on my part. An overwhelming gift: somewhat like the feelings at the moment of reception of the Host at communion, only sustained, not highpointed for a few moments, but sustained in all the things that I do—in the shaving, the dishwashing, the sleeping and eating and coffee making and medicine taking. It is such a prayer that any more formal prayer seems not only superfluous but actually diminishes the intensity: though certainly we have the more formal verbal prayers, at Mass, etc. They anchor the rest, I am sure, and keep the structures solid. For in all this there is a sense of solidity, of reality—no hint of any escape from reality; no need even for such a hint. The dissonances between reality of the things of the earth and the body, and those of the spirit and nerves, simply are resolved and cease to exist.

Later: 5:45 a.m. Have read the journals, and transcribed some of the parts I need onto cassettes. Extraordinary moments. After that, I turned off all the lights, put on the Mozart G Minor Quintet, and listened on the porch, above the sounds of the night. The slow and final movements of this quintet come the closest to expressing in sound the felicities of solitude and silence of any music I know. I turned on the recorder to capture it, to capture the sounds of the crickets and insects, the music, the monastery bells from the valley below.

Late afternoon, around 4:00. A superb stillness, the countryside radiant and calm with that peculiar quality of a Sunday afternoon. I have spent the day working and resting a little, preparatory to the lecture tonight, which is a great irritation to me, and hopefully the last interruption I will have. I do not mind the lecture, but I deeply mind what it does in interrupting the feeling of continuity in the work.

Later: 5:00 p.m. Hot as summer. I took a short walk in the woods and returned here sopping sweat. Now a slight overcast and the beginnings of a breeze. But no, an instant later the sun cast long slants of tree shadow across the field in front of the cabin. If it does not cool down, the lecture hall will be a sauna. We leave at 5:30, so I must soon get dressed. This is the devil of it. For an hour I could not work, knowing the work would be interrupted with the need to dress and leave this beloved hermitage. To go, as Tom said, "and face humanity."

Removed my pajama shirt and sit here trying to dry out—not wanting to put on fresh clothes while still damp. My skin dries, but the scapular lies cool and soggy on my chest. I take it off and hang it on the doorknob to dry out.

Photographed the outhouse this afternoon: a small, upright cylinder, neatly painted grey, half hidden in the trees and near a spectacular scarlet-leaved thorn tree. Opened the door to look in—a hole in the ceiling let sunlight in to glisten on dead spiders in their stale webs. I looked carefully before stepping in, fearing that king snake of which Tom wrote.

But today the king snake was not there, only the dead spiders and their lusterless webs trailing across the crude toilet seat—surely a penance in itself to use. But the thing that struck me as most final was the long nail—rusted and bare—driven into the rough planks beside the hole, obviously to hold the roll of toilet paper.

Now, dressed and waiting for Brother Patrick to come for me. Am over-warm. Late afternoon, soft and beautiful. I think of Tom lying in his grave in the cemetery down in the valley, lying beneath the great cedar tree he loved so much. Here comes Patrick now.

Midnight. Just back from the talk. The Sisters were marvelous, the dinner superb, the audience one of the most concentrated and attentive I have ever encountered. As a result I talked an inexcusably long time—from 8:00 until 10:30, without realizing it, as though the audience mesmerized me. Feel terrible, as though I had been sledge-hammered, and am deeply embarrassed to get Brother Pat in so late—though he was most gracious and generous about it.

OCTOBER 13, 1969

Slept finally around 1:00 a.m. and awakened at 8:00, feeling as though I had not rested at all, feeling as though I had been through some fatiguing exercise yesterday, with soreness in muscles and mind. Prepared a large cup of strong coffee, and now I am shedding the fog. We put off Mass until this evening. I will resaturate myself in the silences and solitude, try to work all day today and tomorrow before leaving for Canada on Wednesday. Feel voided, numb, unable even to complete the Morning Offering or the simplest prayer as yet. Well, it will return, the energy and enthusiasm will come with the work and the day and the deeply curative silences.

Now, with the sun full out, with too much muck and fatigue inside me, I decide to put on a recording of Bach, and it blazes out full of humor and vigor, catches my lethargy and pumps life into me. What a marvelous recording by Marie-Claire Alain! This glorious lady plays the Marcussen organs in Aabenraa, Denmark, and Schleswig, Germany. Unbelievable how this work bounds out, fusing with the trees and the haze and the glistening dew-wet grasses, transfuses strength and health into every fiber of my being. Must record this and carry it with me . . . on the tape, I mean. I am glad now for the deadness that led me to put the recording on—otherwise I would never have played it and never have come to know really that such a recording was in existence. I have been seduced (that's the word) by Marie-Claire Alain's recordings of the Handel Organ Concertos. I am even more so by these Bach performances.

Later. Turned on the tape, put the mike in the window, and recorded the Bach while I sat out in the hot October sun and worked on the journals until the heat got too much, and I feared the sweat dropping from my eyebrows and nose might fall on the pages. A lot of breeze this morning, despite the heat, and the trees roared as in a rain. The tape picked up that washing sound, and also the bird songs and monastery bells.

All the goodness, the energy, the peace and happiness has returned in force. I could not help an old puritanical feeling as I sat on the porch surrounded by this glorious Bach and matching beauty in the woods: the feeling that there was something vaguely sinful in taking such pleasure, such sheer enjoyment in this work. It is the happiest work I have ever done in my life, the most satisfying, the deepest adventure. *Black Like Me* was crushing and depressing as a lived experience. *Hermit Like Me* is enthralling as a lived adventure. More than enthralling . . . nourishing in the most robust and jubilant way; overwhelming in its graces, especially when guided by such a hermit as Thomas Merton as I penetrate his interior and exterior existence through these journals of his; studied right here on the very ground where he lived, and there lived also by me under his tutelage; or through him, because we are vastly different men, though similar in our love of the silence and solitude.

Now Marie-Claire Alain plays the "Fantasia" and "Fugue in A Minor," and the dim memory becomes fresh. Of course, this is the work I used to play in a two-piano transcription with my mother a thousand years ago. We even played it in recital a couple of times, and hearing it in this magnificent performance on this great organ, I wonder how we could have dared try it in a two-piano transcription. In those days, we never had heard it on an organ, certainly never in a performance such as this. If we had, we surely would not have attempted any transcription.

I keep reading references to Tom as a musician. Must ask Brother Patrick about this. Tom and I frequently discussed music. He even mentions in his journal that I was going to attempt to get him tapes of Lourié's [Arthur Lourié, French composer] work, but he never gave me the impression that he was a musician at all, a trained one, I mean. In the journals I find frequent allusions to music, sometimes with brief analyses, so certainly he knew music, and it meant a great deal to him. But was this just picked-up knowledge or did he have some formal study? Did he know harmony or counterpoint? The question sounds sappy. It makes no difference. You can certainly be a musician without any such studies. I just need to know how the term is being used.

In the meantime, I am getting high on these glorious performances by Alain—now the "Imitazione" in B Minor (from the "Fantasia con Imitazione" in B Minor). And now the Fugue in D. There is nothing for it. I must replay these later with the tape recorder on. Perhaps late this evening when the stillness returns. Now the wind is too loud in the trees, and I have had to put on a fan here by the desk—all of which the mike would pick up.

I slept in until 8:00, so we will have Mass here tonight at 6:00, Feast of Saint Maurice. I asked Brother Pat to buy a feast-day cake for Brother Maurice (Brother Pat has to go into Bardstown in any case); and then we decided to make it a little more of a celebration, so he will pick up fried chicken legs and some potato salad in addition to the cake. He and Tarcisius will leave them off up here, and right after Mass we will surprise Brother Maurice with the "feast."

It pleases me—Brother Maurice, so quiet, so unobtrusive, who thinks of everything for me, as he did for Tom. He keeps the place clean, supplies the water, brings up the milk and provisions, comes every morning for 6:30 Mass, and is so unobtrusive you don't realize he is here, or that he is the one who gets all the physical things done. After Mass each morning we have a quick breakfast, the dishes are done, the floors swept, the desk washed down, and they are gone almost before I finish brushing my teeth—and it is Brother Maurice who gets it all taken care of, but with a genius for effacing himself and his actions. I only realized lately how marvelous he is in this. He could do these things and never give Tom the impression that he was there.

Father Flavian is an enormous help, more than he realizes. He has a "cool head" indeed, is very careful (without being asked to be, at least not by me) about seeing to it that I am protected. He handled Monsignor Horrigan masterfully over the telephone. He also prohibited all visits up to the hermitage at any one time, on the grounds that it disturbed those monks who make retreats up here, when in reality it was transparently for the purpose of stopping those sudden visits to me. When I am here it gets known, and retreatants were just showing up. Now Father Flavian says no one can come. Though I do not want people denied the privilege of a visit to Tom's hermitage, too many were coming not for that but to see me, and that was a boner. Yesterday I saw some blue shirts in the woods—but they did not come up and, in fact, kept out of sight. Turned out to be three young Franciscans from Cincinnati. They turned back after glimpsing the hermitage through the trees.

So, on November 9, there is a 5:30 dinner, the appearance at 8:00 p.m., and a reception afterward, honoring me—great Lord and what a groan. If they had any idea of really honoring me, they would leave me free to do my work. But no, I will accept (as I already have) and do my best to feel good things about it and act in good grace. I hear the echoes of all the women in my life: my grandmother, my mother, my wife, and my daughter; they have always told me, when I have started grouching about such activities as "receptions," to "be nice." I will be nice, counting on at least a thunderbolt of grace from God.

9:00 p.m., and I am ready for bed. Rain pours lightly but loudly on the browned leaves, and the air, so hot a couple of hours ago during Mass, has turned rapidly cold. Beautiful. At no place else does the rain smell so good and sound so wonderful. No wonder Tom loved to sit by the fire and read and listen to it.

Beautiful, happy Mass tonight. In preparation for Brother Maurice's feast day, I laid out the table, hid all the good things (cake, chicken, and potato salad), and put on the table a bowl of the foulest old tuna salad, with wilted lettuce, blackening, left over from a couple of days ago; and some macaroni in a bowl I found at the rear of the box, left over from God-knows-when. When Father Tarcisius, Brother Pat, and Brother Maurice entered, I greeted them warmly, wished Brother Maurice a happy feast day. He looked forlornly at the table and walked sadly into the kitchen.

At Mass, he chose the reading about God's providing ample wheat and honey "from the rock." Splendid Mass. Then I gave him his presents—the vile little cigar from Father Tarcisius and Brother Pat, and a photograph (of himself) from me. He looked more and more forlorn about my "beautiful tuna salad." Finally I took him off the hook, brought in the good food, and he was overjoyed. We all ate well, but mostly it was the delight of the feast day, the happiness of being together up here at Tom's hermitage.

Rain is blowing in now. Must go close some windows. Stepped outside to see that the temperature has plummeted thirty-five degrees—from eighty-five down to fifty now, which means I will have to sleep under covers tonight and then have a fire in the morning when I get up at 3:15. They will come at noon for Mass. Splendid. That lets me work almost eight hours undisturbed. More than eight really, though I am slow getting started. Now, must get to bed—joy of anticipating sleeping under covers and hearing the rain.

OCTOBER 14, 1969

Cold and damp at 5:00 a.m., with a raw north breeze: down in the forties. I have a good three-log fire blazing now, to take off the chill and dry out the room. It lights up the room so warmly I hate to turn on the lights to type and read. Rain drips steadily into the water barrels and lulls out all other sounds except the bells from the Abbey. Slept deeply from 2:30 until 3:30. Woke up to build the fire and drink a cup of hot coffee, sitting in front of it with my feet on the hearth. These are hours of the rarest happiness when the silence, the dripping of the rain, the popping of the fire, and the blackness of night become prayer, and you are just there involved in all of that, your whole being saying the wordless amens. Fragrance of the fire: charity of the logs that consume themselves for your warmth; charity, too, of the night and rain and chill and silence out there in the woods beyond these walls.

I think of Casals, rising every morning and going to the piano to play Bach "to cleanse the atmosphere," and how there is no need for anything to cleanse the atmosphere of this hermitage.

Nature cleanses it, the fire and its fragrance join with the silence and the solitude and their prayers, and everything is overwhelmingly not in need of any kind of "cleansing." The feel of this thick, glazed ceramic coffee cup against your lips (no razor-thin china here) and the hot coffee meandering down into the belly—all of this takes place in the prayer, pumps the most robust happiness into perceptions.

Lord, when I think of my first visit here alone in the hermitage—the forlorn kind of terror at the immensity of the solitude when I carried in me still the spiritual and nerve-seeped smog of the cities, and wondered if I could bear this kind of solitude, I am astonished.

All you had to do was let it work on you, let it saturate you and rid you of the junk in your body, mind, senses. (Tom always called it an "emptying" that took place initially.) Then the felicity of the very same elements that terrified you took over and filled you: the silence, the solitude, the discomforts, even, banished all hints of loneliness.

The loneliness just does not exist. There is no corner of the being left for it to hide. The joy is pervasive in its quiet and strength: it is there in all you do, in what Thomas Merton called the "rituals" of closing the windows, washing the coffee pot, sweeping straw (for starting the fire) from the hearth back into the fireplace, boiling water for the coffee . . . studying and working. The rituals of caring for the body and caring for the cabin, sweeping dust from the little chapel with its fragrance of incense and cedarwood altar . . . doing this by the warm, reflected light that makes the ikons seem alive, like beloved persons awake and watching you in the dim light.

A pure sense of companionship inundates the hours and dilates the affections. It diminishes with the presence of others. It is flawless only in solitude. No matter how loved the others who come here (to say Mass, to bring supplies), the flawlessness is turned down a bit. It flames back when solitude returns. From time to time, in the predawn hours, especially during the cold and rain, thoughts turn out to the animals that live in the surrounding woods—warm in their nests and holes. The large squirrels yesterday already had thick coats and looked fat and sleek. They do not distract. Only people distract (or people's noises, airplanes, distant guns), and diminish the sense of union with the Christ of the silences. This is no complaint, Lord knows, only the statement of a fact. One loves and wants to see people, but the truest and deepest sense of wholeness comes when the solitude is truest and deepest: when one is emptied of all the junk, and simply functions as a part of nature and silence and odors and feelings, at one's own natural rhythms of spirit and body. Then, tension and guilt become words so strange you think you should look them up in a dictionary.

There is no somberness in this, nothing of the "serious," nothing of the piously structured or planned, no managing of the spirit at all: that would be fatal. No, there is only the most basic cooperation, going along, letting it handle you as it will (and it handles you magnificently if you don't push or try to direct these things).

Tom lived in these predawn hours in secret prayer. The Psalms. There is that, but also, as he knew, the psalms of the rain, the psalms of the odors and crackling of the fire, the psalms of the stars and the clouds and the wind in the trees—all equally eloquent. And also in this context, the psalms of one's coughings and sneezings and coffee drinkings. The psalms of one's sleepings. The psalms of one's heat rash—for in this nothing need be hidden from God, and nothing is lower than any other thing. All things are taken up and become whole in contemplation. One does not waste time sorting them, grading them, evaluating them. They are there as reality, and that is that. They do not offend God, and one does not worry at such times about offending anything or anyone else.

But just the same, after all this about silence . . . now the hooting of an owl out there in the rain . . . in the immense hush of morning in which there is yet no hint of dawn . . . I put on a little Bach that goes right with the atmosphere. The Bach joins me here . . . it comes to be with the fire in the hearth, with the rain, the darkness. It does not come to create any kind of atmosphere, but simply reflects the felicity of this solitude.

Now, later: the first light of dawn. Rain falls steadily. Trees and distant hills emerge from grey mists. White smoke from the chimney drifts southward under the tall pine trees. I have just stepped outside. The thermometer is still in the low 40s, the air fragrant with the smoke and soaked woods.

Now, later again, at 11:00: the day has hardly lightened. It remains dark and chilled, wonderfully kind to the senses. I have worked splendidly all morning. Have just stopped to do more of the "rituals"—filled the kitchen sink with water and soap which promises "blazing whiteness even in cold water." I put my one dress shirt in to soak because it occurs to me—with what regret—that I must leave early in the morning for Canada. As damp and cold as it is, the shirt will have to "drip dry" a long time.

Much later. I can hardly bear to think of leaving this place and this work. Have not come to a good stopping place. But the time is ending here. We will have Mass tonight (around 6:30) in the chapel here, and then Brother Paul is coming to show me the film of Tom's Bangkok conference, a quick supper and we will be done for this trip. I must get to bed early. Am very tired, and also because I must get up early in the morning. I need to leave here by 5:45 to catch a 7:55 flight to Canada.

6:00 p.m. . . . . shaved . . . almost slit my throat and bled like a Kentucky stuck hog. But to bandage it with the materials here took some doing. I look like a war-wounded, *gueule cassée.* The sun is out, but the evening remains cold. Clear day tomorrow for flying. I had really hoped for a blizzard that would ground all planes and allow me to stay on here.

Fourth Visit

NOVEMBER 5, 1969...

NOVEMBER 5, 1969

Wednesday. Returned here to Gethsemani last night.

Cold. Brother Patrick met me at the gate, and we drove up the hill to the hermitage where Brother Maurice was waiting. Brother Maurice, who thinks of everything, had the table set for three, some hot chili and rice, a blazing fire in the fireplace. We ate a big supper and then spent the time until 10:00 looking at the photos I brought of Tom's Asian trip. They cleaned up the dishes, brought a load of wood for the night, and then left, very late for monks who usually retire around 7:30. When I went back to get into my pajamas, I noted that all of the clothes I had left here had been washed and ironed and were stacked neatly in a box on a chair. It is another world where time is taken to do these things, where there is the thought to do them.

I wanted to write in this last night, but now I am caught in the new time (usually it takes much longer), and my body told me 10:00 was late, late. I put on my pajamas, went to bed, piled on the quilts and blankets, and slept immediately and profoundly—awakened at 5:30 a.m., which seems *late* here where the normal waking hour is 3:00 (but which would seem painfully early anywhere else). Up, put the water on to boil, built the fire—a good big one warming the room now. Live coals in the fireplace before I started the new fire. Now, with a large cup of coffee, the fire crackling at my back, night blackness over the frosted hills and woods surrounding me, I begin work. I feel the outside drop away, the nerves recover a normal health in the silence and solitude . . . the sense of spontaneous prayer in all activity, or lack of it, in all things, returns.

At 6:30 trees begin to detach themselves from a predawn sky that is overcast; the scene is all monochrome, cold, absolutely still. It lightens rapidly, with no color. It is a time to sit and let the stillness instruct the senses: to think whatever thoughts come. To let it work on you.

Later: nearly 7:00. Have had the lights off, drinking coffee by firelight and the grey light of dawn. Just checked. The temperature outside is thirty-eight, while inside the cabin the fire has brought it up to sixty-five. It is now light enough to see the brilliance of color in the leaves outside. The trees close to the cabin, the ones Tom planted for their color, are almost intact; but the larger ones in the distance are almost bare of leaves, which makes the massive pines that much more luxuriant in appearance.

I have created a problem here without realizing it. Piedy, Susan, and Mandy are coming for the weekend to participate in the affairs surrounding the official opening of the Merton Study Center drive. They will stay here in the guest house (a kind of motel across the way). I suggested to Brother Pat that I would go down and stay there with them on Saturday and Sunday nights.

Well, it appears that although they are "dialoguing" about this (letting men spend the nights with their families in the "women's quarters"), still, except in extraordinary cases, these quarters are separated and segregated, and there might be some squawk from the elderly lady who runs the women's quarters about having a man sleep in there.

"If it's going to cause any problems," I said to Brothers Patrick and Maurice, "then I'll just sleep up here at the hermitage and let the ladies sleep down in the 'women's quarters.'" They said they would feel Mrs. Gannon out about this, see what her reaction was. So, the big question now, "down at the Abbey," is whether or not Griffin gets to sleep with his wife during her visit here. Mrs. Gannon, who can be the most charming hostess in the world, apparently sees all sorts of complications in breaking with this older tradition of separation in the guest quarters. Understandable in times when there are a lot of guests here; but at this time of the year, there are none. I suggested to Brother Pat that it might be simpler if, for those two nights, we just took motel rooms in nearby Bardstown and left Mrs. Gannon without such conflicts. He thought that was unnecessary.

I recall when Robert and Gaby Casadesus went to visit Solesmes and stayed in the hotel across the street. I asked, in some surprise, why Robert did not occupy "la maison rose," and he replied: "I'd rather sleep with my wife than alone in the guest house."

I feel rather bad about inadvertently facing the community here with a problem that has its ludicrous elements: how to let a man sleep with his wife when both of them are here together. The community favors it, but the dialoguing has not come to a final decision in the matter, and the lady in charge of the "women's quarters" has not been consulted in sufficient depth about it.

I started to say, and then bit my tongue: "Would it help if we took an oath before Mrs. Gannon not to 'do anything' during our joint occupancy of one of the women's quarters beds?"

All kinds of speculation arise from such a situation. I recall the sign in the motel room at Monterey years ago. "Immorality in this room is strictly prohibited." And although there is nothing remotely immoral in a man's sleeping with his wife, perhaps such a sign in the guest-quarters rooms might assuage the situation. My temptation is to send down all sorts of memos to the community about this. Perhaps a sign: "Make Prayers, Not Love." But no, that is more obscene than any, because it implies a contradiction between praying and loving.

I must get off of this kind of speculation. It is too wild. On the contrary, I am going to play the role of "victim," quietly, with dignity and serenity and piety, so that all through the community they will look at me when I go down for conventual Mass on Sunday, carrying my head high, and say to themselves, "There goes that poor man who was defrauded of his marital rights because we did not finish our dialoguing about desegregating the guest houses (or more exactly the 'men's quarters and the women's quarters') in time to allow him these rights, these God-given rights." And they will cast stricken and sympathetic glances in my direction.

On the other hand, there is something a bit jarring about the very idea of people sleeping together on monastic properties, even outside the enclosure, no matter how God-given these marital rights might be. Something pretty tactless about it, and I am sorry I ever brought it up. I do hope they will not discuss this in chapter—whether or not an exception should be made to allow Griffin to sleep with his wife—because all these implications of marital rights will be there beneath the surface of the discussion. Since they vote on everything now in the community, I do feel embarrassed that 120 Trappist monks will have their contemplative silences disturbed by the intrusion of this kind of issue and be obliged to cast a yea or a nay vote on whether my wife and I sleep together or apart during our *nights* here (no problem about our being together during the day . . . that's perfectly okay). The community vote, of course, would be yea . . . but that leaves Mrs. Gannon with the final decision in any case.

So now, early in the week, the drama has begun. All kinds of speculations enter. They will know that I have been up here a week in the solitude and silences—a week without lovemaking, and so *surely* it will happen if they allow us to sleep together. Also, the proper atmosphere of the monastery is to create a lovingness which would make union, sanctioned in the sacrament of marriage as a virtue, that much more inevitable. But can anyone that crippled-up really do anything? they will wonder. Then they will remember that when I was here three years ago, I was in a wheelchair and managed to get my wife pregnant. So now that I am not in a wheelchair, I could certainly "do things."

I have a horrible feeling that my sappy suggestion that I would like to sleep with my wife while she is here has created a major issue that cannot now be stopped, and that the whole community is involved in whether or not we "succeed" (sleep together) or "fail" (sleep separately). It may become harrowing by the end of the week. I will be quiet, say nothing more, let events take their course. This is one of those unstoppable melodramas that sometimes occur in religious communities.

Brother Patrick's final comment last night was, "Don't worry. I'll try to be diplomatic and see what I can work out for you. No, I'll ask Father David (guestmaster) to handle it—he's very good about such things."

Brother Maurice added positively and firmly: "Sure, I don't see any reason why you couldn't."

Tom is surely laughing in his grave.

At 9:30 the sun is out so brilliant it hurts the eyes—a great surprise after the somber morning, because it suddenly appeared a moment ago. Beautiful and brilliant.

Someone has cleaned the windows and done such a superb job that I have the feeling there is no glass in them at all. Incredible views out all the windows of the motionless scarlet and vermilion leaves of the underbrush through the woods.

Late evening. The fire blazes, the countryside is soft and radiant with the setting sun and the beginning of a brilliant dusk that makes the leaves almost glow in redness. Still, absolutely still. Nothing moves as the light fades rapidly. Incredible silence and peace. Soon they will come, and we will celebrate Mass here. Must close this down for the moment so we can use the table for supper. A good fire blazes in the fireplace behind me. It is almost hot in here.

Magnificent moments as the day turns to night. I stood on the porch, with all the lights out, in the tremendous stillness, and realized that only in such solitude do the realities come starkly clear, and only in their clarity is man overwhelmed by God's mercy. I perceive something of what Tom perceived profoundly. How to portray this incredible, mercy-filled starkness?

Tonight, feast of St. Martin of Porres. We celebrated a beautiful Mass, deeply felt because Brother Martin of Porres came up and joined us. He helped fix the water and was very exhausted. We had a sliver of cake and made the occasion as festive as we could to celebrate his feast day. Then we went through the photos.

The room is quite warm tonight. It is 9:00, and I am ready to crawl into the bed. We had a great chortle out of the sleeping situation here, which they saw as more and more ridiculous the more we discussed how I had received permission to sleep with my own wife. Brother Pat told them this morning that I had offered to get a motel in Bardstown. "And call a press conference," I interjected. And how all this would look in the national press when it was learned I had been denied the privilege of sleeping with my wife here.

Cannot resist this quote from *The Geography of Lograire*, that amazing final poetic work of Thomas Merton:

"50. So Christ went down to stay with them Niggers and took his place with them at table. He said to them, 'It is very simple, much simpler than you imagine.' They replied, 'You have become a white man and it is not so simple at all.'"

NOVEMBER 6, 1969

6:00 a.m. Still and calm. The stars are brilliant in a sky that begins to lighten in the east. Last night Brother Martin de Porres hooked up the heater, so the room is not as chilled out as it was yesterday morning.

A restless night, night of nightmares. An interminable one in which I was in a cheap hotel room somewhere trying to telephone my wife, but the lines would get crossed, and always there was another conversation between two gossipy young people, discussing in the most banal way their friends.

"Yeah, Louise and Pat have started going together now."

"Don't you think Eldridge Cleaver is *weird*?"

And the hour grew later, and I was consumed with loneliness and sickness not to get the call through to my wife. I never have such dreams ordinarily. Why here? Tom had them too—he talks of them a great deal in his diaries. Perhaps it is part of the purging that takes place here . . . the "emptying," as he called it . . . where the unconscious pours out.

No need to hide it here: here one is called to face squarely the realities of oneself: of one's body, one's mind, one's conscious and unconscious life; not deliberately—it is just part of the solitary life, part of the natural transparency of self that is accomplished in silence and solitude when one does not try to direct or guide it, but simply goes along with it. These dreams of deep anguish are part of the filtering process that takes place within—removing the impediments to love, the inner murkiness.

As man has to be converted over again each hour, so man has to be aware of his profound vulnerability each moment, because the world demands in each an illusion of strength that amounts to an illusion of invulnerability: thus the illusion of growth that is not authentic growth at all. Here, where man gives himself over to the times of nature, to the inner silences as well as the surrounding ones—where a man just gives himself over—the growth is more natural, not that unspeakable hot-house growth of the world. The reality he faces is the reality of his vulnerability, which is why he can hardly escape the awareness of God's mercy: here, in the solitude and silence, the world's image, the "mystique" of what a hermit should be simply falls away, and what *is* is so far removed from the "mystique" that one becomes attuned to what is. Then one becomes deeply irritated with the mystique, with the demands that one play "roles" in all contacts with the public that demands one act out the mystique rather than the reality. This is a basic conflict that Tom knew well, and why his refusal to "edify" anyone caused some discomfort when he was placed back into merely pietistic situations in his human contacts.

He reacted uncomfortably to any contact that suggested: "Edify me. Help me to become what I think you are." Because he knew that what they thought he was in no way coincided with what he knew himself to be: a unique human individual struggling to make himself ever more conformable to God's will *for him*; not part of some great stereotype that could conform to holy role playing. For him to become liberated from everything that was not God required modes that might in no way be right for another: to liberate the other from any desire to "become what he thought Father Louis was," to liberate the other from everything that impeded him from functioning as the unique person with the unique vocation that he might have. "God wants you to be yourself and to grow." God does not want you to become a part of some mediocre monolith.

Everyone who got to know him was aware of this: he never sought to change another into a role that conformed necessarily to his reality. Those who had the privilege of a relationship with Tom found that he fixed on you and did not fix you on him. His gift of himself was always concentrated on the other, never on himself. Only after his death did many of his friends know a great deal about him. His hidden life was quite deeply private and hidden. No one, not even those who were very close to him, really knew his "secret prayer." He revealed those facts of himself that were proper to each of his friends: but underneath this was his vocation as monk and hermit—something between himself and God alone, something that had to remain secret because these things become distorted when known.

Writer. Two parts of him: The writer who deliberately set out to write books, articles, etc. The writer whose books were the overflow of his "meditations on paper." His diaries, completely free and undisciplined, provided the germ of much of his writing.

Poet-Metaphysician. He listened until he heard the essences: his late poems, and those profoundly felt, are the ones devoid of the cliches and other weaknesses according to canons of criticism. As a result he was sometimes the despair of connoisseurs who have all these criteria worked out: connoisseurs of the spiritual life, let's face it, who had less profound spiritual experience, but who had theologized more; and who, like other connoisseurs, had acquired their prejudices and criteria at a speculative level rather than an experiential one. Thomas Merton sometimes threw such men into distress because his lived experience would not always correspond to their structured analyses.

Fifth Visit

DECEMBER 5, 1969...

DECEMBER 5, 1969

Arrived here at Gethsemani around 7:00 last evening. Brothers Maurice and Patrick and Father Tarcisius came up and we celebrated Mass and then had supper. Since December 3 was Father Tarcisius's birthday, I bought some eggnog in a little store on the way and also brought him a book. Brother Maurice has cut a great supply of cedarwood, which is neatly stacked up on each side of the fireplace. Cold here—around twenty degrees, but with some sun this morning. Great joy to be back.

Picked up Thomas Merton's 1966 journal from Tommie [Mrs. O'Callaghan, a Merton trustee] yesterday at the airport. When they left after 10:00 last night, I began reading and could not stop; finally dozed off at 2:00 and slept until 9:30 this morning. Very unhappy about that. Want to get back on the schedule of rising and working at 3:00 a.m.

Did not keep this journal faithfully last month. Piedy, Susan, and Mandy came for the appearance at Bellarmine. A great time. Now, an overwhelming workload, and I must get at it.

A good steady fire going now—not one of Brother Maurice's holocausts, but a good easy fire. The smoke perfumes the woods like pinon. A strange, hazed, whitish sunlight breaks through thin clouds.

Now—late in the afternoon—past 5:00, and dusk is long and grey over the land. It is cold outside, up only into the thirties today. Good day's work, but Lord there is so much of it to get through. I feel great—happy and full of contentment. This work is intense, but without strain, and by late evening I am completely and healthfully exhausted. Then the Mass and supper and bed.

The fire going steadily all day, the room is now up to seventy degrees F., and the bedroom is up to about fifty-five. The little electric heater, by which I dress in the morning, went out when I took it into the bathroom, so I will not have that to break the cold in those two rooms until something can be done to repair it.

Night—8:30. Beautiful Mass with the new liturgy, utterly simple now. We used the new hosts—a kind of wheat bread (flat) that is full of the fragrance and taste of the fields, marvelous in its symbolisms. We had it last night, and ate it by sitting around in a circle, as though not a real supper, but a simple, symbolic bread-breaking. But it is clumsy when simply put into the mouth by the celebrant. Today they called and got permission from the archbishop for us to take it in our hands. So Father broke it, put it in a basket on a linen napkin, offered the basket, saying, "The body of Christ," and we took our own, saying, "Amen." A marvelous and beautiful Mass.

DECEMBER 6, 1969

Sleepless night, and now at 2:45 a.m. I give up trying to sleep and get up to begin the day—at least I will surely sleep tonight.

I retired early enough . . . at 9:30 . . . and just lay there. I had begun to doze when I smelled smoke. I got up to investigate and found that one of the logs in the fireplace had rolled forward on the hearth. I fixed that and returned to bed. No sleep. I lay there, perfectly peaceful and perfectly happy and still no sleep. At midnight I got up, remembering a passage I needed to check from *Conjectures*; checked that in a few minutes and returned to the kitchen; drank a glass of milk thinking that might put me to sleep. Returned to bed and lay there wide awake, but in deep physical repose. Got to wondering what I could possibly say to the community here when I talk with them on December 10 (anniversary of Tom's death). What could I say that would be interesting, that they do not already know? That will not insult them with its idiocy? Prayed even, for sleep, but no sleep at all. Checked the clock: 1:20. I knew I was messing up. Hanna and Bob Shepherd [old Merton friends] are coming at 11:30. If I slept now, I would be even more groggy and would sleep late and not get any work done before they got here. Well, no great problem, I told myself, and relaxed deeply. Wider awake than ever. At 2:20 I renounced the effort, got up, fixed hot coffee, put on a dozen eggs to hard-boil, went through my larder to see what I could serve the Shepherds for lunch. Not much—some sardines, some ripe olives, some good olive oil. So I decided to make a mayonnaise to go with the sardines and to go with the fruit and cheese (found cans of pineapple, peaches, and have a few bananas). Contemplated making *oeufs a la russe*, quite seriously, until I realized I have no gelatin, no meat stock, no carrots, and above all no little moulds to put them in.

So now, I sit here and prepare to work on the journals. The eggs boil away in the kitchen. I have a metal cup here with two eggs warming up to room temperature to make the mayonnaise later. They are remarkably beautiful in this light. Must photograph them.

Now, about 4:00. I have let the fire die so I can remove some of the ashes. Chill around my legs. Must clean the fireplace and build a new fire. Stepped out on the porch. Thirty degrees F. outside.

Later. Filled the bucket with ashes, tried to pick it up and got burned. Carried it out with a towel and have a good new fire blazing.

Note that in the early months of 1966, Tom lived extraordinarily halcyon and grace-filled days here as a hermit. Tremendous journal entries.

Later. Stopped to have some breakfast—hard-boiled eggs and a glass of milk. Very good. Have drunk too much coffee in these early morning hours, and the egg and milk soothe the nervousness caused by the coffee—a question not of nervousness (for I am at great peace), but of irritated nerves in the belly.

7:15 a.m. And now, as I suspected, I am getting bleary-eyed and very tired. Ate two more hard-boiled eggs and a glass of milk and feel drowsy. Will surely have to lie down for at least a little nap. Will set the alarm for 10:00. Must shave and dress and get things ready for the company at 11:30.

Monochrome light over the countryside. Is it clear? I cannot tell. It may be. Right now it looks snowy.

6:00 p.m. Strange day. Great fatigue and a couple of cat-naps after all night working. Very nice visit and lunch with the Bob Shepherds. We have arranged to go to Louisville on Tuesday to hear John Jacob Niles's settings of some of Tom's poems in a private concert at the Niles home—not Louisville, of course; it is near Lexington. Hanna and Bob Shepherd are two of the most comfortable people I have ever known—absolutely natural and unaffected and charming.

Now, it is completely dark over the countryside. I await the arrival of the monks for Mass here. Feel that I will certainly sleep tonight.

Tomorrow and Monday should be quiet and solitary work days. Although I have done a great deal, worked all night, still today has been a kind of mess of unsustained work, and as a result I feel groggy, stupid—but deeply contented. Such a marvelous place, particularly in the early long hours before dawn, and these lovely silent and still hours of early evening.

I put on Bach—the ravishing performances by Marie-Claire Alain of the eight little Organ Preludes and Fugues. The grey cinderblock walls of this hermitage seem to absorb and echo the joys of this robust music. The whole place dances. What a blessing, too, to have Mass each night with this marvelous new liturgy.

Later. Beautiful Mass and a good simple supper—prunes, bread, butter, milk, a hard-boiled egg, some ripe olives. Now at 8:30 they have gone, and I am ready to retire. A warmer current outside (forty degrees F. on the porch), and a light rain has begun to fall.

DECEMBER 7, 1969

5:00 a.m. Back to a better schedule, finally. Read a little last night, but was asleep before 9:30. Good, comfortable sleep, waking occasionally to hear the rain that fell all night, and is still coming down.

A good slow fire burns now, a few moments later, and the wind blows around the windows. I turned on the porch light to see that rain had blown over the concrete almost to the door. I await the dawn to see what the country looks like after such a night's soaking. Odd, but in a place like this, such a sight can create an anticipation of some excitement—or rather the anticipation of such a sight. In the solitary life, such "little" things become joys—they are not swamped by a lot of other distractions and the fatigue of nervous attrition. In the world, often at least, it will simply be rainy, nasty weather, good or bad for the crops. Here, it takes on another character altogether: it is a kind of music; it is God's gift to us, along with the wind in the tall pine trees. You don't evaluate it according to anything else (whether or not you would prefer it *not* to be raining)—it is as welcome as the sun. It is one of the things one embraces, as one would embrace the sun. It is just there, and you revel in its sounds and smells and feels, and wait for the daylight because that will bring a new scene, a new dimension. It really is of no great importance, but the anticipation fills you with eagerness.

7:15. Still dark. I open the door and hear the rain fall with a gurgling sound, like a brook nearby. It has probably soaked the ground and is running off. Decide to have a breakfast for a change. Will stop and cook some eggs.

Now, a pale grey dawn over the soaked countryside. The rain increases the sense of privacy, of isolation. Temptation to turn off the lights, but it is still not light enough outside to permit any kind of work without the supplementary illumination.

Almost noon, and the rain continues its steady fall, without wind and almost without sound—more visible than audible. The clouds hang low and the knobs across the valley are blue-black. It looks as though it could really storm this afternoon. I will be glad if it does. Am going to call and suggest Brother Patrick not come up at noon. He will have a real problem, I'm afraid, getting up the hill after such a soaking.

DECEMBER 8, 1969

Immaculate Conception. And the anniversary of Thomas Merton's arrival in Bangkok, and the date of his last journal entry, and the date of his last letters to me and to some of his other friends; letters we received, of course, after his death on the tenth.

Jim Andrews of the *National Catholic Reporter* came for a

retreat. When I discovered he was here, I had Brother Pat invite him up for Mass and supper last night. We have talked a number of times on the telephone, and I had been much impressed with him and wanted to meet him. He came and shared Mass with us in the little chapel here. He took some photos, had supper with us, and did a little interview about Thomas Merton and the biography. He will stay on until Wednesday.

Later—7:00 a.m. The sky begins to show some lightness. I turn off the light and eat breakfast (banana and a glass of milk) by the firelight. Perfect quiet in here. I open the door and hear roosters far in the distance—no other sound at all. It is not raining, and there is no wind in the trees.

Later: Streaked dawn—so perhaps it is clearing. I am disreputable—need a haircut and must find some way to take a bath. The bathroom remains so cold and there is so little hot water, it takes some managing. Today may be clear and it may warm up. The dawn looks promising.

Later: 8:00 a.m. Have washed a couple of the windows that got a little grimed over from the wood fire; and have also done my "laundry"—washed the underwear and socks, and have them hanging on chairs outside where they will take a long time to dry, because the temperature is only thirty degrees and the humidity must be very high after all the rains. But the sun is out and there are only thin clouds.

DECEMBER 9, 1969

6:00 o'clock. Mercifully back in the hermitage after a great day in Lexington at the home of Rena and John Jacob Niles [the Kentucky folk musician], where he gave Brother Patrick and me a private concert of his Merton Songs—his two cycles on the poems of Thomas Merton, performed with incredible beauty by Jacqueline Roberts, soprano, and Janelle Pope, pianist. The settings just floored me. I had been led to believe they were rather like Delius, which I did not find at all. They are deeply felt settings, with marvelous melodic lines and splendid accompaniments. I did not know that he was a trained musician until afterward, when I learned he had studied with Vincent d'Indy. I really did know, with the first notes, that he was a thoroughly schooled technician. These are not folk songs, nothing like the marvelous things he did before. They are art songs of high quality, particularly high melodic quality. They remind me (not harmonically or melodically) of the great cycles of Schubert or Schumann. They come from deep within, give an impression of great naturalness and spontaneity, and contain settings like "For My Brother Reported Missing in Action" that are simply overwhelming.

I was so devastated and startled that I felt the strain tremendously. But I began to get myself together on the second part of the cycle, and managed to do some photos of the extraordinarily expressive Niles face. He is seventy-six. After the two cycles, he got out the dulcimer and sang us a few songs with the two young ladies: "Amazing Grace" (which I have never liked, but which was fantastic in his version); then "Go Way from My Window" and "I Wonder As I Wander." All of these are his earlier compositions, as well as "Black Is the Color of My True Love's Hair."

I am going to write John Reeves at CBC, Toronto, and see if we cannot do a documentary with these songs and this man. It will have to be TV though, because one has to see him.

DECEMBER 10, 1969

First anniversary of Tom's death.

Last evening we celebrated Mass late—beginning at 8:00 p.m., because Dan Walsh could only get here at that time. He and Father Tarcisius concelebrated a memorial Mass for Tom. Today at 11:00, Father Flavian will come up and celebrate the anniversary Mass. Tommie O'Callaghan will join us for that and then a little lunch. Colonel Hawk [Rogers, Bardstown restaurant owner] is sending a baked hen. I am making mayonnaise and a salad. We bought a crummy-looking apple pie in Bardstown yesterday to serve as a kind of dessert. Was very tired from the trip to Lexington, but the melodies of the Niles-Merton songs would not let me sleep. I read in the journals and marked passages (or noted them on a paper) to transcribe. Day of great stillness now at 9:00 a.m. Nothing moves. Heavily overcast skies. A cold winter landscape—no sound at all, not even birds.

DECEMBER 11, 1969

Yesterday was full. Father Flavian came and said a very beautiful Mass for the anniversary of Thomas Merton's death. Tommie O'Callaghan joined us (Brothers Patrick and Maurice, too) and remained for lunch. In fact she brought a great deal of food, and since we weren't expecting it, we had prepared lunch too (Colonel Hawk's hen—which he didn't let us pay for), and a green salad. We stayed at the table here in the hermitage until about 4:00, when Tommie had to leave. The rain poured, and Brother Maurice took her down in the jeep to her car. We had a good talk, a good quiet day in commemoration of Tom's death; but it left me very exhausted—much more so than a day's hard work would have.

Then, last night, I went down to speak to the community, to tell them what I am doing up here and how the work is coming. The ground is so soaked and the rain so persistent, we did not know if we could get down. Actually the jeep went off the path and almost turned over. We had to get out and let Father Flavian get it out, which he did by maneuvering the car onto a new path. When we got down to the Abbey, my black suit was streaked with mud and my shoes were heavily mudded. I took off my pants and shoes and left them in the guest room to dry. Then I lay down and dozed. Brother Patrick quietly came in and brushed the dried mud out of the suit and cleaned up the shoes—over my protestations. "Let me do that," I called from the little alcove where I was sleeping, but without the strength to get up and go do it. He insisted that he was glad to do it, no problem, etc., and I went on to sleep for a quick but deep nap.

When I woke up he had gone, the suit was hanging up on the wall, and my shoes were beside my bed. I hurried to dress. We went to the chapter room where Abbot Flavian gave a brief introduction, and I spoke informally for thirty minutes. They halfway wanted me to stay down for the night (because of the dangerous condition of the trails leading up here). The thought of missing a night in this hermitage was painful . . . especially since I feared I might not sleep down there (different bed, much more heat in the guest rooms), and then not be able to get up at my usual hour of 3:00 and begin work.

Brothers Maurice and Pat brought me back, creeping up in four-wheel drive. We made it fine, had a little light supper, and they left me at 9:30. I went to bed immediately. Read *Zen and the Birds of Appetite* until the pages swam in my drowsiness, and turned off the light at 10:00. Profound sleep. Woke up to a cold cabin, got the fires going, got hot water on for the coffee, and came to life.

Now at dawn, perfectly still, perfectly silent, a grey and misty scene from the front window.

Later. I ordered a little AM/FM radio to get the news and weather yesterday. There is one good FM station in Louisville for classical music. It comes in clear and fine. Now, however, I almost wish I had not. The news is a terrible intrusion. I have decided to keep the radio completely silent except for the 6:00 a.m. news, and perhaps a newscast in the evening. They are predicting some possible snow mingled with the rain. But decidedly this is no place for a radio—even turned off it is a symbol of a connection with the outside, lessening the sense of isolation and solitude.

Strange day. It is almost 4:00 p.m. now and I am utterly exhausted. And have been so since shortly before noon. It is not a natural exhaustion, but some sort of awful physical depletion, as though I had worked too hard too long—and I have not, in fact. Though I find that company (like yesterday), even when I enjoy the visits (as yesterday), ends up being in such basic conflict with the rightness of this silence and solitude that I feel a terrible strain even when I am not nervous or uncomfortable. Every such day is not only a day lost, it is two days lost, because it almost always takes me at least part of another day to get over the physical effects. What I really feel the need for is prolonged time in bed. In fact, I have spent a good part of the last two hours on and off the bed, reading *Zen and the Birds of Appetite*, then sinking (in a way that nearly frightens me) into naps to which I cannot abandon myself, from which I find myself struggling back. I feel the need to rest until the strength returns, and at the same time the need to remain conscious of these precious hours of silence, these precious sights of the country, this magnificent and curative solitude.

Now, I am up, have added water to the chicken carcass I am boiling for soup, have fixed myself some very strong coffee, and try to come back to life. Everything is a great effort. If I were wise, I would probably take a couple of aspirins and go to bed and sleep it out.

In all of this there is a profound infusion of happiness, even physical happiness—ravishment, really, to be in this hermitage, with a good cedar fire behind me, so dark I have to use the lights already at 4:00 p.m., isolated and surrounded by these rain-soaked, absolutely still woods and the fine mist that obscures them except up close. The leafless branches of the tree at the front porch glisten with drops of rain that cover it like crystal jewels.

DECEMBER 13, 1969

My mother's birthday—her sixty-ninth. No way even to get a telegram to her. Will offer the evening's Mass for her today—in gratitude for all she is and has been, in gratitude for all her sacrifices and dedication to this family.

Am working too hard to be a good hermit at the moment . . . at least not a good Trappist kind of hermit. No complaint; I am having a glorious time; but yesterday did not even have time to make these journal notes. The only real problem is that I have not been getting proper sleep: working until after midnight (after 2:00 this a.m.). Father Tarcisius told me a "good" Trappist gets seven hours. And it is needed. I feel the tiredness which would be really bad in the world, which is bad enough here, though its effects are actually minimal because of the great happiness I have in the silence and solitude. But how I wish I could have had more time in these days to experience the silence and solitude in a more attentive manner! Only today and part of tomorrow left on this trip, and still so much to do. I set myself amounts to get done. Brother Patrick brings those things up, and then I sometimes find they take longer or involve a lot more time, and at the end of the visit I try to come to a good stopping place. Yesterday, Brother Patrick brought more materials, but seeing that I was at work and preoccupied by it, he quickly took off after lunch. I was working on that difficult section about the calligraphy, trying not to use the word Zen (which carries such a tone of false meanings to most Western minds, even those who think they practice it). I got it done after at least seven or eight rewrites.

Beautiful Mass last night. Brother Paschal joined us again and for the last time. He is in retreat this week prior to his ordination to the priesthood on December 20, after which he will go to the Trappists in Chile. He has been coming in the evenings from his hermitage (Father Flavian's) for Mass and supper. A wonderful man. I realized only as he left last evening that we were saying goodbye. He will be ordained and gone to South America before I return.

We are really being poor these last days. I spent all my money on provisions and equipment (new electric toothbrush, an electric beater for the kitchen, etc.), and we have about run out of provisions and money both. I am down to $6 which I must hold for tip money for the return trip to Texas. They will provide whatever is needed in the way of food from the monastery of course—no danger of starving; but still I begin to eye the peanut butter jar.

Just went in to make more coffee and glanced at myself in the mirror in the bathroom. Disreputable. I just get right out of bed and go to the typewriter without even running a comb through my hair. At midmorning, I begin to repair the things—brush my teeth, take the diabetes medication, but have not taken time to shave in three days. The bathroom is too cold for any but the most necessary activities. I will shave a bit later in the morning when I have hopefully developed more "strength of character" (as my grandmother used to call it). I think of Dom James's motto, "All for Jesus through Mary with a Smile," and feel horribly inadequate at times like this when it takes what I conceive to be heroic courage even to go to the bathroom. Down to twenty degrees last night. Not much warmer yet this morning. Thank God at least there is a bathroom, and I do not have to go out to the little outhouse in the woods. Anyway, I am disreputable and must find time and strength and courage to do something about it. There is just enough hot water for a very careful quick bath. If you don't manage it right, you end up under a shower that is surely colder than any Finnish snow that could be experienced after sauna.

But the day is clear, brilliant.

I dedicate these days and all my awareness in prayer (and my unawareness, too) to my brother and his wife, who is very nearly dead from cancer, imploring God's mercy and consolations on him at this agonizing time for both of them: of course, it is harder to look on. She is so deeply sedated that, although she is in agony, she perhaps, I pray, does not realize it too much.

Later. Nearly noon. Managed to get a call through to my mother, to wish her a happy birthday. We talked mostly about my brother and his wife. She dies with such slowness. It is such an agony for him. I should be at my brother's side. My mother reassured me that Jackie and Ham are doing everything to help. Mother feels the same way as I do—that we should be there even if we can't do anything; but Edgar said there was nothing we could do and he would hardly be able to see us. She lingers.

Masha, on unlimited morphine, suffers still ungodly spasms of agony. The tumor on her side is now so huge they cannot put a gown on her. In spite of all the sedation, she is perfectly lucid—even wants to go home, which is now impossible, of course. She is making the arrangements with Edgar and Jackie—asked them to take all of her jewels to Jackie's house, see that the bills were paid, etc. Her only direct reference to it, however, was to ask the other night: "Why does it take so long to die?"

Such things destroy me.

Sixth Visit

JANUARY 15, 1970 . . .

JANUARY 15, 1970

Back in the hermitage, almost 10:00 p.m., and no hours were ever more joy-filled. I got in from Boston, after endless delays, around 7:00. Brothers Patrick, Maurice, and Father Tarcisius brought me up in the four-wheel car through the moonlit, snow-covered countryside. We unpacked the car, came in where a fire already flamed in the fireplace, got things unpacked, and said a beautiful, joyful Mass in the little chapel, made doubly eloquent as I realized their "surprise" for me would be the reserved Sacrament. They had got permission. Snow reflected the moonlight outside our windows. Inside, the great happiness of Mass in that chapel and the realization that I would have the reserved Sacrament with me up here alone during the next days of solitary work. No need to try to explain the transformation of this Presence from the magnificence of the earlier solitude to the absolute felicity of this one. Great God, an overwhelming happiness floods through these hours before I retire. To help celebrate the event, they bought some chicken and dumplings (canned), and we had that with some peas for supper. Very good. We talked, we had a glorious time, always aware that in the tabernacle in the next room was the reserved Sacrament, lighted by a dim little altar lamp.

How I have longed for these first moments alone in this cottage—now more isolated than before by the heavy snows. A good cedar fire in the fireplace warms my back. The house is clean, the dishes washed and put away, the night a marvel of serenity. I wanted only to make these brief notes before retiring so I can get up on time (at 3:00 a.m.) to begin tomorrow.

JANUARY 16, 1970

Slept the alarm through, and now I drink the first coffee, looking out to the first dawn over a landscape of whitest snow that glints where the light strikes it just right . . . a still and silent landscape that goes in harmony with the tremendous happiness I feel here . . . the overwhelming contentment. Coffee water boils in the kitchen with a steam-shedding sound, the reserved Sacrament dazzles the atmosphere from the chapel beside me, the day comes alive, and within me it births in a kind of timeless Eden.

The only movement outside is that of birds and the drip of ice from the eaves.

Later now, the sun is full out and the light brilliant.

Later—afternoon—2:15: and nothing much gets done because I sit here in this magnificent silence and watch the sun move tree shadows across the snow, interrupting this only to go into the chapel and stay with the Blessed Sacrament. Just sit there and watch the white, reflected light against the white-washed stone walls of that tiny room. I did go out for a while and photograph at close range the snow, the deer tracks, the bits of golden weed stems that pop up in isolated little patches through the snow, smelling the pines, smelling the wood smoke (so like piñon) from my fireplace. I spent a long, long time, until finally my feet were frozen.

Now, later, almost 5:00, and the sun has disappeared. Dusk is near—utter stillness outside, grey snows, greyer skies, a monochrome landscape looking even colder than it is. I have built up the fire that warms my back as I watch the cold landscape turning toward night. Soon the light will be gone and the jeep headlamps will come up the hill to bring Mass and supper.

Long, long twilight. It is 6:00, and the light has scarcely dimmed outside, though some color came into the sky through the woods to the west, a brilliant vermilion glow, startling in the greys. Now, however, it fades rapidly, the snow seeming to become whiter as the sky darkens and the woods become black masses of silhouette. I have had to turn on a light but will turn it off again soon. The moments of early dawn and late dusk are similar in the qualities of silence they evoke, and everything in me defers to them. I understand it is supposed to turn colder with snow flurries. How glorious if I should get snowed in here.

8:20 p.m. One of the most beautiful Masses I have ever experienced, full of scriptural passages about the snows and the creation of the elements by God, full of the fragrance of breads, like the remembered foods of one's childhood. We were drawn deeply into it. At the intentions, Father Tarcisius improvised one of the most extraordinary petitions I have ever heard, and I am really sorry I could not have anticipated this and recorded it. My petition was simply that some of the peace and happiness we experienced would go out to others. Then we had supper, and now they have cleaned up and gone, and I am tired enough, I think, and hope to go to bed and sleep immediately so that I can get up at 3:00 tomorrow and get a good start.

JANUARY 17, 1970

Saturday. 4:00 a.m. Up, coffeed, but still asleep on my feet. Visit to chapel, Morning Offering, in semi-drowse. Fire lighted, but cabin still cold. I sit huddled against the cold. The moon has gone down so it is really dark outside, after a night of radiant light reflected from the snow. Can I stay up? Dear God, that warm bed drags me back. No, I stay up, waiting for the body to come to life, waiting for the room to warm. After being up a half hour, everything within me still dozes.

Now, at 5:00, the fire blazes, and I am easily awake and into the work—the fog of drowsiness replaced by the clarity of happiness. Wonderful warmth against my back.

At 9:45, the palest sunlight filters through the clouds.
Breakfast—two eggs, two pieces of whole wheat bread fried in the skillet. Now, some strength returns. Need to clean up a bit. Got right out of bed, and have not now, five hours later, even brushed my teeth or combed my hair or washed my face.

Beginning of the monastic retreat today, so times have been moved up; they will come for Mass and supper a bit earlier. It is 5:15 now.

Brother Pius came up and brought me the Leica M3 with 35 mm Summicron lens so that I can make some more interior shots of the hermitage. I have shot one good roll already, and will wait and see how the light is tomorrow. It is foggy, hazy, now, with moisture falling. Probably will become snow flurries tonight. I have just shaved, taken a sponge bath (too cold to bathe completely), put on a fresh undershirt and my pajamas.

One of my teeth is sore (one of the capped and gold ones), and I fear a lack of Vitamin C—also great fear of losing it, which will be serious. There seems to be some infection, and it has loosened in the socket a little. I have no Vitamin C in pill form and so have been drinking pineapple juice and will start slugging the orange juice.

JANUARY 18, 1970

Sunday. Slept until 5:00. Got up, and trembling from the cold, put on water to boil for coffee, lighted the fire, visited the chapel to say the Morning Offering—and had trouble concentrating enough to get through it, but the ardor of my feelings in that presence made up for the stumbling words, I suppose. Now, with coffee too hot to drink, I huddle here at the typewriter and try to come fully awake. My tooth throbs—some infection there for sure. I try to pay it no attention because I have so much work to do today.

Stepped outside—it is thirty degrees and raining—the cold penetrating—and hurried back in by the fire.

Turned on the transistor radio to hear the news and weather. It is supposed to get much colder, down to zero or five degrees below tonight, high tomorrow between ten and fifteen, with snow flurries. So, I will have to get in more wood when daylight comes. There is not enough inside to keep the fire blazing for the next twenty-four hours, which will be necessary to handle that zero temperature. In a sense I am delighted. I will experience what Tom so frequently experienced and about which he wrote in such detail in his journals.

The fire pops loudly and roars up the chimney. It warms

my back and relaxes the muscles in my neck. I pass the chapel door to enter the bathroom. In the darkness the flickering vigil lamp from the chapel reflects from the bathroom walls. I sit and watch it as a kind of visual conversation. It speaks to the eyes while the rain speaks against the windows to the ears; it speaks warmth in that cold, cold room with its cold, cold fixtures. It reminds me visually of the companionship I feel here in the tremendous solitude of this mountain cabin. It leads me to attempt to state verbally what is so constantly my feeling here—one of overwhelming contentment; no, more: one of deep interior jubilance, as though my heart and lungs and spleen and liver and bladder and intestines and genitals were instruments of an orchestra playing the fugue from the Jupiter Symphony within me.

Later: dawn's first hints. The time of celebration here is this moment of first light in the morning, and the last light of evening. Suddenly the snow begins to appear on the ground and trees begin to be silhouetted against the sky—nothing more. The silence is so deep I do not disturb it even with the sound of a flushing toilet. I go outside, into the lightly falling rain, return inside, turn off all the lights, and watch the day begin.

8:30; and the snow is falling steadily now, powdering over the older snow and turning the branches of trees white again. Very preoccupied with thoughts of my wife and children, and longing to be with them. No matter how happy I am here, and I am deeply happy, my thoughts are with them constantly, and with a perpetual hunger for their presence. After a while I may call them.

Stepped out again to check the thermometer; it sinks . . . now in the mid-twenties. How I wish I did not have so much work to do and could just sit here and watch the countryside as the snow falls silently and steadily on it.

The snow falls harder now. It is good to take care of the things necessary for such a time—the things of the body, enough to keep one functioning. Little by little I bring in logs for the fire and stack them against the wall. I get the stale bread out and toast it so later I can sprinkle it out for the birds. Marvelous to be out, wrapped in sweaters and scarves, gathering in the wood that will sustain this cabin this night, and keep enough warmth so that the pipes will not freeze. And I have to start planning some kind of supper. Brother Pat got some ground meat yesterday, so I will try to cook it into something hearty with a thick gravy that we can put over rice. Better start that soon.

I put out the bread crumbs, but the birds have so far ignored them. Wonderful contentment in the work. The snow falls thick, and a first bluejay has come to eat the bread crumbs now. He calls out, raucous as a crow, perhaps to let others know he has made a find, perhaps to warn them away from his find. His call does not sound friendly. Two splendid red cardinals hop around in the hedgerows, coming no closer.

Now they have approached as far as the tree, within a few feet of the bluejay, right here outside the window. Splendid, two magnificent red splotches against the snow. Odd, now, within five minutes a dozen or more have congregated. Now the five or six males have been joined by many females with their duller coats and their orange beaks and the glow of red on their breasts. They eat first the crumbs I threw on the ground, and now two have ventured on the edge of the porch where I put most of the bread.

I drink orange juice all the time, trying to fill up on Vitamin C to stop this mouth soreness. I have a slight fever, undoubtedly from the infection. I have taken two aspirin. Some of the windows are beginning to steam up a bit, which means it is rapidly getting colder outside. It is 10:00 a.m. now, and still no breakfast, except the juices and the coffee. Good to fast. I will hold off until noon.

The morning moves in delight as the snow drifts down steadily and thickly. I alternate between working with great contentment on the texts for *Visual Merton*, making photographs out of the windows, fixing myself now a cup of rose-hips tea. Have no idea what it is, but I know that Tom used to slug it hot and strong, and this is the kind of day for it. Step frequently outside: the wind blows lightly from the north, causing the tall pines to moan and sing. A great deal of white light reflects into the room, with the firelight, to give it some life. Now the birds are truly venturing onto the porch, but I see my mistake. The papa cardinal chases the others away—I should have spread the crumbs out more. He hogs the little pile. I will take the broom out and spread them all along the front edge so others can get to them also. The rose-hips tea is good, fragrant, without having too much taste.

Now the bread crumbs are spread out all along the porch, and many birds partake. The bluejay just simply grabbed a large piece and flew away. The redbirds are congregated and sharing. The joys of a hermit! We share a festival of good food for them and hot sweet tea for me in this cold and snow. They come, fill their craws, then fly away, and in a few moments they are all back again. Now, two of them fly off and tangle in the air, whether fighting or mating I am not enough of a bird behaviorist to know . . . but surely not mating in such weather. Perhaps the one is trying to take the food from the other. I'd prefer to think they were mating.

3:15. Heavy snow and huge fire. The birds have cleaned up the food I threw out, so I will have to put more. Brother Pat came for lunch, a nice quiet time. Now I have worked some more, photographed the birds quite a lot, got the room good and warm, and then took off my pajamas and washed them and then washed my hair. I sit here stark naked, clean-headed, with the pajamas hanging over the back of a chair right in front of the fire, where they dry rapidly. I have heard dogs barking frantically in the woods and just now a shot, so someone is up on the mountain hunting in this snow. The air outside has the purest fragrance of cold snow and wood smoke from the fireplace, but I cannot go out now until my head gets thoroughly dry.

Now, more hot tea; this time a black one, very good indeed. Toasting stale brown bread for the birds, and will toast a piece of white bread to go with this tea. These are actually what are left of Tom's teas. He had many, and especially mentions liking the strong black ones.

Much later. Almost dark. The snow has stopped and the air grows colder, but it is nice in here. Cooking the meat has helped keep it warm. Not only have the birds come for the bread, but also a beautiful, sleek grey squirrel, nervous as hell; but he braved the dangers and came right up on the porch, grabbed a good big piece of bread, and took off at full speed.

The day ends, and it has been a marvelous one, full of peace and activity, with no sense of rush. I hope I can get to sleep early tonight, so I can get up early again tomorrow. Must leave in the afternoon for New York, but would like to keep that early-rise schedule.

JANUARY 19, 1970

Monday. It only got down to thirteen degrees last night, and this morning it is fairly clear. Up early, doing mostly copy work, and then began to get things ready to leave this afternoon. Sponge bath, soaking feet, etc. . . . a portion of the body at a time in a little plastic tub here in front of the fire. Washed my socks, and have them draped over a chair in front of the fireplace. Feel fine, but the shock of going from this isolated hermitage to New York City is not something I anticipate with any joy . . . to say the least. But then, by this time tomorrow morning, I will have finished with the appearance on the *Today* show and can be on my way home to my family. I dread to travel after such an appearance. Too many people recognize me.

FEBRUARY 24, 1970

Back in the hermitage and to work after too long an absence from this blessed place. I have been to Europe, got back home a week ago, and arrived here today for a good long stay of at least ten days. It is terrible to say but there are only two places where I am truly at home, where I want to be, where I am completely happy and right: within the rooms of my own home with my wife and children, and here in the solitude of this hermitage at Gethsemani. Only these two places. In all others, no matter how pleasant or enjoyable, I am not at home; I am vaguely miserable.

Joy to return here. Arrived around 7:00. We came up in the Bronco (the road is terrible) to find the hermitage warmed with a good wood fire and immaculately cleaned by Brother Maurice. We said a beautiful Mass, a requiem for Brother Dominic who died this morning at the age of ninety-three, having spent seventy-four years as a monk here at Gethsemani—a peaceful and happy death. The burial and funeral Mass will be in the morning.

Then a good supper of bread and butter, chicken soup, milk, and they left me at 9:30 to go to bed. I have been getting things ready to get to work in the morning. Now am in pajamas, making these few notes, allowing myself to sink into the glorious silence and solitude, letting it work on me, filled with happiness and serenity.

The fire burns warm at my back. Splendor of the solitude. Now to bed. The Blessed Sacrament is newly reserved again in the little chapel. Tremendous contentment in that awareness. I am deeply tired, deeply relaxed, deeply happy. A perfect combination for going to bed and anticipating a good sleep.

FEBRUARY 25, 1970

Up at 5:30, but not awake. Turned on stove under water kettle to boil the water for coffee, staggered out to prepare the coffee, then in to visit the chapel long enough to offer the day and give thanks for being here and to pray for Brother Dominic who will be buried this morning, and pray for Masha in her agony. Then built a fire. Turned on the transistor radio to get the weather report . . . past stations that blared heartbreak blues or over-jubilant country music and switched it off again . . . too much sound for insides not yet awake. Then on again: weather to be cloudy, cold, and drizzly. Fine. Off now to the warm silence, hot coffee, and a good wood fire at my back. I feel myself gradually coming awake, out of the dense stupor of heavy sleep, to merely heavy drowsiness. I let it take its own time, this wakefulness, let it grow gradually in the magnificent silence of the predawn hush.

Later—7:30. A grey morning, damp, silent except for one glorious, rich bird call (I think it is a mockingbird). I have turned off all the lights, and the cabin, fragrant with the wood fire that burns gently, almost silently, is suffused with soft grey light. The trees and hills fade into early morning fog in all directions. No light was ever more beautiful, no silence more comfortable. No wind stirs. The trees are still, in a stillness full of expectancy.

I have sprinkled stale whole wheat bread over the front edge of the porch so that the birds and the squirrels can come for a feast. Checked the outside thermometer: it is just above the forty-degree mark.

I do nothing. I take Merton's advice and do nothing, just let all this saturate me, wait for it to tell me what to do. I watch, experience, listen to the things about me. I empty myself of everything, knowing that when the time comes, the energies will rise up out of this quiet. I am just here, seated before the windows that give out to the woods on the sides, to the woods and pastures and knobs in the front, always aware of the sacrament in the tabernacle in the next room, with its faint odor of flickering vigil lamp.

A fluttering motion catches my attention. Already a bird has come to eat . . . a scruffy, brownish bird, absolutely silent. The food has been discovered. This bird will somehow communicate that fact to others, and in a while, the porch will be lined with them. They take a piece of dry bread, fly to the branches of the trees a few feet away, then return for more.

Stillness, stillness . . . the softest light reflects from the grey stone walls and grey cement floors of this room. Everything waits, suspended in calm, and underneath—a profound ravishment of the senses, the nerves, as one senses the perceptible inner healing.

You wait, Tom said. You don't go rushing after what is already there. You wait, give it time, give it time gradually to reveal itself in you. Nothing is lost. No time is wasted. Give yourself the time for these things to happen.

I wait, giving myself to the views and fragrances and silences. Tree branches move, the tall pines sway as a breeze touches them, black against a hazed white sky. In here, warm, cedar-scented dryness; outside, the chill dampness, fragrant with winter's clean odors, fragrance of hinted rain.

I do small things, things that require no thought—make up the bed, feed the fire, straighten the room.

Later—8:30. Chill, so I add another log to the fire and it cracks loudly in the silence. I have fixed breakfast on the two-burner electric hot plate: rye toast (toasted on the hot plate by placing it on a bent wire grill, made of a fine-meshed wire); and two eggs fried in a little butter, a glass of milk. So dark in the kitchen I had to turn on a light. Brought the food in and ate it before the fire. Then washed the dishes in hot suds. Brother Maurice has some soap powder in a bowl with a teaspoon in it, labeled *Tide* in black on the bowl. You put in a couple of teaspoons and run the sink full of that tainted well water. Now, everything is clean and shining, the rooms straightened and swept, the lights all turned off because the larger windows in this room allow enough light to work by, and the electric light spoils the beauty of it.

Now, the new log has caught flame and burns with a nice silent steadiness.

11:30. Read—begin to read the journals for final note-taking. Then, feeling drowsy, I put on a sweater and went out to take a slow walk through the woods. Silence all around except for the wind high in the pines, giving a washing sound like the distant rumble of surf. Walked in the damp bed of leaves until I was frozen through and then returned here, nearer and nearer with the smell of smoke from the chimney growing stronger . . . a lovely fragrance in the woods. Into the hermitage, feeling the warmth from the fire, and now, with my sweater off, I absorb the heat with gratitude.

Down in the Abbey, they are all gathered and chanting the requiem Mass prior to burying Brother Dominic in the monastic cemetery that lies just outside the chapel side door. The peace of his life, and the quiet joy of his death, his entry into eternal life, permeates the atmosphere of the morning.

At noon the temperature has dropped into the low thirties by the porch thermometer (which read low forties much earlier this morning). Well, let it fall. The porch is stacked with a good supply of wood. In such a place, the more miserable the weather, the greater the sense of isolation, unapproachability, the deeper the contentment. I will get some supplies this afternoon. They are low right now—plenty of milk, water, and eggs, but nothing much else.

5:00 p.m. now. The sky has cleared, the sun has come out, and the temperature drops rapidly.

Physically, I have fallen to pieces—an overwhelming fatigue. Perhaps it is the total relaxation. I keep getting on the bed, falling into a deep sleep, waking up in a few minutes, staggering in here and feeding the fire, doing a little gesture of work, and then needing to lie down again. I feel as though I could sleep a month, almost drugged and full of stupidity. It is almost shocking. Always when I come here there is something of this, but never this devastation. I realize that the trip to Europe, the intense (but happy) work since my return, getting up at 5:00 each morning and not getting to bed before midnight, are slapping me down now that I have this total relaxation in silence.

FEBRUARY 26, 1970

5:15 a.m. Calm, full moon, and the outside thermometer reads ten degrees on the nose.

Have a roaring fire in the fireplace and am drinking hot coffee, so it is comfortable in here.

Slept profoundly from 8:30 last night until a few moments ago, so feel completely restored except that my spine is stiff from the cold, but warming nicely—the fire really puts out a splendid warmth right now.

Now have turned off all the lights and type by the firelight and reflected moonlight. The countryside is still under this white light, almost glowing, with no hint of dawn as yet on the horizon.

7:00 a.m. The softest dawn, pale pink and orange suffusing the sky, turning the hills in the distance a greyish blue. Nothing moves. Time to fix some breakfast.

Breakfast of eggs and toast and milk. Now the sun sends long slants of light through the trees, frost glistens on the grasses.

Later—nearly 8:00. Have done my cleaning up—swept the floor, wiped off the tables with a wet sponge, made up the cot, washed the dishes. Now, though the temperature remains at ten, it is almost warm in here—the fire does a marvelous job when there is no wind. Begin to work once more on the journals of Merton. Must try to find a way to go down and photograph the grave this morning.

At home it is almost 7:00. Piedy and the children are just getting up. Always they are in my mind. I follow them through the day.

9:15. Again this strange collapse of energies with no similar collapse of enthusiasm. Suddenly a great inertia sweeps me and I have to lie down, and then I sleep for half an hour, deeply, as though I had had no sleep last night (when I had marvelous sleep). I awaken full of fatigue and heaviness. Well, I go along with it, knowing it will pass when all the clatter of purely nervous energy has passed and finally a natural energy replaces it. This is my second day here. I suppose it has been too long. The first few times I came it took two days, but when I came here regularly, usually all of that was gone after twenty-four hours. The surroundings outside and the quietness inside are beautiful—no shadow hangs over these hours. I view them like a person in some final illness. But this is not a final illness, it is only the transition that takes place coming into such total solitude from a life ordinarily filled with stimuli of another sort—movement, noise, people.

Though it is distressing to feel so weak, I have had enough experience with the hermit life now to know that it is part of the initial "reforming" of force, and that when the energies do surge forward, they will be splendid ones. So I accept this, go along with it, let it tell me what to do without any forcing on my part. Beneath it all, I am aware of a great and nearly sublime happiness.

Now, at 11:00 a.m., another sleep. I work for half an hour and then sleep deeply for half an hour. Strange. I have just been out on the porch for wood and to feed the birds and squirrels; a beautiful young grey squirrel came up on the porch to eat the larger pieces of bread.

Now the squirrel is back, less and less timid, and the trees are leafed out with birds of all descriptions and sizes—marvelous red cardinals, mockingbirds, bluejays, and a huge red-headed woodpecker. The mockingbird swoops down, chases the small squirrel off of the porch, but he is back up eating again almost before the bird lands back in his tree a few feet away. At first, every time I made a move, the squirrel ran. So I froze when he came on the porch. Now I can move gently, even turn on and off the typewriter (the click used to send him scurrying), and type without his running.

FEBRUARY 27, 1970

Friday. Up at 5:00, after a good night's rest. Sitting here with hot coffee and a good fire at my back.

Went down yesterday afternoon to photograph the grave and ran into Father Francis (he used to be guest-master here and is now a diocesan priest). He told me a good anecdote on Tom. He said that when he first came here as a novice there used to be a custom: when you broke anything, you went and knelt at the refectory door holding the broken item penitentially up in your hand so that all could see you and what you had broken as they entered the refectory.

Father Francis had asked which of the monks was Thomas Merton, and Merton had been pointed out to him somewhere on the grounds. The second time he saw Tom was when he was in that penitential stance at the refectory door, but Tom was holding up a pair of longjohns, split down the middle, and with no penitential expression, but an "impish" gleam on his face. It broke Father Francis up, and was typical of Tom.

Did not get so cold last night, down to only thirty this morning on the porch thermometer.

Talked with Piedy and Mandy yesterday. Mandy wants to see me (Piedy, too), but when I told her I would be here another week, Mandy said, "Well, I think I'll just come on up there to Gethsemani, that's where I always go."

"I wish you would," I said.

"All right, honey. I'll be there tomorrow. Don't you worry."

I told this to Father Tarcisius, Brother Maurice, and Brother Patrick. Last night at Mass, during the intentions, Brother Maurice made his and then added, "And for Mandy, that she may have a safe trip if she decides to come here tomorrow."

Our Masses now are utterly simple and very beautiful.

Violence is the solution without intelligence or wisdom. I am profoundly opposed to violence, not so much to men who do violence, but to those who drive men to do it, or lead men to do it. An explosion of violence, caused by constant frustration of justice, is not the fault of the one who explodes; it is the fault of those who condone the frustration of justice. Any man can be driven to violence, even those who most protest violence.

FEBRUARY 28, 1970

Dunstan Coleman came up for Mass and supper last night with Father Tarcisius, was deeply taken with the way we celebrate Mass up here; had a good little supper and then talked until 9:00. I got into work and did not go to bed until after 1:00 a.m.

Could boot myself. I'm feeling the effects today—slept until 8:00 and still have not got well into the work; so nothing was gained by staying up so late, and now I have to try to get back on my early-rise schedule. I missed the hours before dawn in which I usually do the best work.

Also read again Jim Andrews's article on Tom in the *National Catholic Reporter*. It is one of the finest things I have ever seen.

MARCH 1, 1970

Sunday. Messed it again. Read *The Waters of Siloe* until 3:30 this a.m., then slept until 9:00, got up and prepared the house for the guests who came at noon. Bob and Hanna Shepherd brought a magnificent lunch, and were accompanied by Carolyn Hammer, and we had Brothers Richard, Lavrans, Cassian, and Patrick join us here, since Carolyn needed to see them on business of some sort. Splendid lunch—white and red wines, marvelous green salad with mushrooms, fried chicken for me, a superbly beautiful glazed ham, and all sorts of other things. Though the day remained overcast and threatening rain, it was strangely balmy. We ate and talked, and Hanna cleaned up everything afterward. Bob and I photographed, and everyone got his business attended to. Lovely afternoon here in the hermitage. I was so glad to have them. They did not overstay, though I would have been willing for them to.

Now it is almost 5:00 p.m., and the quiet has returned. I have got back into my pajamas, feel the fatigue of the day, but it is a happy fatigue. Must begin making my notes for the history and background of the order, and above all need the statutes, which were published here, I understand, in 1946, so I can probably get a copy. Am almost through with *The Waters of Siloe*, and must make a quick run-through tomorrow to write up the background materials I need. That is certainly one of the clues to Tom: his ability to distinguish between the spirit of the contemplative aspects of the order, and the practices that could be an end in themselves, and frequently were.

Tremendous quiet now.

MARCH 2, 1970

4:45 a.m. Strange night of sleep and awakening and sleeping again. It rained gently, and there was great darkness. I would sleep and then get up to go look out. Whenever I opened the door, the drone of rain and the dampness gusted in, and I could not make out even the dimmest silhouette of a tree, though the sound of rain in the trees has a special flatness that made me aware of the surrounding forest. Then back into the bed, under the blanket, and into sleep.

Because of the absence of all light, every time I opened my eyes, the flicker of the vigil candle in the chapel caught and held my attention. I looked down over the foot of the cot, through the door, through the small kitchen, to that glowing, flickering rectangle of doorway into the chapel, and felt the deepest union with it, with Christ in the tabernacle, and Christ in the silences, and in the surrounding rain, and still dazzling silently within me from the communion earlier in the evening. Those moments, and they were only moments between sleeps, were so filled with awe and wonder and contentment, and yes, the most perfect delight, that I returned back into sleep with the happiness of a child, and each brief awakening was like a gift as my attention was caught again and again by the candle that kept vigil and communicated to me—riveted my attention on the divine presence sharing this shelter with me this night, in these woods, in this chapel. There was joy in everything, the peculiar unconstricting warmth of the blanket around me; in the feel of the clean cement floor when I went to the bathroom next to the chapel (just cool but not really cold to my bare feet; that sensation of a floor absolutely clean from a recent mopping); the delight of making my sleep-filled way in the darkness, turning on no lights, guided and oriented in everything by the glow of light from that chapel doorway. A sense of total freedom in God's presence, the need to hide nothing, be nothing, act in no special way—like the freedom of very small children in their parents' presence.

Now, sitting here long before dawn, with the vigil lamp joined by the light of my fireplace, the felicity continues as I make these notes while drinking hot coffee in a cabin that seems to continue to sleep around me—an illusion given by the fact that after I built the fire, I turned off the lights again. They are like a visual noise, as out of place here as any other noise in this predawn silence and solitude. The illusion of visual silence is not disturbed by light from candle or fireplace: it is smashed by the electric light, so I leave it off for the time being.

This morning there is another happiness—I am to go down and see the bakers prepare the bread, and help them with the baking. (I want to come to know all the activities, as Thomas Merton did.) If I see that it does not disturb them, I will photograph them. They have agreed; I am the reluctant one, reluctant to introduce even the click of the camera into their contemplative labor.

The house was beautiful last evening. I put away everything—arranged the books and papers where they belong, and then mopped the whole place with a huge, heavy institutional-type mop. In the grey light from the windows, the place shone with a kind of repose, a plainness and lack of ornament (the ornament of disorder) that was extraordinary. And what weakness, today every muscle aches from wielding that mop. Well, I must do that more often. Usually Brother Maurice has it all done before I am even aware that it needs doing. Much of that quality remains this morning, softened and warmed by the fireplace and the rustle of rain (heard but not seen in the blackness outside).

I make these notes a little at a time, spending long moments between sentences or paragraphs, just experiencing all this, letting it do with me what it will; aware that I am experiencing something so simple, so profound, so fundamental and out of time that the contemplation of it, right now, is the most important thing I can do, the only natural thing I can do, the *only* thing that matters for the moment. It occasionally fills me so completely that I come to jot down a note. The note is the overflow, thin and hasty, of the wealth that God pours into these hours before dawn in these woods.

Making the notes is not to capture the moments. There is no reason for the notes, because they can only hint at the reality. They are made as part of the nature of the hours, and because this is the way this man and this moment function—they are as natural as breathing. There doesn't need to be any reason; they are thoughts.

We celebrate the hours; God, for whatever reason, gives these hours so overflowing that every act, every movement enters into the celebration, like silent music. I stop drinking the coffee—it is not right for the time. I make hot tea with great care, warming the pot first, and that in the preparation and in the taste fits the hours better. And the fragrance is more attuned to the fragrance of rain in the forest and the fragrance of the cedar log fire that provides the warmth and the light. And when I open the door to hear the rain, the rain now smells of the fragrance of this wood smoke that drifts downward from the outside chimney.

At some core of myself, I am dimly aware that God gives all this as an awesome gift, for his own reasons or for no reasons. I do not question any of it, do not wonder why, what it is a preparation for. These thoughts are there, but I do not let them come to the fore. I accept this immense joy, this tremendous gift, and ask no questions, fritter no attention away from the thing itself. But it is shattering, just the same, to sit here dumbly and be the recipient of such divine generosity.

This is the most silent hour of all. Even the animals sleep now, even those nocturnal prowling animals sleep now, and the humans of this valley (except for the monks, who are awake and chanting the office) are in their period of deepest sleep. And that deepest silence is necessary for us to hear that deepest of all musics—the music of rain falling steadily into the deep leaf mulch of the surrounding forests. This pure gift of God.

Later. I went out on the porch to see if there was any hint of dawn. Nothing but the louder sounds of rain running in rivulets now in the gullies. No star visible, but below, tiny points of light from the Abbey seen through the trees, lights as small as distant stars in this rich blackness, and as bright, telling me that in the Abbey they are already about their various tasks.

I think of my wife and children asleep in their beds. They are with me like the flickering vigil lamp, in every waking moment, and probably in every sleeping moment as well. There is—on the surface—a kind of tearing: the unblemished joy of this solitude in this hermitage, and the constant longing to be with my wife and children. But by some extraordinary fusion, it is only surface; at the depths of me there is no conflict at all. The two are harmonized: here I am with the Christ of the silence and the solitude day and night; there I am in the presence of the Christ who dwells in my wife and children, day and night. The longing is to be there and to be here. At base, there is no contradiction in those longings, which are finally only one longing: a longing God fulfills with such gratuitous magnanimity that a lifetime of babbled prayers could not begin to express the gratitude that fills our secret hearts.

Later. Although I pour words on paper, there are no words to formulate prayers. I go sit in the presence of the reserved Sacrament in the chapel and cannot sustain a verbal prayer, which is, of course, not important. I fix my attention dumbly on the incarnation, the crucifixion, the resurrection, and just rest silently there, not even meditating, utterly dumb and mute and in no way worried about that, either. Something happens, I am sure, though I have no idea what it is or how it happens or any consciousness that it happens. But there is ease.

Hunger begins to bother me as the sky finally lights, not in the east but all over, just a bit, detaching the shapes of motionless trees from the blackness. I go fix a piece of toast and a glass of milk.

Now, with the first light, a movement on the porch attracts my attention. The small grey squirrel is there looking for the bread crumbs I usually put out. I forgot this morning, so his sniffing is fruitless. As soon as he goes off, I repair the oversight. Was he watching? I suspect he will soon be back and find the food.

Now, at 7:30, I am ready for Brother Patrick to take me down, though he is not due until 8:00. I have cleaned up things, straightened the bed and prepared the camera and dressed. Heavy overcast, but the light is luminous, without shadows.

1:30 p.m. The morning spent with the bakers—Brothers Donald (in charge), Mark, Robert, Conrad (the interior cellarer whose office is in the building). Beautiful morning. The sky overcast, but good enough light to make for a beautiful light inside. I photographed all aspects of the bread making, from beginning to end, and while the bread was rising, documented the fruitcake-making process, equally as interesting. I shot exactly one hundred frames, ran out of film, had to dash to Bardstown to replenish my supply. While there, I bought a six-pack of beer for the brothers, and they enjoyed a can each during the last break before putting the fruitcake into the oven. Then they sent me back up to the hermitage with one of the hot loaves out of the oven. Splendid.

Brother Patrick brought me back up just as a new rain began to fall. Now he has gone, and I am in my pajamas once again, very tired, very happy. I sit here and watch the views of rain that dims the distant mountains, and listen to its steady droning on the roof and in the trees.

Though I hate to miss a moment of this, I must take a nap. I am simply too done in not to. Have a great deal of work material, so perhaps if I take a nap now, I can get up early enough to get some of that done before they come for 6:15 Mass.

4:00 p.m. Slept over an hour and woke up to heavy rains. Worked. Now it is almost 5:00, and the rains have stopped for the moment. The whole country, in a light fog, but with sun invisible above, giving warm tones, looks like a landscape from Renaissance Italy. Great tiredness and pain from this morning's photographic session and round trip up and down the mountain, but this is nothing . . . it does not even touch the joy of these hours . . . it in no way distracts from them or dims them.

MARCH 4, 1970

Incessant, steady rain all night and continuing into the dawn of this day. It falls straight down. It makes the silence and the solitude more profound, and is therefore a celebration of quiet, a perfecting of joy.

Later. The squirrels were late in coming, but this moment (almost noon) when I returned to this room from the shower there were three of them. What are they doing—spreading the message? Or did they send a first emissary to see if it was a trap, and finding it safe, send a second, and today a third. They are all small, young, surely from the same nest.

Shaved and took a good bath, and now feel better. Here you bathe by wetting yourself, then turning off the shower before the hot water runs out, soaping thoroughly, then rinsing quickly.

4:00 p.m. Steady hard rain all last night and all today. I realized that I have worked almost without stopping since 4:00 this morning, so I stop now to make these notes, too groggy to do anything else. And hungry.

I did remember this morning to put out the dry bread, and now three little squirrels come up on the porch to eat, plus hundreds of birds. But it is the squirrels that delight me most. They are much less nervous now, and finally have concluded, I guess, that nothing here is going to hurt them.

The joy of this place—especially in time of rain. The rain falls heavily, but straight down, without any wind or slant, and the cabin is filled with a soft grey light that is warmed in here by the small flame in the fireplace and in the chapel by the vigil lamp before the tabernacle.

I ache now, and must go lie on the bed for a while. I have never in my life worked so effortlessly or known such sustained joy, especially since they let me keep the reserved Sacrament here in the hermitage chapel. Last night, awaking in the blackness of the blackest kind of night, hearing the rain drum against the flat roof, the flicker of the vigil lamp caught my immediate attention. Looked through the door of the sleeping room, across the little cooking room, to the chapel door, all aglow with the light of that candle, and thought I would die with happiness. I uttered no words, just watched it with the deepest felicity until sleep returned. Usually I get up when such a thing happens and go sit for a few moments in my pajamas and bare feet in the chapel, but last night I just lay there and watched it. Thoughts of the Christ in the tabernacle mingle with thoughts of my beloved family asleep in their beds, my friends, my compadres, my godchildren, all the monks in the Abbey down below the hill.

I am openmouthed with bewilderment that God should

flood me with such fine gifts, and I utter prayers of thanksgiving to Tom for being the instrument that brought me here to be where Christ obviously wanted to find me, in the silence of these woods, at this time. All of it lingers when I go home to my family. The overflow of it is sensed by my wife and children who seem to take as much joy in it as I do. These are rare days in our lives. We do not know why God does this, what he is preparing us for. We just live in the moments without thinking anything or planning anything or trying to understand anything.

9:00 p.m. Brother Patrick did not get back from the eye doctor's in time for Mass and supper. Brother Frederic came with Father Tarcisius and Brother Maurice. After supper, Brother Maurice took the scraps out and saw a fox. Then, when they went out to get into the Bronco (they came up some back way in the car) and turned on the strong headlights, there was one of the foxes—a beautiful, huge grey animal right close to the hermitage. He trotted away slowly, giving us a marvelous view until he disappeared unhurriedly into the pines. What a beautiful one. Maurice thinks a whole family of foxes come up and eat the scraps every night. I searched through the supplies, found a meat patty and put it on the edge of the porch, and left on the light. But of course I have no hope they will be bold enough, or incautious enough, to come right up on the porch the way the squirrels do. In any event, it pleases me to know that such handsome animals are so close by. They will wait until all the lights are out and it is completely quiet to come for the meat.

Now, it is late (for me), and I must hurry to bed.

MARCH 5, 1970

Thursday. Up in the middle of the night. Went to check on the temperature outside. Turned on the porch light and opened the front door. There, at the edge of the porch, another and smaller grey fox. We eyed one another a long moment, and then he turned and trotted away. I put bread out and got up an hour later to find it all gone. So the foxes come up at night, the squirrels and birds during the day.

Chilly this morning. I am seasoning the skillet Father Tarcisius and Brother Maurice found for me yesterday when they made my purchases of supplies. A flat, low-rimmed iron skillet perfect for the *crepes*. I washed it good, then heated it red and let it cool, then filled it with oil and let it set all last night. This morning, with the oil still in it, I heated it to boiling, and now it cools out on the porch. When it is good and cold, I pour off the excess oil, then wipe off all I can, and glaze it in the heat once more so nothing will stick when I cook—and then hope no one washes it after I am gone.

MARCH 6, 1970

Friday. Worked hard all day yesterday and wrote very little in this notebook. The weather has cleared and turned colder—down to thirty degrees now, but a brilliant light. Three squirrels again this morning. Am reading too much (and too late) at night and keeping a slight headache from that. They fixed us a meatless pizza last night, and I rolled with heartburn all night. One of the Fathers died yesterday morning, an older one; he is to be buried today. We had discussed Trappist funerals in some detail, and so last night, helped by the pizza heartburn, I dreamt of death—and not pleasantly, either; not the releasing death of Trappists, but miserable and tragic death. At 3:00 I woke up with severe stomach cramps, plugged in the hot plate for heating coffee water, and then dashed to the bathroom with an assault of diarrhea.

Now, a second trip and two coffees later, I feel weak but quite all right.

Frost remains white in the shadows and a ground fog rolls like white smoke in the sunlit areas.

Brother Pius came last evening to join us for Mass and supper, and then gave me a quick haircut, so I feel less barbarous. The last cut I got was in France, and fortunately it was a short one.

Later—2:00 p.m. While Brother Patrick and I were having lunch, Piedy called to tell me that Dr. Franz McKee [Texas doctor] had been horribly murdered last night. Two men (at least) came into his house and waited for him, having crackers, sausages, and soft drinks until he came in. They struck him over the head with a candelabra, crushed his skull and then shot from close range, the bullet going through his body and into the floor. He was Father George Curtsinger's close friend. They were asking prayers from us here in the community. I promised them we would pray for him and his family tonight at Mass.

I called Father George, and when he answered and recognized my voice he blurted out, "Oh, Franz, I'm just sitting here completely numb." He must have been numb to call me Franz. I suppose he is—as I am—completely horrified by the killing, and the fact that there can be men so dehumanized they would do this kind of thing.

Later—I have tried to work, but nothing really sticks in my mind except the shattering horror of Dr. McKee's murder. So I just stopped reading and started copying things that I am going to need. I feel so for the children of Franz. My God, what they must be going through. Not so much the death of the father, which can be understood and accepted, but the unspeakable manner of it which they will know all about, because Piedy says all the details have already been given twice on TV.

And all of this is made more poignant by the extraordinary beauty of this sunlit afternoon, the marvelous beauty of the redbirds eating the crumbs on the porch, the breathtaking sight of a first crocus in blossom near the closest tree, that one brilliant pair of yellowish-orange blossoms that are so perfect on the short-stemmed green leaves that come barely an inch above the dried grasses. They opened at noon, and now at 4:00 they are tightly closed. My thoughts are glued to prayers for Dr. McKee and his family and friends, and for the souls of those poor dehumanized beasts who could so deliberately plan and wait to kill him.

To get some health into this horror, I have made the sauce for some *crepes* tonight, and will begin cooking the *crepes* around 5:45, so they should be done when the monks arrive around 6:00.

APRIL 18, 1970

Back in the hermitage. It is dusk, 6:30, and I have finally finished unpacking and getting my work pages in order, and getting everything ready to go. Arrived around 3:00 and came directly to the hermitage with Brother Maurice. We had a snack with Brother Patrick, and then they left me to get settled in. A glory to be back here. Everything has turned green, the redbuds are in bloom, the air of evening still and fragrant with spring.

Tonight at the Abbey they will vote on the proposition for a small community in North Carolina. If it is yes, then we lose Brother Maurice, which greatly saddens us, but I think he is eager to go, so we just pray for God's will to be done.

Father Tarcisius spent a week up here and did an amazing amount of work. They have put in new shelves for the kitchen (in the hallway), and he repainted very beautifully the chapel. They will come to say Mass at 7:30 tonight, because of the voting.

I am done in. I only got two hours of sleep last night. Had to get up so early to drive to the airport this morning. But I feel fine, except for the lack of sleep. And just to be here makes me so happy nothing could dampen that. Bought some new kitchen utensils in Bardstown so I can make the new rice dish; bought a lot of supplies, in fact. Food prices here are really horribly inflated. I spent almost $50 on supplies, and did not get much at that.

But no worry. I am here for a week of solitude, and at this completely serene hour of dusk I am filled with the greatest possible happiness.

The windows are all open (Father Tarcisius also replaced the screens which have been down for the winter), and the temperature must be in the seventies. Will go look. The outside thermometer reads exactly seventy degrees.

APRIL 19, 1970

Sunday. The rains did not come. This morning a hazed sunlight makes all the new leaves on all the trees transparent, and picks up the patches of redbud blossom throughout the surrounding woods. I put stale bread out before dawn, and in a moment the squirrels were on the porch, absolutely tame. Now, in the great stillness of this lush, green Sunday morning, meadowlarks and mockingbirds sing above the drone of bees. It is warm, almost eighty degrees on the porch thermometer. I hear the bells from the Abbey below calling the monks to tierce, and then they will chant the conventual Mass. I do not go down except on the last day of my stay here. If I go early, everyone knows I am here, and then the guests on retreat find out, and the interruptions come. No, we will say Mass here this evening at twilight.

I am in a drowse as I watch wild lilies open up at the edge of the porch. Last evening, two days late, I finally steeled myself to remove the bandage from inside my mouth. It was such a shock I had to take darvon. I went to bed at 10:00 but could not sleep. I lay there, watching the vigil lamp's flicker from the chapel, waiting for the rain, wondering how I could be in such misery and at the same time so transformed by the joy of these radiant silences. I listened to the whippoorwills chanting in the darkness outside.

Then I abandoned the attempt to sleep, got up and fixed a *riz à la dauphine* (in honor of Mandy), working with great care to keep my mind off the wound. That took me until 1:00 a.m. I then took a large glass of raw eggs and milk, drunk through a straw, and that let me sleep until six this morning. I hurried to the refrigerator and saw that the *riz* set beautifully. We will serve it for dessert tonight.

Brother Patrick called early to ask if Dom Colomban [Bissey, the Father Immediate of Gethsemani], who is here on a visitation from France, could come say Mass in the hermitage and have lunch with me tomorrow. I, of course, agreed. Fortunately I bought some nice chickens in Bardstown, on my way here yesterday evening. I got them out, cut them up, salted them, and they are wrapped in a kitchen towel now. I'll make *coq au vin* for Dom Colomban and Dom Anthony [Chassagne, Abbot of Mepkin, South Carolina]—start it this evening and finish it tomorrow. So, in the kitchen the chicken is wrapped in towels, carrots are peeled, small whole onions are peeled and soaking together with the carrots in clear cold water, the mushrooms are washed and draining. It takes longer to do things here, because there are only two burners on the hot plate and they heat erratically. We'll have the *coq au vin*, boiled parslied potatoes, green salad, *crepes* Grand Marnier. Maybe I can work up some kind of *hors d'oeuvre*, though the cupboard is virtually bare.

Now, later, it is noon, and although the sun remains bright a wind blows through the woods, causing the tall pines to sway. It sounds as though I were near a seashore, hearing the wash of waves. But it does not dishearten the birds that sing on and on with a kind of exultation that is contagious.

Later—5:00 p.m. Long afternoon's work, and now the wind is howling, the sky heavily overcast, and it is beginning to rain. The trees sway so dangerously they look as though they might crack in two. What a marvelous place to be in a storm! The porch, which was swept clean before, is now covered with debris, large chunks of bark from the trees, leaves, straw have blown up on it. And still the birds sing, though I can hear them only faintly above this roar of wind in the forest. The temperature outside is seventy-five degrees. I have prepared most of the supper and sit here with a large mug of strong coffee. I hear a crash and a huge explosive crackling, which surely means that one of the trees nearby has been snapped off by the wind. I wonder if Father Tarcisius and Brothers Patrick and Maurice will be able to come up for Mass. If not, what shall I do with all this food I have cooked?

Now one of the squirrels has come, and sits not three feet from me on the other side of the window. It is the first time they have come in the afternoon or evening, and I was just feeling sorry for them, wondering if they were holed up against the storm. No, he is here, and he stands upright, holding a large chunk of dried bread in his paws, and nibbles rapidly and delicately at it. He is very curious about me. I keep typing to accustom him to the sound. He comes closer, his nose almost to the window and peers at me, then goes back down on the porch for more bread, climbs back up on the woodpile stacked against the window and eats while watching me. What a beautiful creature he is, and what joy his presence brings me. He is completely unafraid, does not tremble at all, though when he first started coming here some months ago, he would dash up, get bread, and fly to the woods, or certainly take off if I so much as made a move. Now I can get up and walk about and type and cough, and he acts perfectly secure. Well, the visitor (or rather the inhabitant, I am the visitor on his lands) is really gorging himself (or herself). It delights me for these animals not to be frightened—or rather to grow out of their fright of me. I hope no one ever comes here with a gun; there are posted signs everywhere. Otherwise, it would be cruel to make the animals trust humans—they would be sitting ducks for a hunter. After eating several chunks of the bread, he has hopped off the porch and disappeared.

APRIL 20, 1970

Dawn, and after the downpours, the morning is clear and so beautiful and still and quiet, the air so washed that all the senses seem equally washed and fresh. I have put out the bread for the squirrels. Birds are as swept up by all this as I am. They chant their roulades loudly from the lush vegetation, with a purity and sensuous echo that gave me the startling illusion that I was at the edge of a rain forest. Surely it would melt the heart of even the president of the National Rifle Association.

Now, almost 5:00 p.m., and this has been a day. The Abbots came to concelebrate at noon. I put on the *coq au vin* to warm up during the Mass. Within a few minutes we experienced the illusion that we were in France, and that slowed down everything. Both Dom Colomban and Dom Anthony are men of great warmth and complete simplicity, so we ended up spending two hours at the table and having a great time talking. The food was good and they, who usually eat sparingly, more or less threw caution to the winds (not caution, but reticence) and took portion after portion. I served the *coq* with mashed potatoes first, then the green salad, then the *riz à la dauphine*, and we managed to get good wines, and then afterward had Grand

Marnier as a liqueur. I took many photos, Dom Colomban told a thousand funny stories. I was amazed at how well Father Flavian speaks French. How vital was the spirit of Thomas Merton, here in his hermitage. We felt his presence almost tangibly. Dom Colomban told me that on his last visit before Tom's death, they had a session up here. A long and very beautiful afternoon.

Now, I have until tomorrow evening alone. The weather is beautiful beyond imagining. The quiet of late afternoon surrounds me. Brothers Patrick and Maurice cleaned up everything, so the house is spotless and all the dishes put away. I feel half dead. Will get into my pajamas and read and make notes from the journals and try to get to bed very early. I have not had more than four or five hours sleep any night for a week now. I relish this prolonged solitude, because a lot of people are coming to see me this week, people doing doctorates on Tom, the priest in charge of setting up the studies center in Wisconsin, etc.

Later—lay down for a moment and slept deeply for an hour, almost as though I had been drugged (am not taking sedation) and wanted to sleep on. Got up and washed my clothes and fixed strong coffee, and now that has awakened me a little.

Now, at 7:30 p.m., all the color has left the sky, and the air chills rapidly in these last moments before night. The country is strange, new pale green leaves on the trees are surrounded by the monochrome grey of the sky and the distant hills. Such a stillness. Even the birds are silent. I have to close the windows against the dampness and chill. I watch the approach of night, with the lights out and only the vigil lamp in the chapel providing a concentration of warmth in its flickering, not in its flame but in what it flames for—the reserved Sacrament. The incredible, absorbing companionship that increases in intensity and joy as the distractions of daylight and bird songs fade. Now, the bells, heard faintly from the Abbey, calling the monks to compline.

Too cold now to sit up. I take my work to bed, hoping I will sleep soon.

APRIL 21, 1970

Worked finally on the journals until almost 1:00 a.m. despite my good intentions of going to sleep early. I recall drifting off to sleep, hearing myself mumble, "Is there any idiocy I am not capable of committing (and do)? Is there any idiocy I am incapable of uttering (and do)?" I slept until 6:00 and woke up groggy and aching, put the water on to boil for coffee, staggered out to feed the birds and squirrels, and was just knocked silly by the glory of the morning. Still, clear, chilly, but magnificently beautiful—with redbuds caught by first sunlight all through the trees, and cardinals, bluebirds, and yellow birds like great brilliant blossoms in the trees. They turned the wordless prayers that simmered low inside me into interior magnificats. A brilliant morning, fresh, sunbathed, absolutely still.

Men who put away everything that is not God run the risk of putting away everything that is not themselves; of putting away many things that are manifestations of God, and putting away God in the process. It is not really a question of putting away anything, but of allowing oneself to be stripped of whatever God wants. Some religions manage heroically to practice an asceticism that sieves out everything except their prejudices and antipathies, which take on the robes of militant virtue dedicated to God (quite sincerely), and so they end up in the atrophy of hating for the love of God. In the religious life they have to act, an aggressiveness that springs from weakness (and weakness can be hard as stone), and their actions are almost never *for* a thing but rather "anti-" things: anti-communist, anti-renewal, anti-everything that is not in conformity with their prejudices. Their cumulative message seems to be not that men should be like Christ, but that men should be like them who are like Christ. What nonsense.

4:00 p.m. Hard work and no time to write in this journal, though I should, regardless of the time it takes. Good session with Father Al Pooler, CP [then director of the Merton Studies Center at Bellarmine College], who came for Mass with us last night and stayed for supper. He is deeply involved in the Merton Symposium projected by the Johnson (Wax) Foundation. Then after they left, I worked until midnight on the rare and precious issue of *New Zealand Art News* devoted to the work of Tom's dad, Owen Merton. Splendid things. I am reproducing all of them and wish I could see more. Am learning more about Owen Merton, and liking very much what I am learning.

Since my return here, the dogwood buds have opened in some of the trees near the hermitage, and on top of one of them now, as I glance up, I see a flaming cardinal perched on one of the limbs with the white blossoms. The sky is much darker, the wind rising, the temperature outside up to a humid eighty degrees with rain forecast this evening. It looks as though it could begin any moment. A tremendous "attentiveness" in the atmosphere. It is like the distinction Tom made about "the tremendous action of contemplation"—where all is attentiveness to what is happening (as differing from just sitting or kneeling or woolgathering).

Now the wind comes rushing through the forest like a tidal wave. Nowhere is rain more glorious than in a deep forest such as this. Put out more bread so the squirrels can come where it is dry if this develops into a storm. They are so tame now they are almost insolent, and they seem much more curious about me than I am about them. I hope they get as much enjoyment out of these funny encounters as I do. At least they get food.

APRIL 23, 1970

A magnificent rain and windstorm last night, and this morning the wind has gone, but rain falls steadily over the countryside and those extraordinary bird songs come bursting from the darkness of the inner forest, loud and resonant over the rumble of rain.

APRIL 25, 1970

Saturday afternoon. And no time to write in this until now. The weather has been bad, which means wonderful up here—completely rained in and cool enough to need a small fire in the fireplace. But this has been a terribly fragmented visit, too fragmented to get the work done that I had counted on getting done. In addition to the Abbots, there have been other visitors (daily), and work to do for them and therefore not for the book. I enjoyed them all—two men doing doctoral dissertations on Tom; they kept their visits short, but still they were interruptions, just enough to mess things up.

Tonight will be restful. Only the Brothers and Father Tarcisius coming for supper, and all of us are so comfortable together it is no more intrusion than having my family with me. Since this will be our last meal together this session (if I go tomorrow—depends on the weather, if it rains any more we cannot get out), I have a good rich *boeuf bourguignon* simmering for the dinner.

But I ache all over, and most distressing of all, my feet are completely numb—something off with the diabetes. They are numb, and the lower legs up nearly to the knees have no feeling at all. Will try to take a little walk and perhaps restore some of the circulation. It is beautiful, hazed and thinly overcast, the temperature up to seventy degrees—dogwoods and redbuds in bloom all through the woods.

MAY 16, 1970

My third day here and only now, in midafternoon of this Saturday, do I have a moment to begin making notes.

Went to Connecticut—twenty-four hours in Hartford, twenty-four more with Nell Dorr [photographer] in Washington, Connecticut. Extremely hot. Stayed soaked all the time. Came to Louisville on the thirteenth, came out here early the fourteenth. When I arrived at the gatehouse, there were three emergency calls. One from Philadelphia. The schools (high schools) are anticipating a "race war" among black and white students at the beginning of the school year. They asked me to spend the first week of school givin̠ ᷆onferences to students in all the schools to try to calm things and turn the tide. Great God. I could not say no, but I did not say yes, either. I said that if the situation really did develop, I would not refuse, but that I would not come unless they felt a real emergency existed.

And then Chicago called with the same damned thing. I told them I had promised Philadelphia the first week or ten days, and they wanted the second. I told them the same.

I cannot go out and do all this. Two or three appearances a day for twenty days consecutively is more than I can handle physically. We will see. I cannot say no to such requests if there is a real need, either.

Well, I got through all those damned calls late in the day, washed my clothes, cooked up supper because Dom Jean Leclercq is here and he was coming to say Mass and reserve the Sacrament. A funny, brilliant man. He told me sadly that he had a liver condition, could eat nothing I had prepared, and not drink red wine (which we had found). Well, I fixed him some peas without butter. He ended up *sneaking* (no other word) three pieces of meat, endless servings of *crème au caramel*, all the peas, and a whole bottle of wine. As we talked, he would fix me concentratedly with his eyes, but my peripheral vision saw his hand moving to take more food and to take more wine.

Splendid visit, and I learned a great deal from him about the personalities at the Bangkok conference and about his long-time relationship with Tom. Have also been reading his book, *Alone with God* (Farrar, Straus, and Cudahy, 1961) so I could question him about the hermit life while he is here. Another session with him tomorrow.

And then, Lord, it has been a whirlwind of work late into each night (1:00 or 2:00 a.m.), many visits. (Great Lord, even seminarians on retreat here before their ordination to the priesthood found their way up and asked for autographs. Wonderful, open young men, but they were a painful interruption to an overwhelming schedule of work that has to be done.) This morning I had to go down to have a session with a French Canadian Sister who is doing her thesis on Merton, Sister Dominique. She works closely with Bishop Alexander Carter, whom I admire so deeply. Good session. Now all that is done, all the visits made, all the conferences. Brother Pat promised me a while ago that there will just be the three up for Mass, and so I feel as though the pressure is off and I can really work and live as a "hermit" completely.

After the great heat of the past few days, it has rained almost constantly the last twenty-four hours and has turned so chilly I have to have a little fire in the hearth; but the view is of lush summer—the high wall of hedgeroses in abundant bloom, the lilies (are they that?—they look like white irises) in splendor in the shadows of the woods, the birds.

MAY 17, 1970

Sunday. 4:00 a.m. Up and put water on to boil for the coffee, hurriedly built a fire in the fireplace (the inside temperature was forty-five degrees). And now, with the deep night outside, rain dripping from the eaves, a good hot log fire at my back, a deep and authentic silence, the jubilance that only really comes at this predawn hour, the jubilance of solitude and silence and uninterrupted hours before me, permeates the atmosphere.

I have fixed the coffee, checked the thermometer (up to the mid-sixties in here, with that beautiful fire), turned off the lights, and write here now by the warm light of the flames—these brilliant orange flames that contrast with the flickering whitish flame of the vigil lamp in the whitewashed chapel beside me. Utter, overcast darkness outside, a chill, rain-damp darkness that does not reveal the presence of a single tree, though the air is strongly fragrant of pine and wild rose blossoms.

I have another week here. Father Tarcisius and the Brothers volunteered the promise, on leaving last night, that after the brief visit planned this afternoon with Dom Leclercq, no one else would be allowed near the hermitage the rest of my stay. So the nearly unbearable joy of this morning is in part due to the moment, but made absolutely pure in the prospect of a week of real solitude. It is always denatured when there is the anticipation of interruption. So, how does one say it?—the visits, the interruptions, have been fine; the people who came were fine and deserved to be here and to participate in the Mass, and it meant much to them because they were all friends of Tom's; and it meant much to me, too, because they are splendid.

But finally this place is an authentic hermitage and is true to itself only when it is inhabited as a hermitage. You accept the other, the visits, you even welcome them sometimes, but no matter how good the visits are, they are a blemish to solitude. And the solitude is where one lives that ultimate harmony of all the sights and sounds and silences and prayers and labors in true naturalness and reality, with perfect interior union with all that is; when that interior union is a perpetual alleluia and magnificat and thanksgiving combined without words; when all activity and all repose and even sleep itself enter into the heart of that awareness; and finally there are no words even to attempt to express it because the words and the concepts represented by words all melt into the heart of it, dissolve, and cannot say it.

Finally the gap between the words and the reality is so immense, one matches the interior muteness with the exterior silence, stops expressing, stops explaining, stops even asking questions or analyzing, and just abandons everything to whatever is happening, because whatever is happening is so sublime one should finally just be the receptor for it and let it do what it will. Then the act of sweeping the floor or washing a dish or making the cot or anything else takes on all that radiance, for everything occurs in that mute attentiveness to the dazzlement. All of this occurs in quietness.

It does not shout; it bursts the heart and the affections and the perceptions, but without sound or movement; it is like a fog of interior joy that simply consumes everything into its radiant obscurity.

I stopped to go take the dymelor for the diabetes. I turned on the electric light—a great gift this light, but in this moment it flared like a harsh blasphemy, and I quickly turned it off to return to the natural light of beginning dawn. Outside the first hint of light. Masses of treetops stand mute and unmoving above the mystery of a dense ground fog. I go out to put bread on the porch for the squirrels.

Outside, I broke the bread into small pieces. Through the window I saw the warm steady light from the fire and outside the cold light, hardly light at all; nearby trees black, unmoving silhouettes, trees a little farther away dim masses in the fog. My flesh tightened with the chill and damp. Deep, mist-filled silence all around, and fragrance of the cedar smoke (like piñon) from my fireplace. Then, finally, deeply chilled, I came back inside to sit by the fireplace and warm my back and then my front and then my feet (on the hearth).

In such hours, words (the way I think) will not do it. They are like rubber balls that a man tries to throw up to the clouds. They will not reach. They come nowhere near saying what is and what happens in these hours.

Later—nearly 7:00. The light is silvery, the fog has thickened so that nothing is visible beyond the hedgeroses. Birds sing gloriously, and now the bells from the Abbey float upward their waves of sound—all of these sounds in the forest that spring like flowers from the silence, embellishing silence without destroying its essence.

Later. At 8:00, and with interior cringing, I turn on the little transistor radio for the weather report—to see if I should keep the fire going, build it, or let it go out. The day will remain chilly and overcast, they say. And then, to my horror, the most incredible music surged, silken, "Rock of Ages" played by Montovani and hummed with a bawdiness that sought to be angelic by a women's chorus. I almost fell down rushing to turn the damned thing off. It was pure pollution pouring from that nasty little speaker. The bastards dress up a nice, simple, plain old hymn in their silks and satins and turn her into a slut; they pimp in the name of religion.

Food now. An egg and a piece of toast and a glass of milk. It acts like a drug on me. With what relish do I go back to the sleeping room behind the kitchen where it is quite cold, straighten the sheets and put a blanket over the top one and prepare to crawl into that for a nap.

Later: Slept deeply for an hour, and awakened to find all the fog gone and a glorious cool clarity over the soaked country, the sky cloudless, the sun gently warming the stillness.

Later: 2:45 p.m. Worked. Then Brother Patrick came at noon to bring some supplies and help me clean up. We cleared out the refrigerator, and he went out to throw the food in the brush for the foxes.

I stood on the porch and told him goodbye. When I turned back to the porch edge to look off into the woods, there not ten feet away was a marvelous large grey fox with rust-colored fur under his neck. I did not move. He leisurely ate, explored, came within six feet of me, stopped and stared, wandered cautiously backward to about twenty feet. I slowly walked back in here and got my camera. He then sniffed around in the grass at the edge of the porch, giving me wonderful close-up views of him which I photographed.

The squirrels came for the bread, and now blackbirds are on the porch right in front of my window as I type, eating the bread, the sun glistening from their shining plumage where I detect blue, almost peacock blue, highlights in the black feathers. A tremendously serene and beautiful Sunday afternoon, the feast of peace, cool and yet full of warmth and companionship with the animals as tame and unafraid as in Eden. Brown bees, bumblebees, wasps, yellowjackets cruise in the humming atmosphere. This morning I even heard a duck quacking from the woods—there must be standing water in there somewhere.

Later. The fox is back, wandering about in front of the porch in full sunlight as unconcerned as can be. The sound of my typing does not bother him. The click of my camera does not either. Well, it is irresistible. I am going to put on some shoes and go out for a while to see if I can find the duck pond. The ducks are somewhere nearby. Brother Hartz told me that yesterday when he was in the woods, he got within forty feet of a deer before the animal turned and walked away. "I suppose," he said, "that after 150 years in these woods, the generations of deer have concluded they are safe here and have lost their fear of man."

MAY 18, 1970

Monday. Forgot to mention that with Fathers Leclercq and Tarcisius celebrating the Mass last night, we had a multilingual one: Dom Jean was chief celebrant. He started in English, then I read the Epistle in French, he read the Gospel in English, we did the Canon in English through the communion. He then burst out in strong Italian for the prayer and blessing and to the end. And I gave the final response in Latin. There was no foolishness in this, except for the last response in Latin. When we were deciding what language to use, I suggested we use all of them (since it was Pentecost), and Dom Jean said: "Fine—anything but Latin." So tacking on the *Deo gratias* was a spontaneous *méchanceté* [mischievousness] on my part. Father Tarcisius got tickled but Dom Jean just rose benignly above it.

Later—almost 9:00 p.m. Late dusk, but still enough light to see the colors of trees, the calm of evening, the warm tones of the sky over the blue tones of the knolls in the distance, and above the tallest tree, in the clear depths of the sky, an enormous, ivory-colored, nearly full moon. A breathtaking moment. They have been up for Mass and supper and have gone now, leaving me in this blessed solitude for another twenty-four hours of the deepest joy. It is balm to my soul. I give it all my attention, all my attentiveness, no matter what I do. I listen with my heart and my soul and my senses to all that it tells me, and what it tells me bursts within me a pure shower of felicity. Now it is 9:00, and I turn off the lights and go to bed, even though it is not full dark outside.

MAY 19, 1970

Tuesday. 6:00 a.m. It gets light. Have been sitting by the fire slugging strong coffee and studying the texts Merton mentions on mental prayer. Cold as the devil. Now, I stop to fix breakfast as dawn brings light to the white hazed knolls across the way. The countryside is still, deeply silent except for one tentative bird—it sounds like a field lark, a song thin and drowsy.

Breakfast—a piece of buttered toast and a glass of milk. If I take more than that I get too sleepy to stay awake and alert to the work.

I put bread out for the squirrels, but the blackbirds have swooped in and taken every morsel.

Now, nearly 7:00. Such a drama. That squirrel came to find no food. He stood up on the logs and stared at me. I went for more stale bread and this time I put only one piece out on the front part of the porch, and tossed the rest on the logs and down behind the logs, in the narrow space between the logs and the front window. The birds will not go in there. Well, the squirrel came right back, got the bread from the porch and hopped up on the logs to eat it. Two blackbirds came to peck the crumbs, and that squirrel trembled violently and dashed down behind the logs. Now the birds have gone and he sits again on top of the log-pile, not three feet from me, and placidly chews the bread. The fragrance of wild roses and pine float in strong on the morning air. Rabbits and three squirrels roam around in the grass just in front, in the sunlight that catches sparkles of dew.

Now, the squirrel has really caught on. When the blackbirds appear, instead of running, he just gets down behind the logs where they cannot follow him with their wide wingspread. I wish I had brought my movie camera. This competition for food, this play of wits, is fascinating. The squirrel is the underdog physically, for they can peck the hell out of him, but he has solved the problem. The minute they disappear he hops back up on the top log, holds the bread in his front paws, and eats until they swoop in again.

Work, and for noon lunch, a glass of milk and a peanut

Griffin at Merton's grave

Griffin working in the hermitage

Griffin cooking on the two-burner
hot plate

Hermitage kitchen

Carolyn (Mrs. Victor) Hammer
at the hermitage

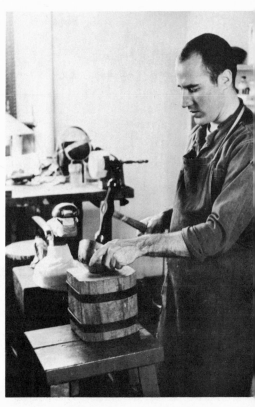

Brother Richard, the silversmith

Brother Dunstan Coleman, Griffin, Dom James Fox

Dom Jean Leclercq, O.S.B., from Clervaux, Luxembourg

Griffin's sons, Greg and Johnny, with Brothers Maurice and Richard

Brother Patrick Hart

Brother Lavrans Nielsen

Brother Ambrose Rico

Brother Maurice Flood

Dom Colomban, Dom Flavian, Griffin, Dom Anthony dining at the hermitage

Abbot Flavian Burns of Gesthsemani

Father Tarcisius Conner

Hermitage chapel

Fireplace in the hermitage

Bedroom in hermitage

Wooden cross outside the hermitage

Scenes from the hermitage, early morning

Hermitage in winter

Griffin sitting on hermitage porch

Wash on line outside hermitage

butter sandwich. The bread is too dry and stale to make eating it more than a duty. They will bring fresh bread tonight. Last night they brought a bucket of the most beautiful hand-picked strawberries from the monastery garden. Now, I take them out of the icebox and sugar them. Tonight we will have them for supper. I leave them away from the cold for a couple of hours to absorb the sugar and make some juice. They sit in white bowls near the window on this desk, marvelously beautiful and marvelously fragrant. The windows are all open now, the temperature up to eighty. Have been sitting on the porch reading.

MAY 21, 1970

Thursday. Up at 3:15, staggered in to turn on the hot plate, and then into the chapel to make the Morning Offering, then into here to light a fire in the fireplace. Now, at 4:00, with hot coffee in me and a good warm fire at my back, I come alive. All is darkness and silence outside, except for one lone whippoorwill that calls out incessantly in a rich music nearby.

Turned on the weather—to be hot and clear. Also heard that Nixon has ordered the flag flown at half-mast all day (rather than the usual half day) for the boys "who gave their lives in Vietnam." Why doesn't he tell the truth? Their lives were taken from them, in most cases at least. There was always an irony to me in this "giving one's life" when if you did not, in the army, you were shot as a deserter or something else. This is why I never took any of the medals in World War II. It is a peculiar sort of bravery when a man obeys orders, often against his grain, with the knowledge that if he does not, he gets it from his own beloved country—imprisonment, death, or dishonorable discharge.

Tonight we will offer Mass for these young men and their families. Last night we offered it for the six killed (shot in the back by police) in Augusta and their families, and the two in Jackson and their families.

Real Catholic right-wingers fascinate me. They rage against taking communion in the hand because "permission has not come from Rome." They call for "obedience to the Holy Father" in all things. But when the Holy Father laments the war in Vietnam and condemns our intervention in Cambodia, they are deaf to all obedience and in fact go right on preaching "kill the Commies and make Asia safe and free," as though this were what the Pope had said. They hold every utterance of the Pope infallible except his entire stance on peace, which they simply pretend does not exist. Selective conscience. Selective deafness.

Today, down in the Abbey, they will sing a peace Mass. I wish I could go. The Brothers are quite excited about it.

Later—6:00 a.m. The first hints of dawn. I have been out on the porch, walking slowly from end to end, saying the scapular and other prayers to the accompaniment of millions of bird songs as everything comes awake now. It was cold. I had to walk to bear the chill, and I got "cooled out" through and through. So now I am back in by the fire, filled with the peace of this utterly peaceful dawn, with the lights off and writing this by the dim light of the fire. I hear the bells now, announcing the beginning of the conventual Mass.

Later—noon. Brother Patrick says the peace Mass was beautiful and very successful. Soon they will have a civil rights Mass, and Father Flavian wants me to address the community on the subject. I hope before the Mass. I think the Mass would mean much more. There is at least one Father here, a right-winger, who told Brother Patrick "there's no such thing as racism, racism doesn't exist," after he heard that Brother Patrick wrote an article about racism.

Getting very hot. The porch thermometer, in the shade, already reads ninety.

MAY 23, 1970

Saturday. Dawn, this day of departure, beautiful cool morning. Always the two emotions on such a day—the heart runs ahead to join the family, while there is at the same time great reluctance to leave this blessed hermitage, these woods and the animals, the solitude and the silence and the companionship of the reserved Sacrament.

JUNE 27, 1970

3:00 a.m. Cool and fresh after hard rains here yesterday. Up at 2:00, and hot coffee. Johnny, Gregory, and I arrived last evening after a good enough plane trip from Dallas. We took a car in Louisville, stopped just long enough for supplies, and came on to the Abbey, arriving around 6:30.

It had rained an inch yesterday, so the road up the hill to the hermitage was impossible. Brother Maurice got a huge tractor, Father Tarcisius and Brother Patrick put the boys and me and our bags into a jeep, and we hitched the jeep to the tractor and managed to get up the road to the hermitage. There were some tense moments. Brother Maurice drove the tractor in pouring rain, but the boys enjoyed the adventure, and Maurice seemed to also. We unloaded quickly and got inside, got into dry clothes, celebrated Mass, and had a good supper of chop suey, fresh bread, milk. And then they brought out the surprise, a birthday cake for me (very good), and some dietetic ice cream. So we had a lovely time.

The rain stopped, and it cleared to a glorious, soft sunset. The boys were fascinated at the ease, humor, and simplicity of the monks, and quite taken with everything, especially Brother Maurice, who is a fine athlete and who is going to stick with them while they are here. The forecast is for beautiful weather these next two days, so they can swim, help with the cattle, etc. They will come up here each evening for our Mass and supper.

Brother Maurice took the boys back on the tractor. I visited with a young black seminarian from New Orleans who had joined us, and everyone left before 10:00, because I was in bed at 10:00 and asleep three minutes later. Slept soundly as the night grew colder, until 2:00 this morning, when the chill awakened me. I woke up feeling rested and deeply happy, so I decided to get up and unpack my work and get to it.

113

This is the hour to work—while it is cool (down to sixty now), and while the silence seems the deepest; there is not even a bird sound in the surrounding forest. I have already put out the dried bread for the squirrels and fox.

Here, already, the luxury of time is back. In the marvelous hours before dawn, there is the feeling of time to do everything without pressure or rush, time to do things correctly, time to do nothing at all except just be, time to take delight, as now, in the sound of coffee simmering on the hot plate in the kitchen; time above all to let the place work on you, absorb you, fill your tissues with the newness of silence and solitude until all the rough edges of the nerve endings are smoothed off.

It is nothing you do. It is what you allow the hours to do to you here.

Now, at 3:30. Down in the Abbey, they are up and singing vigils and getting ready to start their workday, some in the kitchens, some in the cow barns, others in the many activities that go into running a monastery that supports itself and supplies all its needs. My sons are down there in it, sleeping well, I hope, since they will not be awakened until 7:00, which will give them just time to make their beds and get to breakfast. Gregory left his camera up here. I know he will be wanting it a thousand times today. I will send it down with Brother Patrick at noon.

Later: 10:10, and the morning remains wonderfully cool, in the upper sixties, with an overcast sky and a light breeze. I have already done a day's work—eight hours. Just heard from Brother Maurice and the boys. They are coming up at noon for dinner with us, and I am really very glad. I miss seeing them. Already Johnny is begging me to let him stay until Tuesday. I will probably do that if he really wants to.

Later: 4:50 p.m., a tremendous day, clear, the breeze cool, the view from this window full of the green and distant blues of the countryside. I became extremely fatigued after noon, and slept deep, dreamless sleep until a moment ago. Now, I feel emptied and exhausted. The change is so great from the world of sound and movement and contacts that my letdown into this is almost a blow. A blessed blow, however, as the body and the

114

nervous system adjust to this completely different set of stimuli. They fall not only into rest, they collapse for a time, try to refill themselves in sleep and in inactivity, allowing the silence and the solitude (poor words, really, for what all this is) to seep in and cure and fill up every tissue of body and spirit. There has been no lack of sleep, but I am taken by the feeling that I would like to return to the bed to "sleep it out." That sleeping room, as Merton noted, "is the coolest in the cabin"—it retains the cool longer than these other rooms. By afternoon, the front room is about the same temperature as the air outside, and there is a considerable drop when I walk from here into that sleeping room. On hotter days, Merton used to take his work back there.

6:00 p.m. For ten minutes now the fox has been out front, fastidiously eating some stale potato chips that Brother Maurice threw out. The fox is about thirty feet away, and is undisturbed by the sound of my typing. I have been studying him through a pair of binoculars. Somehow I am surprised that a fox would like potato chips. Now, he has taken a large chip in his mouth, listened attentively, and walked into the woods. I suspect he heard the approaching jeep, long before I hear it.

9:30 p.m. The fox heard Father Timothy's footsteps rather than the jeep. Wonderful Mass with Father Timothy celebrating, the boys, Brothers Maurice, Pat, Martin, and Nat, and a good sort of catch-all supper afterward. They then went out and practiced throwing Greg's frisbee, and the rest of us tried. Greg, Maurice, and Johnny are real masters and do beautiful things with it. It was so marvelous to see them up here in the clearing in the forest playing with that marvelous object. Brother Nat got good at it, but Patrick, Martin, and I remained hopelessly unskilled. Now they have gone, late dusk is only now settling over the country, and I am ready for bed. There is something profoundly satisfying about going to bed for the night while there is still daylight (though faint) in the surrounding woods.

JUNE 28, 1970

Sunday. Up at 2:00, worked a couple of hours, and then returned to sleep until 5:30 when the cold awakened me. Now, after three cups of hot coffee and with a sweater on, I am almost comfortable. The sun is just rising, the temperature is in the low fifties. The birds murmur in the forest, and Sunday really begins.

I think with affection how much man's life is spent in a preoccupation with the things of the body—searching for a place to shelter it, to sleep it, to nourish it, to take care of its chill or its heat. I have been so tempted to light a fire in the fireplace, because it is really more than "brisk" this morning, but I know that it will be hot later in the day, long before the fire will have burned itself out. So I sit here huddled in this sweater, with hot coffee beside me, and watch daylight begin to penetrate the shadows of the forest and listen to all the birds come alive, not in those loud, liquid, flute-like calls of evening, but in chirpings and introspective roulades and trills.

Hanna and Bob Shepherd are coming today for lunch. They are bringing the food, and we will celebrate a noon Mass up here in Latin at Hanna's request.

Later—7:30 p.m. The company stayed until 4:30, when I was completely played out. They are wonderful people and brought a great picnic lunch. As soon as they left I lay down for a nap and was in deep sleep when Greg, Johnny, and Maurice came up to make some popcorn at 6:30. I was glad to see them. Got up and had some coffee and visited until a moment ago when they took off with a bag of popcorn for the night. They are due at the cow barn at 7:30 to see them milk. They are going to try to get me a small bottle of fresh milk. Now, I am still so sore and bone-tired I am going back to bed, even though the sun is still well up.

JUNE 29, 1970

Monday. Noon of a strange day, marvelously beautiful, but strange because I can hardly do anything but sleep. I slept twelve hours last night, did not get up until 5:30 this morning, prepared the beef for tonight, then the boys and Maurice came up at about 8:30 and I fixed them bacon and eggs for breakfast. They left shortly after 9:30 and I fell onto the bed and slept deeply until 11:00. And I still do not feel as though my sleep is out. The weather is beautiful. I feel only an irresistible drowsiness—more than that, a desperate need to sleep, a feeling of great weakness.

Brother Maurice is taking the boys in to catch the flight back home this afternoon. I do hope their stay here has meant something to them besides just the "fun." Brother Maurice has been marvelous to them.

JUNE 30, 1970

Tuesday. No time to write in this all day, and now at 6:10 I make a beginning, realizing I will have to stop soon enough for Mass and supper.

Sisters Mary Luke and Jane Marie [Sister Mary Luke Tobin was the only American woman auditor at Vatican II; Sister Jane Marie Richardson attended as her secretary] came last evening for a conference about Merton, brought me tapes and other items dealing with their relationship to Merton. Father Flavian came up to celebrate Mass and have supper with us. The meat was tough as hell and I was embarrassed, but "it had a good flavor" as the Sisters said consolingly. And everything else was beautiful, including the conversation. They are remarkable, both of them. The two foxes came out and put on a real show, which greatly entranced them (and me, too).

Brother Maurice got the boys off safely, and then at Mass made a beautiful intention of thanksgiving for the love they had brought him (and that he brought them). Piedy called today to say the boys were really overwhelmed by the visit, and talked her arm off half the night telling her everything they had done and how great the monks were.

Now I hear the truck coming through the woods, so I had better get some pants on. I am sitting here in tee shirt and underpants because of the terrific heat of today. The wheelchair is an enormous help. I have nothing like the pain of the past weeks, and it is because I spend part of the day in the chair, which permits me to go right on working and is a much better solution than the bed. Today is the first day I have really felt great and really worked well. The heat is fascinating. It fascinated Tom who referred to it often. It does strange things, brings a strange kind of joy to the life of the forest, to the hermit life. It is very uncomfortable, almost suffocating, but you feel a deep kinship with the panting foxes and squirrels and rabbits that seek the shade, and you hear the oboe tones of locusts in the trees as even the birds fall silent in such burning heat.

JULY 1, 1970

Wednesday, July 1. Cool, splendidly cool, now at dawn. The sky is clear, but a mist hangs in the still air over the countryside. Sometime in the middle of the night I was awakened by the near presence and powerful fragrance of a skunk—the first I have smelled here. It must have been right under my window, because when I came to the front door to see if I could see it, the fragrance was much less. Bells from the abbey—faint on the air, a good and deep silence except for a loud crow's cawing in one direction and the bawling of a cow far more distantly in another.

It is supposed to be very hot again today. I wonder if I should close the windows at the beginning of the sun's appearance and try to keep this cool air inside and the hot air out.

Now, I must get to work.

JULY 2, 1970

Thursday, July 2, **Visitation.** It is blazing hot in that lush tropical way that the South can get in the summer—all the plants and trees are green. The temperature is near one hundred degrees at noon. I have worked in the early cool of the morning. I have taken cold showers and remained naked except for shoes and scapular, which is the only thing that makes sense in this heat and isolation. In only a moment the clothes are sopping and have to be washed or they sour. But now I am dressed. One hundred Contemplative Nuns are here for Mass and some kind of a spiritual luncheon picnic, and since they will surely drift this way to see the hermitage, I am going to have to stay dressed until about vespers time, when they will leave. I have it pretty well cleaned up. I went out a while ago and cut small white wildflowers and some very beautiful yellow lilies and made a bouquet for the chapel.

A strange and marvelous moment as I placed the flowers

118

before the reserved Sacrament, sat on the chair for a short visitation, felt marvelously happy and at peace and clear within myself. Sat there and smelled the cedar of the altar, and experienced the snow-whiteness of the walls as a kind of dazzling light, and was aware of the sweat that literally flowed out from me, from my hair, down my face, into my eyes, down my belly and legs, sopping in God's presence in the silence of the forest, listening to the rasping of the locusts—everything conjoining into a harmony that made me reluctant to go dry off. The squirrels, foxes, skunks, snakes, and even the birds pant in the shade of the noonday heat. I hear no sound except one high, thin field lark's song and the locust's sawing, and no breeze moves a single leaf in the forest. A great sun heat, a deep quiet, a profound joy, a fasting hunger in my belly, a child's desire to eat and then to nap on dry warm sheets that will soon be cooled by my sweat and the fan.

A movement attracts my attention. Two large butterflies brave the heat to come suck the sweetness from those yellow wood lilies. I think of Gerald Vann [English Dominican priest] and his love for the woods and the lilies of the fields and all the plants and animals. He is buried now at Newcastle-upon-Tyne in England.

Later—4:30 p.m. Temperature is 99 in the shade. Just talked with Dom James in his hermitage, and he said it was 110 in the sun.

JULY 3, 1970

Fierce hot day. They say it is the hottest day in four years, and that tomorrow will be the same. Oh, me . . . .

At that moment I heard something and saw the electric typewriter blaze in my hands and got a huge jolt that brought up an involuntary scream. In a moment I was on the floor with the wheelchair on top of me, utterly bewildered. Lightning had struck that lead-in wire with a crack, gone through and made jolting contact with me. My eyes were blurry when I climbed to my feet, and I was amazed to discover that the shock had deprived me of control over my functions, and without my being aware of it I had messed my pajama pants. The clock was still going, now it was raining and blowing outside—hard. My typewriter was buzzing. I cautiously turned it off. It was 11:20, and I had promised to make lunch for Brothers Patrick and Maurice who were bringing up Amiya Chakravarty for a visit with me.

I went and cleaned up the worst of the mess and put my pajama pants and slippers in a rain barrel with some strong soap. I lay down for a moment. I put on shoes and socks so if another bolt struck I would not be grounded. I tried to call down to Patrick to delay the visit with Chakravarty, but the phone line had been knocked out.

Now, later—at a little past noon. I have bathed, shaved, washed my hair, washed my pajamas and slippers, cleaned the mess from the room, and expect my guests any moment. A new storm is brewing, a vicious one with high winds and much lightning. I am getting some sense now. My sight is bleared and the skin is off my left cheek. I have done nothing to prepare dinner and am so shaky I cannot right now. I realize that the wheelchair saved my life. I was in it, with my feet on the footrest, the whole thing insulated from this stone floor by rubber wheels. Even at that I got a great jolt, but at least I wasn't grounded. If I had been in my desk chair with my feet on the floor (I was wearing only cloth slippers), the full power of the lightning bolt would have gone through me. Also, the typewriter is metal but the keys are plastic, and I am sure that helped. What continues to surprise me, because I never was actually unconscious, was that I did not realize until later that my bowels had moved.

Now, later. The storm got so bad, the winds so high, I was sure this cabin would go. I went into the chapel with the Blessed Sacrament determined to die there, if die I must. I am sure these tornadic winds and rains have caused great damage to the countryside. Now it seems to be settling into a steady rain. Perhaps the worst is over.

Fascinating, in a way, that my first involuntary reaction was a loud scream, like the one Tom gave. This makes me feel absolutely certain that the shock killed him, and not that he had a heart attack and fell against the fan. I feel a strange, almost tender union with him now in that moment of the jolt, the scream, the blank-out and death. I returned from the momentary blank-out, but he did not.

Later—almost 4:00. Chakravarty came and stayed 2½ hours, an immeasurably moving encounter—this scholar saint, so full of compassion. We talked of his years with Tagore, his long association with Gandhi, his friendship with Schweitzer, and some of our common friends. A tremendous communion together. He let me photograph that most beautiful face, and of course, we talked mostly about his relations with Merton— what a touching, simple, great soul. He said he had always lived in the shadow of great men, and never wanted to steal their light (which is why he was reluctant to be photographed, implying I should have photographed them, not him).

Later—night. Chakravarty spoke in chapter down at the Abbey at 7:00, so Father Tarcisius and the Brothers came for Mass at 7:30. Father was very concerned about my near-electrocution.

Then we offered our Mass intentions.

A beautiful Mass. I prayed especially for Chakravarty and for Tom, and quite especially in thanksgiving for having lived through the experience of the electric shock, quite especially because it allowed me to live something of Tom's physical immolation. Now the soreness is here to remind me—some pain in the chest and the left side of the neck and the base of the skull and around the left eye—probably due to getting knocked out of my chair more than to the shock itself.

Later still—things are pretty well messed up. I cannot recall anything specific about Chakravarty's visit. I lay on the bed trying to sleep and also trying to remember what I wanted to transcribe. And I know he was here, and remember him, but am blank about some of it. The electricity knocked out the heating element on the hot water heater. And when I went to turn on the little transistor radio, it was dead, too. It was not even on when the lightning struck, but it was plugged into the same high wall plug as the typewriter, and it was sitting on the metal stove. It hums, but does not work. It obviously got burned up somewhere inside. I can smell the odor. Over and above these things—the soreness, the almost uncontrollable diarrhea—there is a kind of tremendous forlornness tonight at the sobering thought that if it had not been for that rubber-wheeled wheelchair, they would certainly be shipping my body home tonight for my family to bury, and thousands of people would be talking uncomfortably about the similarity of Tom's death and mine. I have in my nostrils the faint arnica odor of pharmacies which is really the smell of burned-out wiring, and it nauseates me.

There is a strange consolation in the fact that the monastery phone system is knocked out. No calls can come in. We will have real silence for a couple of days.

Later. Sometime past midnight, and I cannot sleep, so thought I would make these notes. Brother Raymond, a Salvatorian [Brother Raymond Taylor, cofounder of the Servants of the Poor], from Michigan originally, and now Wisconsin, has come to accept some kind of artwork from Brother Lavrans. He came up here. He resembles someone I know, and I thought I knew him. No, but in a few moments, we knew each other deeply. A most marvelous visit. I will never forget him and will pray for him especially because he has long carried both the white and the black man's special burdens, and everything he said went deeply into me.

I am still messed up from the shock; the undersides of both hands are completely numb, as though they were asleep, and all the muscles in my belly are slack and I cannot tighten them. Strangely, at the moment of the shock, Father Flavian was saying Mass. Perhaps his prayers saved me.

In any event, Father Eudes, the M.D., wants to examine me tomorrow, and that is probably best. Father Tarcisius will come pick me up at 5:45 a.m. By then we will probably be able to sort out what pains came from the fall and what came from the electric shock. I am not clear. I have trouble pronouncing words and I got names mixed up tonight—called Brother Maurice Brother Marty, called Brother Lavrans Brother Flavian. A good night's sleep should fix me up all right.

JULY 4, 1970

Up at 4:30, relieved to find myself intact and quite all right. The soreness now is just muscular—the stomach is okay. I feel a real sense of gratitude to see this day on this earth. Only got four hours sleep, but I can get a good nap later in the day. Will go down for the special Mass for racial justice.

Still dark outside. A fine breeze in the trees.

Later—10:00 a.m. Mass, and I got sick, but managed to stick it out. Father Eudes examined me. Things are all right. The shock was apparently to the left side, and the place on the face is a flash burn, and not an injury from the fall. The muscle spasms are part of it, so is the loss of yesterday's events as far as the memory is concerned. He gave me some muscle relaxants and wants me to stay in bed today. He had me cancel my talk for the community tomorrow. I will give it next time.

Later—nearly 12:00. I slept an hour, and then could not sleep longer, but too addled to work. So I came in and listened to the tape Brother Maurice made of Chakravarty's talk last night on Merton. It is a lesson to me in beauty and delicacy—a masterful talk. How I wish he could write the biography. I pray for his kind of sensitivity.

Later—almost 6:00. The day remains cool and beautiful. I have slept two hours. A lost Fourth of July as far as work is concerned, but a beautiful and recuperative one, and I feel as if I am now getting my mind back from that accident yesterday. I know I went to Mass a million years ago this morning, that Father Eudes preached and then examined me and gave me medication. I am aware now that during the blank-out, Brother Maurice came and put clean sheets on my bed, cleaned the bathroom, brought milk, and cleaned the cabin. I was never even remotely aware of it until now, when I see the evidence of all this. What a remarkable man he is—to do all these things while I am right here, and my never seeing him or realizing he is doing them.

9:00 p.m. The Brothers and Father Tarcisius came up to bring more medication from Father Eudes, and also to have some supper with me. Beautiful evening, very quiet and serene and untaxing. They have just left. I stood out on the porch a moment, noting the temperature at sixty-eight. After the jeep had got beyond hearing, I was turning to come back in and take the prebed medication when I heard a trumpet from some distance, in the direction of the monastery, playing a few bars of "Down by the Riverside." Then silence. Then a couple of riffs. Then silence and a tentative scale. Strange sounds in the night—undoubtedly one of the monks out on a path somewhere, practicing his horn as quietly as possible. But surely if I heard it here, the sleeping monks must have heard it too. Many of them retire at 7:30 or 8:00, and it was after 9:00, really the time of the old "Great Silence." Only those few notes, and then silence again. The sounds would have been beautiful—blending with the forest, unharsh, if they had not been so startling, so unexpected at this hour and in this place.

Now, I am in a quandary. I cannot remember at all if I took my dymelor tonight. If I did not, I am in trouble. If I did and then decide to take another, I am in trouble. Father Tarcisius would know, but I have no way now of contacting him, and don't want to wake anyone up at this hour. I will just presume I took it, and then if I get shaky during the night, I'll know that I didn't, and take one.

Father Eudes sent up a note with the medication:

John:
Take (1) blue-white caps about 7 p.m.
     (2) red capsules about 15 minutes before going to bed.
     (3) if you are having cramps take 2 aspirins or 1 emperin every 4 hours.
     (4) if you need me any time, even during the night, call at #244
               Sweet dreams!

The whole community knows about it now, and are very concerned. Father Flavian is going to speak about it briefly at chapter in the morning, especially since I was scheduled to speak, and now cannot, because of the memory lapses and general muscle spasms and the medication I have to take for that.

So I expect there will be all kinds of lightning rods and such put on the hermitage right away to protect it from such accidents again. Father Flavian's is thus protected, and so is Dom James's hermitage. Apparently Father Eudes was over in Father Flavian's hermitage for a day of solitude, and that place got a hit or near miss, too, but was saved from any damage by the lightning rods or whatever.

Have been to bed, but now at 11:00 I make these notes because if I don't make them I fear I will not retain them. Each time I get just to the edge of sleep, the left side of my chest begins to quiver and it irritates me back to a kind of desperate wakefulness. I turned on the light, read the pages of notes concerning the recent (June 21) death of Brother Elias (at age thirty of lung cancer) and the texts he chose for his last Mass, and the homily Father Flavian preached at the funeral Mass. Remarkable pictures of something almost unknown to the world—the special way that death is handled in a Trappist monastery: the great beauty of Elias's acceptance of his suffering and last agony, the manner in which God's grace showed through him to all the community in the last months, and particularly the last hours before he was released from the mystery of life, the mystery of dying, into the mystery of whatever his existence is now.

It has helped me greatly to read these pages, which I read with the slow concentration of a child, aware that they were not being retained. It has helped me to renew what in a sense I already knew, that I should not be distressed because since the shock yesterday (or the day before) I have been unable to connect with anything at Mass, or with prayer; as though the words were bouncing off of the stone wall of my unfeelingness. I knew it was all right, but could not help feeling some lack in all this. Reading these pages, the extreme docility of Brother Elias's acceptance of real suffering . . . well, it makes me know that it is not important how sensitive we are to the events: what is happening within us at the reception of communion is happening whether we can feel anything or not. And so I can go sit like a dumb stone in the presence of the reserved Sacrament and offer that dumbness and unfeelingness itself as my prayer, with the suspicion perhaps that *that* is the most valuable and valid prayer I can ever really utter.

Now, I must go to bed. Now I am truly ready—and past

ready for sleep—but I knew that if I did not make these notes, worthless though they may be, they would vanish forever from my recollection.

I turned in my wheelchair to go to bed and felt a breeze through the front window, and realized that I had come in here to write a line about that and got off onto other things. I had really come in here because lying on my bed after reading the pages about Elias, I realized that the night air from the forest had chilling undercurrents, and I was filled with delight to think that I would have to sleep under covers tonight. It seemed to me so wonderful and joyful that I came in here to note it down, and then forgot it until now. It is like the joy of those first chill nights of autumn, the special joy of feeling chill air on the face, but feeling the body warm under sheets and blankets; and this chill air is special, because it is filled with the fragrance of pine and cedar trees in the surrounding forest.

JULY 5, 1970

I am up at 7:00, grogged from the medication, but feeling all right. I take hot coffee and sit here watching the stillness of an overcast morning on this green land. Squirrels and rabbits are in the grass near the porch, foraging for the bread scraps (at least the squirrels are; the rabbits seem to be just sitting in the grass). I think of Father Flavian talking in chapter this morning, and am deeply grateful to Father Eudes for not permitting me to attempt it. I am much recovered, but not in any condition to give an "address," even to such a sympathetic and charitable audience as the monks.

Everything is seen in a special light this morning, in a special way, as though a semi-opaque haze had been removed from sight. I have heated water to wash the dishes, filled the sink with cold water (about halfway), put in the dishes, and then poured the hot water from an aluminum kettle. Then I filled the kettle to heat more water—the spoons, the grey light on the dented aluminum, the thin suds, all of these things viewed as in a great painting . . .

Brother Pat just called to check on me. Splendid man. I told him about the trumpet, and he said that was Brother Michael who goes to one of the barns at night to practice, and that they cannot hear it at the Abbey, but apparently he was playing in this direction and the sound carried across the valley. I told him to tell Brother Michael I enjoyed it.

Nearly 10:00. And I am messed up again about whether or not I took the dymelor this morning. Father Eudes just called and wanted to know if I recalled his coming up here the day before the accident (because the shock affects only recent memory). I was startled. I had no recollection of his having been up here, but of course now I do. He wants me to give this diabetic medication to Brother Maurice and have Maurice administer it until I get a little better memory.

As I was writing that, Brother Patrick came up with some fresh rye bread, a gift from Brother Donald who is concerned about the accident. What a touching gesture. Also some carrots and radishes and onions from the garden. I have washed them and put them on the drainboard to dry. By the soft grey light that comes in the kitchen window, they are extraordinarily beautiful.

Brother Maurice picked a cup of fresh blackberries from the bushes against the stone wall Tom made. I recall now that I came in here to get my camera and photograph those few ripe blackberries and the many, many red ones (which are the unripe ones—one of the old Fathers here used to warn the novices: "Don't forget—the red raspberries are green.").

Later: Why am I ashamed of this memory blank? I am, though, or at least I am embarrassed. I find myself wasting a lot of time. I go to make up my bed and something distracts me between here and there, and half an hour later I pass through the kitchen and note the bed has not been made. The simplest things seem overwhelmingly complex. I got out the eggs and just now went in and saw that everything was set to make the mayonnaise—eggs, oil, lemon—and I had not made the mayonnaise.

The supper is cooking now, at 4:00. It has been a nightmare to prepare it, to remember what I have put in and what I left out for later. I hope to God it is not a total mess. Brother Raymond is coming tonight, I think. I should go now and take a nap. I do not know if I went to Mass this morning or not. No,

I think it was yesterday. We will have Mass here and bless the ikon that Brother Lavrans made to present to Brother Raymond.

5:00 p.m. Very still and overcast—no bird songs, no sound at all. I have washed out two undershirts, and they hang now on the trees. Immense desire to nap. But an even greater desire to sit here and look at this forest, to miss nothing of this silence. Still, I should go take a short nap before they come up for Mass.

9:45 p.m. Beautiful Mass. We (Father Tarcy) blessed the ikon, which is certainly one of the most beautiful I have ever seen. I photographed it in color, and do hope I got something good. Brother Raymond and I connect unbelievably—it is as though we were really brothers, or had known one another for a long, long time. What good friends I have here.

JULY 9, 1970

Thursday. A morning of the most extraordinary beauty. After rains last night, the sun shines brightly, but a wall of fog stretches beyond the hedgerow, obscuring the distant hills and the masses of trees. All is still, sparkling, fresh.

Last evening I read the *Journals* (Vols. IV and V) of Julien Green [French novelist], which had so fascinated Tom, and which fascinated me also, but less so. They are journals (at least these two) that are written with the foreknowledge that they will be published. They are full of integrity, nevertheless, and frankness, but they have a polished quality, a studied quality that lacks spontaneity. However, Green's encounters are fascinating—it is a splendid history of the Paris and the people of the art and musical and literary worlds who were and are his friends. I also enjoyed (without always admiring) his constant references to music he heard. I found that in the early days of the war (1939) we reacted to the tragedy in a similar way: neither of us could bear great music—it made us feel too much. You needed not to feel this deeply. He could not listen to a single note of Schubert, and the late Beethoven quartets would have shattered him. I remember writing in my own letters or diaries of that period that I could not hear anything serious or moving, but would listen to Offenbach or something of that sort—music that did not get below the surface of the skin.

How late I come to these things. How many years of reading I have missed.

It is 3:30 now. Clear, warm (but not hot) day. Many things to throw in these pages, and since I have worked hard all day until 2:00 p.m. (when I napped), I will try to get them down.

Naomi [Burton Stone, one of the Merton trustees] called, very stricken about the accident. I was surprised and alarmed to discover I had written her twice when I only thought I had written her one brief note (disturbed because it meant I have not got back everything yet). It is strange to do something as complex as write a letter and have it completely blanked from your memory. I was terribly moved that she would call. I guess the second letter really worried her. I did not (I think) keep a carbon, so I don't know what I wrote her.

One of the things that tires me with the Green *Journals* is the realization that so many of his encounters (with Gide, with Roger Martin du Gard, etc.) become a kind of peacock's dance in which each man is aware that the other is going to go home and write up his version of the encounter in his journal, which will one day be published. It seems to me that Tom would have tired of this fast, but I have to realize that, as Father Eudes emphasized, at this time Tom was living down in the Abbey, mostly with men who had no interest whatsoever in the literary life and gossip of Paris, and that Tom was fundamentally lonely in a special way. And the Green *Journals*, so skillfully evocative, really took Thomas Merton right out of the roughness of the community life, into Green's carefully appointed apartment, or into the studies of Gide, François Daudet, or to intimate dinners in Green's quarters with Raissa and Jacques Maritain, etc., places where the "French" part of Thomas Merton was really at home. Also Green's quest for solitude in the heart of Paris, for the perfect quarters perfectly furnished where he could work without distraction of noises, etc. All of this spoke to Tom in a most special way. Why should I question any of this? In my younger days, I burst with the excitement of such visits, such

129

dinners, such concerts (dinners with Maurice Raynal, the Cas-
adesuses, Maritains—the whole thing), and would burst with it
again, and do whenever I go.

Now, 6:15. Time for them to come say Mass in Tom's
chapel. The sky is lightly overcast, the air is cool, and a deep
hush lies over the countryside. Not a bird sings. No sound at all.
No leaf stirs. Profound peace crowds out and makes silly all the
things that bothered me an hour ago—the panic of having more
work to do than time to do it during the remainder of this visit.
All of that seems, for the moment, to fall into place and to be
utterly unimportant. The moment is important—the moment
of total silence and total solitude and total attention to the great
healing that imperceptibly takes place within the deepest re-
cesses of being.

This was the moment Tom craved and needed and knew he
needed, the moment when the soul is completely liberated. Now
a faint breeze comes. A cottontail moves in the hedgerow, but
the birds remain silent. A desire to go from this profound peace
into sleep. An unbelievable moment, a moment when I feel
fused entirely with the forests and the light and the life within
the forests and the silence and the freedom and the tremendous
repose. A moment when the soul desires nothing more, but the
body desires to go spend the time in the presence of the Blessed
Sacrament. Strange—the soul is already there so does not need
to go, but the body wants that. The body drags me there, if only
for a moment.

JULY 10, 1970

10:00 a.m. Up since 2:30—coffee and work and deep felicity in
the silence of this countryside. The sun is out clear, but the
mountains are hazed. The air is quiet and cool. I stop the work
to make these notes and to clean up the cabin. And I put on the
recording Brother Patrick brought me last night, the 1951 Bu-
dapest Quartet recording of the Beethoven opus 18 Quartets,
just reissued on Odyssey. I had forgotten what tremendous performances these were, though I used to own them. The later
recordings by the same group were not this spellbinding. And
what music to hear in the silences of these forests.

Theological speculation about marriage by men who have never been married always fascinates me. How rarely does it bear any resemblance to the intimate reality of this relationship between man and woman and their children! All the hearing of confessions, all the transference (of mystical love toward marital love), all the "family counseling," etc., does not place the theologian in the sure earth of the experience. Gerald Vann had the deepest knowledge of any theological writer I have ever read in this area. Aquinas, too, had an extraordinary knowledge. This is brought home to me by reading Louis Bouyer. Bouyer is a man of deep sensitivity, but his writing on marriage is so speculative, I recognize no connection between it and what marriage is in my (and others') experience. Usually such speculation degrades marriage in a subtle way. (Vann never did.)

How often do such writings, which start out as serious speculation, end up giving us a little pat on the back and suggesting that it is really okay to have chosen second best as a vocation, and assuring us that there is nothing, really, *wrong* with it (which degrades, because we never for a moment thought there was until they assured us there wasn't). The worst is when they imply that we could really reach great spiritual heights by the practice in marriage of a kind of celibate and monastic asceticism, keeping always in mind that you maintain the proper hierarchy of values in loving God more than you love each other and in willing to drop everything if God calls. What monstrousness.

I was asked by a priest in an interview not long ago what I would do if God faced me with a choice between him and my family. "If I ever suffered such an illusion," I told him, "I would know I had cracked up and gone completely wacky."

It is really this: that they suggest you should be temperate or "moderate" in love, keeping everything in good order in separate compartments, each partner going his own way into the stratospheres of mystical growth and coming together "reasonably" for procreative purposes, to pay the bills, to sign the income tax returns, and perhaps to eat (sparingly).

Great Lord, this is as absurd as the suggestion I always hear that we should be moderate in matters of justice: to be moderate in matters of love is simply not to love. To be moderate in matters of justice is to be simply unjust. These are the tepidities, among others, that Christ vomited out of his mouth. To my poor mind and heart, such attitudes constitute the deepest and most maddening obscenity I know. (Maddening because couched in attitudinous terms which can, for most of us, obscure the blatant stupidity that is really there as the essence of the speculation.)

I wish we could have more children, but for the basest motives, because it occurs to me that I would like to name a child of mine Mea Culpa Griffin just in order to edify the above speculators about marriage and Christianity and *fausse conceptions de la divinisation*. And of course, if they were twins, the other could be Felix C. Griffin (or F. Culpa Griffin).

Later. Have got into some clothes and shaved. My eyes feel bleary from so much reading; they burn as though I had got soap in them.

While shaving I allowed the thought to come and remain a moment before rejecting it. Why did God allow me to live after that electric shock? One should not entertain such speculation for a moment, because there is no way whatsoever of thinking with God's mind in this. I cannot help but suspect, however, that perhaps it is because of the work to be done on Tom's biography, which, if it can be done properly, is a work of great potential importance. It confirms in me at least, in a sense, my intuition that this must be something other than a "critical evaluation," and more like an exposition (à la Beethoven); that I must take in, absorb within me everything I can, understand everything I can, and then allow and trust that what filters back out is as near to the truth as I can get.

I pray to the Holy Spirit to direct me in making it purely the life of Tom and not the life of Tom *as seen by* anyone, or as analyzed by anyone. This does not mean that I get out of it or stay out of it (which is not too difficult); it means something difficult, but to be attempted nevertheless. It means that I give up what I am, all my characteristic notes (particularly those wherein we differ) in order to feed into myself, into my actions and reactions, so much of what he was that for the time I am writing his biography, I will in effect be writing a kind of autobiography of him, hoping to select those highlights that he might very well have selected, to see as important what he saw as important. Perhaps all the years when I moved more and more deeply into an almost innate tendency to abandon what I am (or to hold it in suspension) in order to "become the other" was merely a preparation for this work. Am I really writing from myself here, or is it the Beethoven that flows through me onto the keys of the typewriter? I think it is the Beethoven, which transforms me, so intimate is the connection. It goes through me and types these notes, the way, inversely, the lightning came through the typewriter to flow into me and teach me how Tom died.

I feel utterly unequal to the task. I trust that the prayers of all his friends and mine, on which I count, will help me obtain the guidance of the Holy Spirit in all this. And I trust most of all that Tom will guide me. In other words, left to my own pitiful resources I could not hope to do it; but I long ago stopped counting on those for anything.

People constantly ask me: "How are you going about writing the biography? What new things have you discovered about Merton? What are you studying about him now?" I give very poor answers, because the questions embarrass me. I absorb his journals and letters and writings, yes, but they are only part of it. What sense would it make to most if I told what I feel to be the truth: I listen to the silences he loved, I let the view of a tree saturate me, I let the hours before dawn pump all their silent musical jubilance into me. That is the deepest and most important part of the research. I light a fire in the winter. That is important. I listen to the rain and wipe up the spots where it leaks in. And that is important.

JULY 11, 1970

Not much sleep last night. I filled my mind with what I have done here, where I am to begin when I return in August, and above all with the awe of my having survived that electrical shock so that I am returning home to my family today under my own power. And the return to life was a return to a kind of freshness of view. I listened to the croaking of frogs at midnight, to the high rasp of crickets in the silent forest. And this morning my sight is absorbed by the freshness of early daylight on this green countryside.

And tonight I will be home with my family, in that blessedness.

JULY 19, 1970

Sunday. Early, and I coffee myself out of the fog of sleep; but only for a moment, because on the FM the Bach "Magnificat" tells me what it is to be alive.

I woke up feeling a great heaviness in me, a great lack of energy and alertness. Then I realized why. It is because the *Newsweek* thing will be published soon, and that sort of thing, no matter how good, wearies and depresses me. I am sick of seeing my name, sick of all publicity. I pray that I will have the strength and good sense to find ways of avoiding any further interviews. I wrote the editors, thanked them for their graciousness, told them of my appreciation for the thoughtfulness of Kent Biffle (their Houston reporter), but expressed my "ardent hope" they would find the material too uninteresting to use.

Now, later—nearly 9:00. I hear the sounds of Sunday morning; the family getting up, water running and toilets flushing in the bathrooms, the smell of coffee and toast. I got up and went to greet them, refused toast, but took some more coffee. It will be hot today. I am back now in the little office, surrounded by the pictures, the filing cabinets, the strong electric light, and the air conditioner hums in the background. I pray for a day of quiet in which to work, and for the energy to dig into it.

Herakleitos: "Bigotry is the disease of religion."

Tom's great, intuitive preoccupation with freedom, with an authentic and maximum freedom. He felt, as I do, that it can only exist with any authenticity in a life of great solitude, as detached as possible from institutions. An authentic solitude does not mean being alone necessarily—it means being left alone in a sense: one can have that in a family, in a community

135

where there is sufficient respect for another's privacy just to leave him a maximum of freedom and a minimum of interior interference. This kind of solitude exists in many good marriages and in a family life that hides nothing, that does not need jealously to guard the moments of privacy, or the interior privacy, because no one is assaulting it really. It requires a love that gives but never grasps, that liberates but never imprisons. Tom was so sensitized to all of this that even benign incursions panicked him. They sicken me. He sought that freedom in total abandonment of all things to the will of God; in a vertical relationship. The horizontal relationships (monastic structures, others thinking they were helping him to attain interior liberty by interfering with it) form the cross (+) of the contemplative, which is why he sought the hermit life, or one of the reasons. I don't mean he sought the hermit life to avoid the cross, but because it was a way to the kind of freedom that does not compromise a man like him. It was his vocation. It is the vocation of a few men, not everyone.

I heard again last night the statement, terrifying in its implications, that one hears so often from good and sincere men: "This is a nation of laws, not of men." Do men prattle this kind of trash (it is becoming more and more a nation of "laws" and not of "men"—that is the trouble) without ever reflecting on what they really are saying, what they mean? They will also say that "laws are for the common good." Of what? Of man, or of laws themselves? This is some distance from the ideal of government "for the people." Was there ever anything more absurd than the delusion that free men should pay taxes to support a government "of the people and by the people" that in fact becomes more and more tyrannical in its repression of men's freedoms? Oh, not so much openly (though there is plenty of that), but quite especially in the area of man's freedom to be private. Simon [Yves Simon, the French philosopher] has a marvelous chapter on "facts" and truth. The computers end up gathering all the facts and storing them in a computer bank, and then giving out, whenever desired, with a whole computerized composite of everything about man: a world of facts, medical, psychological, spiritual, intellectual, material. At the press of a button they can cough up all the facts, plus a judgment, and you are there not in truth, but in computerized fact with all your driving infractions, overdrawn checks, religious practices, prostate surgeries, sexual practices, etc., in a mangled and dehumanized composite for anyone to see. All of this in the guise of "the common good." The totalitarian state is the logical result of this concept of "the common good."

Dick Gregory last night commented that he could not understand how nine- and ten-year-old children could find heroin pushers in almost every city, but the FBI can't find them.

SEPTEMBER 16, 1970

Wednesday. 4:10 a.m. and cold up in this forest this clear moonlit morning. Woke up at 3:30, heated water for the coffee (the hot plate does not heat the way it did, and it takes a long time to boil the water), took my medication, and now am seated here at the worktable with a blanket around my shoulders and the hot coffee beside me. Except for the high rasp of crickets, the woods are still and silent. A great sense of liberating solitude.

Flew into Louisville Monday, went to the O'Callaghans' for a dinner with Madeline and Eugene Meatyard [photographer] and Guy Davenport [novelist]. But it was my first day to remain up all day, and though the dinner was splendid, I was too tired to think of many questions to ask about Merton. A good first meeting, however. Spent the night at the airport motel and drove in here yesterday morning. Stood the trip and the long day and the drive without the appearance of any pain. They have provided everything I could conceivably need here at the hermitage—the wheelchair, the meals (prepared in the infirmary kitchen and brought up), and even a hospital bed so I can lie propped up and read during the day. [Between his tenth and eleventh visits to the hermitage, Griffin had undergone surgery.] They checked with the infirmarian to see that they have a good supply of probanthine in the event I should need to take a larger dosage by shot. Certainly I can recuperate here better than anywhere else in the world, certainly much better than in any hospital. And they manage all this without really interrupting the solitude.

Father Tarcisius and Brother Patrick met me at the gate and brought me up, had lunch with me, and got me settled in. What a joy to see them again. They returned with supper last evening, and we said Mass in the chapel off the kitchen, reserved the

Sacrament—a quiet, beautiful Mass. We were much aware of how we miss Brother Maurice, who has gone to the new foundation in North Carolina. It is almost the first time we have celebrated Mass here without him.

Worked yesterday afternoon and was ready to sleep by 8:00 p.m. Went to bed while it was still daylight—dusk light, really. Awakened to take my medicine at midnight, and did not need to turn on the lights because a full moon lighted the countryside and the cabin's interior. Filled with great joy and a sense of relief that the trip did no harm, and that I can stay here and work; that the pains did not come to send me back to the doctors and the hospital. Talked with Piedy three times yesterday, so she is reassured. Slept profoundly until this early morning. The full moon is still quite high above the black masses of pine trees; the air is fragrant of pine and cedar.

Now a new sound—a rooster crows from some great distance. I glance at the clock and see that I got up an hour before he did. Well, his matins are much louder than mine. He must be the Caruso of cocks. Such lung-bursting fanfare, like one of those Venetian brass voluntaries of Gabriel.

Later—almost 6:00. No hint of dawn as yet. The most marvelous adjustment I have to make here is to the new concept of time. In these long hours before day, time stands, and there is plenty of it to do all things. No need to hurry. It is a tremendous gift, and always it takes some readjustment. Time to go sit in that chapel before the vigil lamp, as long as one wishes—a half hour, three quarters of an hour, all day, if that feels right. No schedule to meet, no appointments to keep. Time to make breakfast and wash the dishes. This morning a hard-boiled egg and cottage cheese and a glass of apple juice. Time to savor that and then go spread stale bread crumbs on the porch for the birds and the squirrels to have when daylight comes. Time to fix raisins in a fruit jar, with some lemon and then boiling apple juice poured over and the jar sealed. They will be right for dinner tonight, and should be good with cottage cheese (the only kind I am allowed now).

The moon is still high at 6:30. The nights are much longer than when I was last here. Now, I have to get back on the bed and study the workbooks Tom left. It is too cool to stay up. A

139

breeze brings that outside chill across my desk. The rooster has stopped, but a screech owl cries out from the same direction, though much nearer.

SEPTEMBER 18, 1970

Friday already. The days go without my realizing it. No time to write in this yesterday—or rather I did not take time. Worked steadily and well. This system of the hospital bed and the cassette recorder is splendid. I get the bedrest without losing the time.

An incident occurred here that could really only happen to a Trappist. A couple of nights ago, around midnight, one of the guests here, an elderly benefactor of the Abbey whose first name is Everett, began to have some pain. Brother Wilfred—who has been an infirmarian (and may still be)—took a look at him and thought it was perhaps a hernia and that they should just go ahead and take him into town to the hospital. They telephoned Father Felix in the infirmary and he agreed, so they called one of the Fathers or Brothers and asked him to pick up a car and bring Everett down and they would meet him and drive in to the hospital. The driver misunderstood them to say pick up Father Edward, an elderly Father here. So he went and awakened Father Edward, told him he had a hernia and that he was supposed to go to the hospital. Father Edward, with incredible docility, said he did not know he had a hernia, but if they said he did that was fine. The driver took him to the car, and it was only when Wilfred arrived that they discovered they had the wrong man. They sent Father Edward, surely bewildered, back to bed, and took Everett to the hospital. Apparently it was not serious because he is already back.

Everyone here is laughing, but also marveling at Father Edward's willingness to go unquestioning and to believe them if they told him he had a hernia. The more you think of it, the more extraordinary it is. Father Edward is a very bright old man—it was not stupidity, not senility, but the formation of his soul that led him to assent so readily.

An extraordinarily beautiful and quiet morning. I fix some hard-boiled eggs for breakfast. Am having trouble sleeping at night. Feel sleepy and exhausted after supper and sleep about half an hour, then wake up. I think it is hunger more than anything else. This diet is unsustaining. (Not the monastic diet, my own diet, ordered by the doctors.)

A cool, overcast morning, but very still, as though all nature waited to see if the rains will come. The air smells of distant rain in the forest—fragrant, but far away. Thunder now, and the shouts of crows—all other birds have become silent. I feel well protected from the lightning. They have put up seven lightning rods. Still, I will turn off the typewriter now and go read in the journals . . . on the bed . . . in my cork-lined shoes . . . on my foam rubber mattress . . . curled up in a prenatal position . . . under my static-master blanket. Some might call this cowardice; I think of it as the virtue of prudence (in the modern sense).

Now, black as dusk and a glorious rain without wind. The fragrance of wet pine and cedar drifts in through the open windows.

SEPTEMBER 19, 1970

Saturday. Splendid rains yesterday. This morning it is dark, overcast, and misty—almost cold. The soaked forest stands silent, unmoving, full of white fog. A fire would be helpful, but I do not dare carry in wood. Had a setback yesterday afternoon; the pains began. I doubled the medication and took only cream of rice for supper. Much better this morning. Went to bed early (8:00 p.m.) and worked on the journals, dictating passages onto the cassette until almost midnight.

Rich materials, but my eyes are so blurred from the increased medication it is a torture to read them. No question but what this medication stupefies me. I was a real dumbhead at Mass last evening, messing up on the responses.

Later—after lunch. Brother Patrick brought up the big envelope containing the bound edition of *A Hidden Wholeness.* He insisted I open it and get the first look. I never saw him so excited. We went through it page by page. Beautiful, simple, unornamented. He was thrilled with the jacket, which I had seen, and both of us were delighted with the binding and the calligraph on the cover. Significantly our first sight of the book is here in the hermitage—the first bound and finished copy lies here on the desk in Thomas Merton's cabin. The book offers me a unique and quiet sense of satisfaction. I am glad it exists, and grateful that it exists in such a beautiful and tasteful presentation. The layout is extraordinarily effective, particularly the lead-in to the calligraphs.

Tremendous heat today. But now, at 2:00 p.m., the sun has gone behind some clouds and good winds are stirring. Hope we get a good storm. Hard to work; at least right after that medication which comes every four hours. It blurs the vision just enough to make reading an effort for an hour or so; and I don't wait, so I begin to have headaches. Now a really cracking one.

Nearly midnight. Cannot sleep again. A cool breeze has sprung up from the south after a hot still day, but the cabin is so full of bugs (why? where did they come from, or how did they get in?) that I have decided to get up and make these notes. Also, the food does not sustain me long. I got hungry. Am eating a bowl of fruit with no-fat (99 percent fat-free) cottage cheese over it.

The little finger of my left hand and the little and adjoining finger of my right hand, plus the outer sides of the palms are still quite numb. I feel as though they were sticks when I type. They were that way when I regained consciousness from the lightning, and that is 2 1/2 months ago now, so I suppose I am not going to get any feeling back. They don't really bother me, except when I type. I have good enough muscular control of them. Well, I will try to sleep again now.

SEPTEMBER 24, 1970

Thursday. Slept deeply and woke up groggy at dawn. A cool, clear morning; a feel of autumn in the air, though the view is spring. Herakleitos: "He that lights up from sleeping is awake."

I light up very slowly. I sit here with hot coffee and let the countryside and the breeze absorb my attention. Deep stillness in the forest. A blank period of time, unmarked by hours and minutes, stretches ahead of me. A sense of endless time and no pressure of clocks. In solitude, time is not brutalized by schedules. Only the cycles of night and day, of morning and after-noon, of the body's hunger and satiety, of sleeps and "lighting up" from sleeps, give any indication of the movement of time. This is one of solitude's deepest blessings, this liberation. It is also one of the things men most fear. Our habitual slavery to the clock is too embedded in us. It has become a support, an empty reassurance that we exist and accomplish things and that there is order in life. Men rely on that illusion, and when liberated from it, from the tyranny of schedule (scheduled time), some men are so bewildered they rush back to it. Some view the liber-ation as nothing more than "having nothing to do"—the sheer-est boredom. Above all they feel guilt not to fill in time, not to organize it into units of activity. What timelessness, solitude, and silence tell (or could tell), their lives have not prepared them (us) to hear.

And yet this is not to repudiate time at all. I am not for throwing out clocks or schedules. I am convinced, though, that there is deeper order in natural time than in man's ordering of it by clocks and schedules, and that nothing is really wasted this way. I have a clock up here for two reasons: to awaken me so I do not miss the hours before dawn, so I do not miss "lighting up"; so I can be awake in order to "do nothing," except join my attention and my silence and my felicity to those hours when the silence speaks most eloquently. And I have a clock so I can cook three-minute eggs.

I do not need a clock to tell me when my body needs nour-ishment or rest or to tell me when it is noon or 6:00 p.m., be-cause I couldn't care less when it is noon or 6:00 p.m. I don't have to have this place cleaned up by any special hour. I alter-nate between "working" at the typewriter or research and doing the physical things, and doing the nothing that is involved in that "tremendous activity" of simply being attentive to the sounds and silences and sights and darkness and light. When the inclination comes I sweep or make the bed or wash the dishes or myself. When the whiskers scratch I shave.

This morning I note that I should clean up the bathroom. The imprisoned bugs last night apparently killed themselves fly-ing around the light. They lie like millions of black specks all over the floor and in the sink and on the window sill. But my system of luring them into the bathroom and then leaving a light on and closing the door worked, to my astonishment, because they did not eat me up all night. This morning my sheets are stained with dead bugs, though, where I rolled on them before I hit on the idea of getting them into the bathroom. They came to me because I turned off all the lights except the lamp near the cot, hoping to read some.

Anyway, in this atmosphere, this kind of cleaning is not work—it is a kind of festival. You savor it. You don't rush to get it done.

Good, now it is clouding over and the wind is getting up. This whole forest seems as eager as I for the first frost; and it can't be far away because birds are migrating with high and distant glee, in great bunches these past few days.

In his last talk to the community before coming up here to live as a hermit, Tom remarked: "You don't go into solitude to practice a lot of virtues—if you did, I'd probably be lost."

And it is true that in solitude, the whole idea of virtues and vices simply fades. You are here, open, you live with the reality of days and nights and heats and colds and forests and animals, attentive to, abandoned to, the "Christ who dwells in the silences," in a place where you do not seek Christ, but where Christ wants to find you. And it is enough just to "be." It doesn't matter if you are clothed or unclothed, well clothed or ill clothed, uttering words or silent. You cannot live it without loving; that would be impossible. And if you love, you are not going to have to worry about committing crimes against man or God, and you are not going to have to worry about what is or is not "virtuous," or stop to consider each act to evaluate its virtuousness or sinfulness. You might scandalize men who have their own ideas about the image of a holy life (which usually means a pietistic one), but you have no worries whatsoever about scandalizing or offending God. So the "practice" of virtues is just no consideration. The very nature of your solitude involves you in union with the prayers of the wind in the trees, the movements of the stars, the feeding of birds in the fields, the building of anthills. You witness the creator and attend to him in all his creation.

This is not for one moment mere pantheism. It is the anagogic way. You do not "worship" the thing, but the creator of the thing. The thing fascinates precisely because it raises your attention through its beauty or interest above itself to the creator, which prevents your fascination from lifting the thing out of the *ordo universali* into some inflated category of its own (which would mask reality). No, you become more deeply attuned to the mystery of reality as it is in the clods of dirt and in the leaves and in the grasses and in the feel of rain or the drink of water. It teaches you things that can hardly be put into words, that can only be hinted by words—to abandon the self-satisfaction of comfortable (and flattering) categories, to accept the unity of opposites (or contradictories) as the natural thing it is in reality, to give up the deeply nurtured need in man for things to be "consistent." This "sleep" of formalism and subjective prejudices that veils the reality, which would seek to separate and therefore suggest "conflicting" opposites, is the most difficult thing to get rid of. True peace, says Herakleitos, is the "hidden attunement of opposite tensions."

Now, have cleaned up the bathroom and brushed my teeth.

If I can work out the above into words and phrases, I will have done much to penetrate what Thomas Merton was. Right now it is too rude and raw—because in my mind I divide it into great leaps from Herakleitos to St. Bernard to Merton. All were aware of precisely the same thing: how to uncover in the realm of the spirit what already exists there.

I am tied to the debris of a language that is not true to the truths of solitude, and am aware of this. (This sentence, for example: I should have said "that is not true to the truths of contemplation"—because solitude is not really it.) For example, I find I use terms like *work*. *Work* is a proper term in the world where one has to go on an unnatural nervous energy. Work, then, is work, even when one "likes one's work." Here the term is misleading. Work is part of the joy of the day. Instead of saying: "Now, I must get back to work," I should say, "Now, I have to return to my joy," except that I never leave that joy during the days and nights (because all things are taken up into this felicity, even physical pains and other assorted miseries like the bugs last night); so how can I "return" to it? I have to be more specific and simply say, "Now I must get back to the writing, or the reading, or the research."

Again, I note I have said earlier in this entry, that I "light up very slowly" (after sleep); when I should correctly say "gradually," because slowly implies the very concept of time that is largely evaporated in solitude.

In all of this, I sense a perceptible diminution of intellectual gifts. I have noticed it for some time. I do not make any great thing of it. It does not really concern me, except it is there and apparent. I am like a man who could once play the clavichord, and whose fingers have now lost their agility, and who hits all kinds of clinkers. What is it? Age? The shock of the illness? I do not know. The above messing up of language is a small example. There are many others. Certainly my vocabulary is reduced. In another sense, which is not bad, the sense of overwhelming mysteriousness grows in me, something that in my earlier years I would reduce to "understanding" . . . to concepts, to synthesis. This facility is almost gone. I am deeply aware of it because I have such frequent contact with such gifted men in whose presence I tend to become almost mute insofar as intellectual speculation is concerned. The things that fill me now cannot be uttered with any accuracy, though I sometimes struggle to utter them. I find that I end up writing about concrete (awful word) rather than speculative things—about the way wind stirs the leaves of a single branch of a tree. I go along with it. I can do nothing else, and I am not at all sure this is not simply right for me at this time in my life.

I have the feeling, however, that this is not "simplicity" but simplemindedness. My thought, which was once structured along philosophical and theological lines, is almost never structured that way any more. It is strange to me, because my whole early life was one of intellectual passion, almost without direction. Pierre Reverdy asked me once why I wandered around the world studying. I answered because I did not know what I wanted to do and felt it was at least a valid use of time (!) to learn all I could in the hope of finding one truth on which to build something.

Now, I have forgotten most of those "learned" things. They are just not there, though I suppose they do exist in me somewhere in the depths of the unconscious (sappy term). What is more, that intellectual passion has been nudged out by another passion: the passion not of bringing things into myself, but of going out and giving myself indiscriminately to whatever is there: to the play of sunlight on leaves, to the sound of a voice or the sound of a soul; to whatever chooses to reveal itself. I used to ask the "why" of all these things and to seek to understand them. The great difference is that I find the "why" never comes anymore, and there is no longer the slightest interest in formal and structured understanding. If some understanding comes (it usually doesn't), then it comes as a sort of unasked-for gift, as an intuition crystallized out of nowhere. It is not that I turn my back on understanding or despise it, God knows. I view my lack of it as a lack. I am simply noting what seems to be happening.

The wind rises. The forest is a great wash of sound, like the roar of a nearby surf. My stomach tells me to go now and cut a small melon and hard-boil an egg—no, two eggs. Three? No, just two.

The eggs are on. I stepped outside to walk around the cabin. At the bathroom window I noted a great many spiderwebs—only on that window. I judge that leaving the light on all night attracted many bugs to the window, and it was a good feeding place. There must have been a dozen spiders at least.

I do not mean, in the above passages, to give the impression that there is a mindless, systematic kind of joy in contemplation. Nothing that simple. Watching spiders consume bugs does not make the heart leap with joy. It is a reality, and that is that. You know, too, that in the calm and silence of the forest, millions of struggles are occurring among the creatures, the ones consuming the others, the ones chasing the others. There is, of course, neither joy nor sorrow in this. It just is. There is "dark contemplation" (*The Cloud of Unknowing*). And one does not seek to savor the sounds and sights—they are there, but they must not be confused with God, or even with the search to be open to God. I called *joy* what is really a kind of overriding felicity and peace and repose. But none of these terms really fit. It is a thing more akin to the hidden attunement which is a unity and a union, in a sense, one that simply lets the soul desire nothing else, lets the body experience and savor without desiring—again the felicity as a kind of fulfillment that makes desires quiet, in repose; that lets the heart rest where it is (because that is where it has wanted to be).

Later. Afternoon, just up from the time I am supposed to spend on the bed. Today, since the clouds thinned and the sun came out, I took the quilt and rested on it under the pine trees. The mulch of pine needles made a good mattress and I am well rested, staring up at rapidly moving white clouds across the blue sky, and the swaying tips of the trees. The breeze continued, cooling the shadows despite the heat of the sun. Now it is clouded over again. Splendid rest. I do not know why I have not thought of this before.

SEPTEMBER 26, 1970

Only a little past midnight. Again, I cannot sleep and hardly even feel fatigue. I worked all day yesterday and finally went to bed at 10:30, but read the brief and eloquent new book by Dan Berrigan, called *The Trial of the Catonsville Nine.* This morning, really yesterday now, I thought that I must send a copy of *A Hidden Wholeness* to the Berrigans in prison. But how, since they are not allowed to receive mail or packages from unauthorized sources. Then Father Tarcy brought me the *National Catholic Reporter* in which there was a story about a service celebrated for them in New York, attended by their brother, Dr. Jerry Berrigan, professor of English at Onondaga Community College, Syracuse; so I wrote to ask him to take or mail the book to them. They were such longtime friends of Merton.

I wondered how he would feel about this book, which speaks so eloquently of the things he championed. He would be protesting the imprisonment of conscience by the state, as I must. He would choose his way, and I will choose mine.

In any event, the imprisonment of men like the Berrigans and their splendid colleagues speaks more eloquently than anything I know at the moment of the cockeyed nature of human justice in its present state; that justice which is not human but for the good of the state, rather than for the common good or the good of mankind. Reading the book, I could not help but wish that I were there with them, that I were worthy of being sentenced alongside them. No matter, people like me will be there for lesser virtues if things continue as they are.

Twelfth Visit

NOVEMBER 8, 1970 . . .

NOVEMBER 8, 1970

Sunday. Returned to the hermitage this evening. The drive from Louisville during the early evening was beautiful—the sky blazing over the silhouetted knobs.

Met Brother Patrick at the gate, and we came up here where Father Tarcisius was preparing supper for us. Pleasant, short meal. They have installed a gas heater, thermostatically controlled in the sleeping room, so the cabin is a comfortable seventy degrees, while outside it is in the forties. I went to bed at 8:00, right after their departure, but could not sleep. It is too exciting to be plunged back into such silence, such isolation, back into this solitary existence in these woods. Finally, after hours of sleeplessness, I turned on the light to see it was 11:30. I was hungry, so I got up and soft-boiled a couple of eggs and drank some pineapple and apple juice.

Now I have just finished boiling the water (to make it safe), so all I have to do for coffee in the morning is just heat it up.

Am sore from the long trip, but feel splendid otherwise. Too sore, though, I now realize, to sit up and type. So I will go back to bed, and this time I feel I can sleep.

NOVEMBER 9, 1970

Monday. An unbelievably beautiful morning—wind roaring in the trees, the sky brilliant in the east before the sun has risen. I see now that the screens have been removed for the winter, and the windows are so clean they look as though there were no glass in the frames. It is almost cold, so I have lighted the fire in the fireplace. It flames fragrantly and warms my back. The trees are almost bare, and those remaining leaves are brilliant. The full-foliaged pines and cedars look almost black in this dawn light.

150

I drink coffee and wait for time to come to a halt so that I can drift into the natural activity that is based not on hours, but on sleeping and waking, and the gathering and waning of energies.

NOVEMBER 10, 1970

Tuesday. It is now 4:00 a.m., and I have a long day's work ahead of me. The fire blazes to my back, the coffee is good and hot, the silence is profound and healing. These hours before dawn are a total blessing. Never do I feel so well, so unharried and unhurried.

I stepped outside for a moment. Water drips steadily into the rain barrels at the edge of the porch. As well as I could make it out, the thermometer reads in the low forties, almost on forty—but the air is still, the darkness thick. Not even a hint of the masses of forest, the fragrance of this fire like piñon on the moist air, mingling with colder odors of wet pine and cedar. Although I know the monks are awake down at the monastery, I can see no lights; and with such murky weather, I have the impression no one is about . . . no one wanders in these woods, no one is near. I am walled into this circle of firelight by the mist, the cold, the forest (felt but not seen), and the animal and insect and floral life in those deep woods.

Coming awake, coming to life and work in such surroundings is like some musical theme that slowly unfolds itself in fragments—a hint here and another there until hours later the full theme is finally joined in its elements. At this hour, it is all intuitive. Out of bed, I heat up water for the coffee—that is the first thing, the important thing. While this happens, I come into this work room and light the fire, trembling with the cold but knowing that soon it will warm the cabin and warm my back. Then put my head out the door to see (or hear and smell) what the weather is doing (always the acceleration of gladness when I hear it rain, because rain is a glory in these woods, and it seems to isolate the cabin even more beautifully). Then a moment in the chapel before the reserved Sacrament—no prayers, just being there and letting things happen. The flicker of the votive lamp on the white stone walls, the hints of gold in the ikons, the smell of the cedar altar . . . but most of all the feeling of some remote life in the ikons (especially in that faint white light), as though they secretly watched, as though they have never in all these centuries slept for a moment. Then, in the adjoining kitchen, to make the coffee and come to the desk to make notes (or to begin them), typing a little, resting long times in between, feeling the hot coffee in me and the warmth from the fire penetrate the chill of my back until the muscles relax into comfort. Later the medication, later the breakfast when the need is felt, later the brushing of teeth . . . all those things happen in their own time, but are not just up and done with. And the same with the work. It goes steadily, but with frequent interruptions, and it goes with no sense of hurry.

I fit the happenings to my body, and the way it works. In the morning I cannot see enough to read, so I write, do those things for which reading is not required, until the medication clears the vision. Then I begin the preliminaries for supper. Tonight we will have chicken cooked in white wine, zucchini with vinaigrette, boiled potatoes, and *crepes*. So already I have made the *crepe* batter and salted the chicken. With only a two-burner hot plate, you have to give things time.

Later. Bells from the monastery announcing the call to Mass. So it is 5:45. I stepped outside on the porch to hear them. The sound clear in the night air. The sky appears to be cloudy, but I saw one star.

The squirrel is back. I glance up from this desk and see him there on the porch in the dim light, consuming the bread I put out for the birds. He stayed away during the summer when the wood stack was not on the porch, apparently finding it too risky. But now that there is a large stack of wood (in which he can hide if necessary), he is back and bold as ever. He looks splendid—fat and sleek and much bigger than last spring when I used to have his visits (or hers, perhaps—I do not know if he is a she or a he).

Brighter sky now, densely overcast, and not a leaf stirs. An air of stillness and expectancy hangs over the forest. I go to the journals and that eye-straining fascination.

NOVEMBER 11, 1970

Wednesday. Up at 3:00, and made a new batch of *crepe* batter for whatever needs might arise. The cabin is warm—seventy degrees, but it is cold and absolutely still outside. I have just put out the stale and leftover bread for the squirrels and birds.

Pervasive contentment after a decent rest . . . the contentment of looking forward to these hours before dawn, relishing them in advance, hours when the silence and the solitude seem to be most profound.

Brother Pat called at 3:15 to check on me as he does every morning, to make sure I have not gone into a diabetic coma or got into any kind of difficulty. But everything is fine, and the diabetes seems firmly in control once more.

Now the sky is beginning to lighten—full of fog and haze. One of the squirrels is there on the porch, not six feet from me. He eats, and I type, and we watch one another. This is a much smaller squirrel than the one yesterday, must be that one's youngster. He looks grey in this dim light, with a white belly. He grabs each piece of bread, sits upright, and nibbles it rapidly. He looks right into the window, standing on the woodpile now. I could almost touch him if the window glass didn't separate us.

Later. Continue working on the journals, reading and dictating the important dates, etc. Calm, quiet, dark morning, but still light enough for me to work here without the electricity.

A moment ago I took a break to fix some coffee and decided I had better wash my pajamas and undershirt; washed them in soap powder and Clorox. Soaked them, rather—quite a while. Now they are hanging over chairs right in front of the fireplace, steaming a little. They add to the air of the room a slightly humid odor of clean, wet clothes, and remind me of the winters when I would visit my grandmother's "wash house" where black ladies did our washing in a nice large, separate one-room, whitewashed and cement-floored. They would boil the clothes in great tubs over fires and scrub them with Octagon soap and a washboard, and then hang them out in the sun if there was sun, or on lines inside the room if the weather was bad. That same clean, damp odor is here in the room with me this morning.

Later. There are moments here when suddenly, even in the calm and silence, the work comes to a temporary pause, and I find myself overwhelmed by a renewal of the silence, the serenity, as though it came in a new wave to flood me with the full perception of it. Sometimes it lasts only a moment, sometimes several moments. Always it is unexpected. It comes to surprise my spirit with a deeper felicity, a sudden glowing wonderment, a focusless love that is intense and without any object or any impediment, clear as spring water. It has a distant religious connection somewhere beyond my thought, though it has no object, as I mentioned; no name, no word comes in connection with it. It is as though everything—every tree and leaf and blade of grass and stone—combines into prayer that has no words, no form, and no need for anything of that nature, and sweeps me into it, transforming the quality of my being, like a modulation from one soundless harmony to another. The harmonic silence modulates in my body; and an unfelt change takes place from the soles of my feet to the top of my head. I have only had this occasionally at the moment of reception of communion in the past; never at any other time or in any other circumstance. It comes to me here fairly often, especially after I have got my system back into the natural rhythms of this hermit life, when things flow as nature wills, when the clocks have stopped hounding the mind.

I do not try to understand this. I only know that for quite some time now I have been given a kind of happiness that seems to me to be supreme, beyond which a man cannot go. I have never experienced it before in this sustained manner, and never dreamed a man could have it. I realize that it occupies the very center of my being and it grows there, virtually untouched by what happens—by my dread of the surgery, my dread of the physical things that happen to me. It is pure gift, beyond my volition, incomprehensible to me. I do not touch it, do not attempt to comprehend it, because I feel I should not tamper with it or try to understand anything about it. Always I bite back the question, "Why?", and I bite back my protests that I do nothing to deserve it. The only thing I do not bite back is my awe and

154

gratitude that it exists. It has nothing really to do with me, and will go on existing or will stop existing as God wills.

All is still, grey, hushed, attentive in the surrounding forest and within this cabin. Only the fire speaks, in its warmth to my back, in the hardly audible whispers of its burning.

I do small things—sweep the ashes from the hearth back into the fire, things that will not alter the intensity of the hush. I step outside to breathe the sanity of thin white smoke from the outside chimney that drifts southward. I hear the rattle of water and go to the edge of the porch to investigate. Beyond a vermilion screen of thornbush foliage, I glimpse a doe urinating into dead leaves. Her footsteps crackle as she moves away, disappearing without haste.

NOVEMBER 12, 1970

Thursday. Much colder this morning. Difficulty coming awake, though I have had plenty of sleep. Up, the coffee made, and a fire built and the lights on, all of them; the bread put out for the squirrels, and still I am in a deep drowse and filled with inclinations to return to that warm bed.

Father Stan Murphy came up last night for Mass and supper—a Mass of perfect simplicity in that primitive little chapel, a Mass attuned to the silences and the forests. Father Tarcisius lives the Mass simply, directly, undramatically, and allows us to live it—not just playact it. He does not just rattle off the texts as so many do, he has no rhetorical inflections either. He says them with such a simplicity and such a sincerity that they sound new and fresh, as though he were conversing, and these were the words that came naturally from his mind and heart.

Later. Now the sun is up, pale but visible through the white haze of a low ground fog. It causes the few remaining yellow, orange, and scarlet leaves to appear translucent against the green foliage of pine and cedar.

Late afternoon. It has been really a ravishingly beautiful autumn day, with the sun full out and temperature up to sixty. But now at 4:30 the sky is once more overcast, the haze is thin over the countryside, and the stillness perfect. Utter quietness of all sights and sounds, given a note of special cheer by the odors, however, for I am roasting a leg of lamb and cooking garlicked white beans to go with it for supper. Father Timothy is coming to concelebrate with Fathers Stan and Tarcisius, and our old friend, the philosopher John Ford, is coming for Mass and supper. They will be here around 6:00, and much as I am looking forward to that evening with them in the cabin here, I relish the moments left before they come, the moments when the silence and the stillness dig deep into me, to bring healing, to bring balm and blessing in uniting me to them.

I have not accomplished much today, though I have done work. I feel such a weakness in my legs, and such pain in them when I get up, that I have spent much more time in bed than I usually do, reading and dictating rather than sitting up and typing. Strange, this frequent conjunction of physical misery and radiant happiness; my spirit is filled with joviality, with a silent laughter, so that I have the impression that I am groaning and laughing simultaneously. The wounds groan, the rest of me is aware of that; but it does not touch the core of jubilance within me, does not diminish it in any way. I never cease to be astonished by how little I actually suffer from what others view as my "sufferings." It is doubly odd, because I empathize with pain in others—let someone get a hangnail and I go into shock; but there is none of that in the pains of this body of mine. I just do not suffer.

6:00 p.m. And now it is chilling fast, and twilight becomes night. The great silence changes. It remains as silent, and as still, but with the arrival of company, I reluctantly alter the atmosphere to something less stark. Others do not like the pure silence as I do. It depresses them, perhaps, or at least makes them uncomfortable, even the monks—some of them: though not the ones who come up here. In any event I change it. I light a new fire in the hearth and put up the phonograph (which Brother Pat brought up two days ago). I put on Marie-Claire Alain playing the organ works of Bach—beautifully played on that ravishing Marcussen organ. And so, when they arrive, they will arrive at a cabin in the forest to be greeted by a fire in the fireplace, by marvelous music, and the odors of good mutton (lamb) and garlic and beans.

And now, in the dim light, I see Father Tarcisius coming from the woods on foot, to help me prepare the table. He is clad in gloves and a woolen cap and warm jacket. God bless him.

NOVEMBER 13, 1970

Friday. Feel better. The diabetes is back down to normal this morning. No sugar showing in the test. Slept very well, and am not yet really awake. A long, quiet day ahead of me in which to work.

An intriguing item from Dr. Paul Cameron, psychologist at the University of Louisville, who conducted a scientific survey among 3,416 people to find out what they think about. Young adults (under twenty-five) think about sex at least once in any ten-minute period, religion once every twenty-five minutes. Middle-agers think about sex every thirty-five minutes, about religion every fifteen minutes. Those over sixty-five had sex on their minds only once an hour, but religion every ten minutes. Dr. Cameron said he did not think his survey had any immediate scientific significance, he was just curious.

Breakfast—a piece of toasted Trappist bread and a cup of very good tea. I can imagine nothing better.

Noon. All morning on the journals and on Gordon Zahn's preface to the peace book [*The Nonviolent Alternative*]. Also returned to the Leclercq preface [*Contemplation in a World of Action*]. A wealth of splendid details, but I still struggle with the bigger lines of the biography—the summation by year. I suppose that will all come when I have each year's notes in the files and can go over them that way, a year at a time. The Zahn preface is a great help, but most of all the Leclercq helps me to see the large divisions and how they might form the structural basis for the biography. Most of the journal notes I copy in this kind of notebook page, but without making any carbon. I note that Tom, attracted to really feminine women, susceptible to them, responds with a kind of glee to his reading references to "momism"—he responded to *The Silver Chord* (?), more than I

157

thought that study would interest him; and to Stern's *Flight from Woman*, etc. And he mentions that the astronauts were really away from mother up there in space.

Evening now. And I feel better. Strange day. I had a weak spell after lunch and could hardly leave the bed until I slept an hour. But the weakness remained. Finally, I got up and took a little walk around the hermitage. Got chilled, came back to bed, and covered up with blankets. Got up at 4:00, took hot tea and toast, built the fire, and now my feet are warm, the work has resumed; I have shaved, the sky has turned dark, and already I have to have the lights on inside in order to type. It is the kind of day that Tom liked up here. How often he describes it in his journals. I not only have the lights on and a good fire going, but I have put on the marvelous records of Bach played by Alain, so the atmosphere within this cabin is full and robust with sound, while outside the forest stands in the stillness of late dusk. I cook the remains of the lamb into a ragout, so the rich odors of lamb, onions, mushrooms, and white wine scent up the cabin joyfully. But how odd, I know that I am deliberately sacrificing the silence that is so tremendous at this hour, and I feel a regret about that; though I love, too, what this glorious music does to the interior of this cabin. It bounces into every room, into the chapel to surround the reserved Sacrament with its marvelous rhythms and harmonies. I have gone into the chapel—that small room, without other light than the flickering vigil candle and the white, white walls, and the smell of cooking and the health of Bach's infinite amiability.

NOVEMBER 14, 1970

Saturday. A morning of such natural glory I can hardly contain my enthusiasm. Have been making notes from the notebooks (Merton's) all morning, and now at 8:00 a.m. I stop to take the medication, brush teeth, etc. I got right out of bed and went to work at 3:15 with hot coffee, but not too much because I ran out. Will have to drink tea the rest of the day. Now, with the light of a dark day, the rain falls gently, almost slowly, straight down. The bare branches of nearby trees are lined with water crystals that catch light and shine against the background of dark green cedar and pine. It falls steadily, making the lightest drone on the roof and gurgling into the rain barrels at the edge of the porch.

I have a good hot fire burning gently behind me in the fireplace. It is cold outside—in the low forties—seemingly colder because of the monochrome light and the dampness; but in here it is dry and warm, and the delight with all this is pure and without blemish.

Already I make the long plans for bathing a little later in the morning. Keep the fire built so it will heat up the bathroom and then get the shampoo ready and the soap and the towel on the cement floor (which is always cold). In the meantime I cannot leave this desk where the view is so entrancing: the downfalling rain, the puffs of white smoke from my chimney drifting southward low under the towering pines.

Now the breeze has come to stir the very tops of the tallest trees, causing them to weave in slow motion with all kinds of inner individual motions of the branches, as though they were moving from muscles within, in a dance, rather than being moved from without by the wind.

It gets colder. Will I have the courage to bathe? Of course, it is worth the discomfort of bathing in the cold room to dry quickly there, and then come in and finish drying in front of the fire.

Later: 4:00 p.m. Tremendous day. The rain has slowed to almost nothing, but the day remains dark and the temperature is plunging downward, into the thirties now. The wood fire goes splendidly at my back, and a cup of hot tea warms me. Something intensely exciting about this cold and rain and silence and isolation. The work simply flows better than at any other time. I have some *crepe* batter mixed to fix *crepes* for supper, and am slowly heating up the lamb stew.

Later. Now, finally, with the temperature plunging, I went ahead and took the bath and washed my hair. And I sit here letting the firelight dry me off, "naked as a pagan Italian," as one of my old Southern aunts used to say, pronouncing it "Eye-talian."

Although it is not night yet, it is almost as dark as night at almost 5:00 p.m. Beautiful. I have the lights off in here, too, and type by the light from the fire.

Thirteenth Visit

JANUARY 12, 1971 . . .

JANUARY 12, 1971

Back at Gethsemani, in the hermitage. It is 2:00 a.m. and I have been unable to sleep, so I got up and fixed some hot chocolate and decided to make these notes. I arrived here around 8:00 last evening. Brother Pat brought me up to the hermitage where Father Tarcisius was waiting to say Mass and prepare supper for us. Overwhelming sense of relief to have arrived, to be here in this calm and silence. We got things unpacked, got my medicine into me, and immediately said Mass in the chapel; here the Sacrament was already reserved. Then Father Tarcy fixed a good supper for us: mashed potatoes, peas, and some little cube steaks. Everything was perfectly arranged; the hospital bed, the wheelchair; they had even raised the water can up high so I would not have to bend down to the floor to get my water. A good fire was blazing in the fireplace, though it is not terribly cold, just down in the low forties. Father Tarcy had even gone into town and bought a few supplies, knowing that I would arrive too late to get any this evening (the meat, for example, and also a pound of butter, and I don't know what else). I have made a long list of supplies for the next two weeks which they will go in and get for me tomorrow.

Mass was very beautiful and quiet. Both of them were sleepy since they usually retire at 7:30, and I was crocked from the long trip. They cleaned up the dishes, put my typewriter on the table for me, and left at 10:00. I went immediately to bed, but could not sleep. The sight of the flickering vigil lamp before the Blessed Sacrament filled me with such contentment, I simply could not sleep. So I got up and fetched the tape cassette Brother Kurt [Franciscan Friar] sent, which arrived just before my departure today, and went back to bed and listened to that, making notes of things I will need to answer, about the transcription of material for the book. Greatly enjoyed this and firmly resisted the temptation to answer it immediately, since he has already had one very dopey tape from me, and I knew this one would be even more so.

I lay there in the darkness, very tired, very happy, thinking of my wife and children, and could not sleep at all. There is as much a shock to the system in coming into silence and solitude as there is in leaving it for the noise of the cities. It takes time for the nerves to settle into harmony with this forest and this glorious isolation.

Finally, at 2:00 I got up, and now at 2:20, with the hot chocolate in me and this diversion of making these notes, I feel relaxed enough to try to sleep again.

Later—8:30 a.m. Slept from 3:00 until a moment ago. And now sit here groggily drinking strong coffee to come awake. A still, foggy morning, quite cold—no visible movement in the woods.

3:00 p.m. I slept an hour, and feel some life in me again.

Am messing up. The fire has not been going too well—mostly new green wood and no kindling. So I went out to the woodshed in my house-slippers and got an armload of kindling and got my feet soaked in the process. Then it seemed to need a larger back log, so I went out on the porch and picked up one and felt my side catch so dropped it immediately. Now a good fire, and I am drying out my feet. I am thinking about fixing some sort of hanging arrangement so I can cook meat over the coals; a leg of lamb would be good, even a chicken, if hung right. Must work that out. They say there is nothing but hickory over near Father Romanus's hermitage. I might manage some sticks of that for the cooking. I'll have to ask Brother Martin to help me rig something.

Later: 5:30 p.m. Long, silent afternoon of work, complete joy in all this. Keeping a small fire going at my back. Read Rice's book [Edward Rice, *The Man in the Sycamore Tree*], which manages to get a great deal of incorrect material and speculation down on paper, but is nevertheless fascinating. Again and again he makes contentions that Merton rebuts in his own private diaries, and more or less leaves the impression that Merton told him these things. This is not deliberate misleading—it is that he listened to Merton with his own interior ear and vision and consciousness and sense of affection. He is unjust in his appraisals of Merton's "privations" here, laying it to the inhumanity of the superiors and fellow monks, angry with the way Merton was treated; and yet Merton himself stopped all attempts to give him "special treatment" and wanted nothing for himself that the others would not have also. The end of the book is very weird and forced. Better to let Merton describe his own mystical experience in Ceylon, which I will do in the biography, and without comment or speculation.

The photos, drawings, and graphic elements are fascinating.

Now it is getting dark. The great hush deepens over the countryside. Soon Father Tarcy and Brother Pat will be chugging up the mountain (hill, really), to join me for Mass and supper. Next week, because of the community retreat, we will probably say Mass at noon, and I will not see anyone from noon until noon. This extraordinary hour of dusk should not really be disturbed; it is something you can only abandon yourself to, with the hermitage lights off, joining with the outside in the coming of night. And then only after it is dark, to turn on the lights, fix a little supper, and work a while longer before going to bed early to awaken at 3:00 in the morning. Only in innocence can it be borne—only in a state of grace; but in that state, it is perfect happiness. Otherwise, it is only loneliness, something all hermits have understood. You can bear loneliness in guilt during the day, but never at dusk, never at the beginning of night. Guilt is the difference, I suspect, between loneliness and solitude. I think Tom knew this, or would agree with that contradistinction.

Some questions about the Rice book:
He contends Tom knew he would die in Asia and was already "transcended" and living in another world before he left on the trip. He says Tom allegedly wrote three "farewell" letters to ladies for whom he had a deep affection. He puts in a great

deal of this kind of information without revealing any traceable sources for his information.

His story about the building of this hermitage, etc., seems utterly incorrect to me. He calls it a big place with "workroom and several other rooms," and he contends that the Abbot was so furious that in revenge he refused to let Tom have the "basic facilities" (toilet, etc.) until just before his departure for Asia. None of this coincides with the truth—that this place was built not as a hermitage at all, but as a meeting place where groups could come and discuss matters, particularly ecumenical matters, etc., and was only later used as a hermitage. He has Tom bragging that he had his novices build a really fine hermitage, when in fact Tom was always apologizing because the hermitage, which was not built for a hermitage at all, was really too fine, not poor enough, etc. And of course the novices had nothing to do with it.

What is certainly unfortunate is that Ed could have got all these things clear and accurate just by asking Brother Pat or almost anyone else here. Why didn't he check these things out?

Now that I have read this, I see that it is not really a question of rebutting anything, but simply of treating this misinformation quite specifically in a correct "version" without comment.

JANUARY 13, 1971

Wednesday. Another night of little sleep. I do not know why I do not sleep. Perhaps I must stop drinking coffee in the afternoon.

Have heard that Phil Berrigan and five other men (four of them priests) and one nun have been indicted by a Federal Grand Jury on charges of plotting to kidnap Kissinger and also to blow up the heating systems of federal buildings. Phil is in prison, but the other six are all in custody. Dan and some others were not indicted, but were named as conspirators. What gives? Could this be possible, or is it some kind of monstrous mistake or monstrous suppression? It is a follow-up of J. Edgar Hoover's charges or allegations made public some time ago.

Dark, calm, overcast morning, full of haze and life. Many

birds move about, tiny ones and cardinals and bluejays. Squirrels scamper across the brown grasses under the trees.

Much later now—after 11:00. Splendid morning, morning of great excitement and happiness. I worked steadily on the journals and on the errors in the Rice text, which must be corrected in the biography. I got so absorbed in this, I did not realize that the mist had turned into a light rain, and only when it really began drumming did I look up to see a marvelously veiled countryside with the rain falling straight down and not a branch moving. I shut off my dictating machine so that no sound could interrupt or diffuse the "talk that rain makes" here in the hermitage. It is now dark enough for the lights, but I do not turn them on. I do the things that need doing: spread up the bed, sweep the floor, tend the soup bones that simmer in the kitchen (along with onion and carrot), and will simmer through the afternoon to make us a good stock for tonight.

Then I decided to see if I could not fix up a hook in the fireplace for hanging meats or a pot of vegetables. I put on my shoes and raincoat and went to the woodshed where I found an old rusted hatchet and a long nail, at least seven or eight inches long. So I hammered the nail into a kind of double hook and found some wire, too. But most important, I found the old, thoroughly rusted iron pot Tom used for cooking in the fireplace when he first came up here. It is a beautiful thing. I put my hook and wire in it and brought them back into the cabin. The hook worked fine. I attached it to the metal hinge on the damper up in the chimney, and then I attached the wire to that, so it hangs down to the right of the fireplace about halfway back. So I can let the fire die to a good bed of coals tomorrow and hang my roast up there to cook.

I don't know how to clean rust from the pot, but I washed it and scrubbed it and then put it on the fire until it was hot and thoroughly dry. Then I poured a bottle of cooking oil into it, made sure all the inside surfaces were covered with the oil, and will let it set on the hearth for a couple of days. That should do something. I know that's the way you season an iron skillet.

Father Tarcisius brought the beef roast yesterday because a Sister from Nazareth who is doing work on Merton wants to come for Mass tomorrow evening and have a conference with us and then have supper, so we will have the roast for that.

Now the cardinals have come to eat the grain I have just thrown out. In this rain-hazed countryside, where all is grey or brown or the black-green of the pines, these scarlet birds are spectacular. They seem to revel in the rain. There must be a dozen of them now on the trees in front of the porch.

We have the Mass at noon today, just before lunch, so I will have solitude for the next twenty-four hours until tomorrow noon.

1:30 p.m. Beautiful Mass. The small whitewashed chapel so dark that the candles glowed brilliantly; and then lunch with Brother Pat and Father Tarcisius, and they have just gone, leaving me alone for another twenty-four hours. Glorious. The rain pours.

This rain lulls and delights. With my stomach full I am going to take a quick nap.

A good nap, a deep and marvelous sleep wrapped up in a blanket, dimly aware that the rain poured against the roof and windows of this cabin as I drifted into sleep. It was still there when I awakened forty minutes later.

Hot coffee now to bring me back. No lights in the cabin except the firelight at my back. I checked the beef bones, and they are making a good broth. I made mayonnaise and had good luck. It is not that these things are remarkable, it is that they are doubly fascinating because you have to improvise constantly here with no utensils, no bowls, nothing except a bare minimum. I made the mayonnaise in a two-cup measuring cup, a glass one. Once before when I tried to make it in one of the metal bowls they use here, it turned slightly greenish. And the fascination, too, with time. You have to think ahead because everything goes slowly. It is not that time gets you, it is the contrary, that you are liberated from its hold, that you have all the time and an eternity more in which to get everything done and that nothing needs to go faster than what the nature of your activity finds comfortable. You have time to sit and watch the rain in the forest, time to sit and listen to the silence, time to smell the fragrance of simmering soup bones (cooked with a carrot and an onion and a large bay leaf and some thyme), time to tend the fire. And every single activity or lack of activity is filled with this felicity that joins you to the animals in the woods, to absent family and friends. Tonight, for example, I know it will turn very cold, and with all this wetness, I plan already to put out dry food for the squirrels, chipmunks, and birds so that they can have a good feed before they go back into the woods to hole up for the night.

Have changed plans for the dinner tomorrow night. Brother Patrick had to go into Louisville on abbatial business and I asked him to find me a large leg of lamb. So we arranged with Father Tarcisius to let us have a few logs of hickory, and I will cook the lamb, suspended over the hickory coals in the fireplace, as they do in some lucky areas of France. He will bring it at noon tomorrow when they return up here to say Mass and bring my other supplies and mail. For supper tonight, I'll make an *oeuf a la russe* with some of the beef stock, in which I'll simmer some carrot rounds until they are tender and then let that make an aspic around a soft-boiled egg (cold) and try some of the new mayonnaise on that.

I make these notes sketchily while the rain pours the hardest. When it lets up, I read onto the cassettes my notes for the book. I cannot dictate while the rain comes down so loudly because it makes the dictation too difficult to hear behind the roar.

Later. Almost dusk at 5:00, though you couldn't really tell since it has been dark as dusk for hours, but the food has been put outside and the animals have rushed to eat their fill and then gone until now only two brilliant cardinals remain to peck at the seeds. They look almost forlorn in this damp and cold dusk. My fire burns low, making hardly any sound. I feel a tremendous drowsiness, but will stay up to eat supper around 7:00 and then get to bed.

JANUARY 16, 1971

Saturday. Long, hard night. I went to sleep early enough, around 9:15, but awakened around 11:30 quite chilled. I got up to check the stoves and discovered that neither of them was working—the gas is apparently out or frozen. So I got more covers and went back to bed, but with enough to keep warm the weight was so great I could not sleep well, and I do not have enough wood in the cabin to keep a fire going all night.

Slept fitfully and then profoundly, and awakened at 5:00 a.m. Very cold inside, and down to eighteen outside. I put on a sweater and built up a fire which now blazes strong behind me. Have hot coffee. The typewriter keys are like ice to my fingertips. But it is interesting.

This is the way it was for Tom, and he stayed up here with only the fireplace to warm the place when it was down to zero outside. The fireplace does an extraordinary job in this room. I still have on a heavy sweater, but my back is good and warm and it seems to me that the room is heating up pretty well.

Some chance for snow this afternoon, and more chance tonight; the high today is supposed to be around thirty. I hope they can deliver more gas up today. My wood supply won't last too many days longer if I have to keep the fire going around the clock, which would be necessary in such cold weather. Tom would apparently build a big fire at bedtime and then go cover up and trust it to burn through the night, because he frequently remarks in his journals that he finds live coals in the fireplace when he gets up (around 2–3 a.m.).

JANUARY 17, 1971

Sunday. Cold. With a bluish tint in the forests and sky that comes when the weather turns snowy. It has not snowed yet, but is supposed to today.

Carolyn Hammer and her nephew came, and brought lunch yesterday. Good visit. She brought me copies of Pasternak's letters to Merton, and also read me some excerpts from Lexi Grunelius's recent letter to her. He had received *A Hidden Wholeness* and commented at length on it. It was really almost as though we were at Kolbsheim. He regretted that Victor Hammer was not in the book, but of course I never photographed Victor and Tom together. I explained to her that the splendid photo she once shot of Victor and Tom will be in the biography.

Problem with sleep. This wound is bothering me, and there is just enough discomfort when I go to bed to keep me awake.

The thing that raises the head of the bed does not work now (it is a hospital bed), so yesterday Brothers Patrick and Richard propped it up with a cedar log, and that helped a great deal.

Today the community retreat begins, so we begin our new schedule. They will come to bring supplies and say Mass at noon each day and leave me alone from noon-to-noon each day.

Pasternak ended up writing Merton notes and cards with no signature, feeling that anything with his signature would be delayed or never get to its destination. These letters (most of them written before the Nobel Prize incidents) are filled with sadness and frustration.

Strange, the connections that constantly occur here. I had a little transistor radio that worked on a.c. current to get the weather forecasts. It was destroyed when the lightning struck last July. Yesterday Brother Pat brought another one just like it that the Abbey had purchased to replace the destroyed one.

This morning, so touched by the Pasternak letters, I decided to write the pages of the biography concerning the Pasternak-Merton friendship. I had written the passage about Pasternak's death, the bravery it took on the part of his friends to come and pay homage as he lay on the bier in the living room of his house; and the bravery of Sviatoslav Richter who was in the adjoining room, unseen but heard by the mourners, playing the last Beethoven Sonatas. Almost unconsciously, I switched on the little FM to see if there would be a more definite forecast of snow. I heard the announcer say that they would now play the Karajan recording of the Mozart *Requiem*. What a marvel in the context of this morning's writing to have this sublime music suddenly come into these woods. I cracked the window a little so the cardinals and bluebirds and titmouses and chickadees and squirrels and hares and foxes can hear this music this quiet morning as they wait for the snow to begin falling. And now, from the hush, a titmouse sits tiny on the bare-branched tree at the porch edge and sings, stimulated, I guess, by the music.

Now, at 10:15, conventual Mass begins down at the Abbey. The bells ring up to join with the Mozart. I decided not to risk the trip down, so they will come up and say Mass here at 11:30. How glad I am that I did not go down now, because I would have spent the time shaving and getting dressed and missed this *Requiem* and missed writing those pages about Merton-Pasternak: those pages that wrote themselves, that simply took hold and wrote themselves, the sentences forming themselves to the cadences of Pasternak's English and to the deeper cadences of Mozart's final pages.

After the Mozart, the FM is turned off. What could follow that final "amen" except the amens of a silent and sublime countryside awaiting the snow, the crackle of cedar logs and their fragrance in the fireplace, the amen of iced-over pools of rain reflecting the blue-grey snow clouds, the amen of a vast interior felicity that is out of all time and place. It is a time to do small things—to spread up the bed, to rinse the coffee cup. A time of interior muteness that is radiant with the sights and sounds of this morning; the faint fragrance of beeswax from that vigil lamp in front of the reserved Sacrament, and that lamp that flickers night and day a golden hint on the whitewashed stone wall beside it.

JANUARY 18, 1971

Monday afternoon. Got into such a binge of work last evening that I did not quit until 3:30 this morning—work on the journals. I woke up at 10:00 and came right back to work, feeling like the devil, but trusting the work to revive me, and it did. When they came for Mass and to bring supplies at 12:30, I had stopped only for coffee, had not combed my hair or brushed my teeth. Distracted during Mass, trying to remember all I was working on, until the consecration when I began to hear what was going on. Then a good lunch and they left right away, taking a list of supplies I need. I am almost out of water, and have very little milk left, no paper towels, etc. Most important, no coffee. But after they left, I found a large jar at the back of a shelf, so am saved.

Late afternoon now, and I am paying for the long period of uninterrupted work: muscles ache everywhere, including the muscle of my brain, but this is no time to stop, really. I give myself a rest long enough to prepare *oeufs a la russe* for tonight's supper and tomorrow's lunch (prepared four of them), and this helps get the kinks out.

I have great difficulty writing even the most necessary letters. It is not that I do not have the time, or that I am constantly at work. No. It is that I have great difficulty coming out of preoccupation with the work—the vast amount of things that I have to keep almost memorized—in order to concentrate on other things such as letters.

Some of the reviews make a point (for example, Ed Rice's book) of stipulating that Tom was heterosexually active before entering the monastery. What has that really got to do with anything, and why make a point of it, especially when none of them really knows this much about Tom? They leap onto it as though it were a lollipop of information, giving the implication that there is something exceptional about a normal young man getting a monastic vocation—or the even more rude and naive implication that monasteries solicit eunuchs habitually. Odd that men who claim to be the most worldly and tolerant and broadminded are the ones who leap onto this no-news as though it were real news. It shows that angelism is not far beneath the surface of men's minds in regards to what a religious vocation really is, what a conversion is, what grace accomplishes. Do they suggest that monastic chastity can exist only in men who are somehow not very capable of unchastity in the first place? Sexually weak men? Impotent men?

JANUARY 19, 1971

A little past midnight. Went to bed at 7:00 p.m. and have had five hours of good, deep sleep, so decided to get up and have coffee and go back to work until about 4:00, when I will sleep again until 8:00 a.m. I just checked the outside thermometer and it is down to eighteen already; supposed to go down to thirteen by morning.

Brother Richard is coming up in the morning at 10:00 to take me down to photograph his silverworking shop, which he warns is "very primitive." In any event, he does magnificent work, and I am eager to photograph him doing it. I need somehow between now and then to manage a bath and a shave. I don't know what to do: build up a fire and get that done now, or wait until later and get some of this work done, or try to get out a few notes that really need to be written.

Well, I have gone ahead and built up the fire to a roaring companion as insurance against the night's great cold. It will warm up the stones and help hold out the cold.

There is deep excitement in all of this, though I suppose it is foolish in a sense. If I want to stay warm, all I have to do is go to bed and pile the covers on, but I stay up and do my little battle to keep the cabin habitable. So I will shave and bathe soon, when the coals have built up, and then perhaps the skin won't chap so much; and then I will finish cleaning that Dutch oven I found out in the woodshed and glaze it in the fireplace (hot iron ought to add a little more heat) and may try cooking a chicken in it. But no, this all turns into too much of a festival. Well, I will do it anyway—such a night in such a forest deserves a festival.

2:00 a.m. Temperature on the porch (which is protected slightly) is fifteen degrees. Temperature in here is sixty-eight. But right in front of the fireplace, it is good and warm.

5:30 a.m. Went to bed at 4:00 and was awakened by the cold a few moments ago. Went outside to check the temperature—down to twelve; still, clear sky with half moon and brilliant stars. Marvelous sight. Returned quickly and built up the fire. Decided not to waste it, so I went in and got some pork chops Father Tarcy bought for me in town. I dried them off good, overlapped them on a big piece of thick aluminum foil, chopped a garlic, an onion, a carrot, a stalk of celery over them, wrapped them tight in the foil, and then wrapped all that in a piece of soaked brown Kraft paper, and wrapped that with two thick, large brown paper sacks which had soaked in hot water, and then triple-wrapped the whole thing again in heavy foil. I brought it in to the hearth, fixed a bed of hot coals, spread a layer of ashes over that, put the pack on that, covered it with a thick layer of ashes, and replaced the burning logs on top of the whole thing. I will let it slow-cook like that until lunch day after tomorrow, when it should be about right. No, it will be lunch tomorrow. I keep forgetting that this is the morning of Tuesday; think of it as still Monday night. It will cook, in other words, about thirty-one hours. It is an old French way of cooking, I tell myself. Or maybe a frontier way—or maybe an Indian way. I am not even sure it will get cooked under all those ashes. Well, it is worth a try—it may be charcoal-burned or it may be raw. If it is good, it should be damned good. You are supposed to wrap it in a dozen layers of wet paper but I didn't have that much. I think a chicken might have worked better, but I don't have any more chicken.

2:30 p.m. The sun is out and snow falls in large snow-flakes. I photographed Brother Richard in the silversmith shop here at the Abbey; a remarkable light, and the utensils were wonderful. Think I got good things.

The time goes too rapidly. Already it is 3:00 p.m. and a great deal of work is stacked here for this afternoon—and I am sleepy. Well, it is not such a desperate sleepiness. It comes from having gone out in the cold and done all that photographing, which greatly excited me. Brother Richard is a good subject in that he has no difficulty just ignoring my presence and going on calmly about his work. And the tools and implements of the silversmith are certainly among the most beautiful I have ever seen—large, sturdy wooden mallets, metal hammers (?) in odd shapes and highly polished.

Later—dusk. I have had a short nap—only about twenty minutes, and then fixed hot chocolate and returned to work. But now, when it is too dark to see in here, and the countryside is still, frozen, and grey, I build up a good new fire in the fireplace and sit here watching the approach of a winter's night. I watch the birds. Many come to take their fill of the grain on the porch before my window. They are only about six or seven feet from my desk as I write these lines. I do nothing but wait, absorbed in the marvelous sight, wait until it gets dark when the new life begins, when the lights go on, when I cook some supper and draw the blinds (not for privacy but to keep out the chill as much as possible).

JANUARY 20, 1971

Wednesday. 11:30 a.m. And the great moment came to take out the pork from the ashes in the fireplace. Decidedly, I need to reread the books about French country cooking, frontier cooking, Comanche cooking, or whatever. I was dumbfounded at the lightness of the package when I dug it out of the ashes. And when I removed the successive layers—the foil got blacker, the layers of paper were black ashes, and lo, the meat and "savory vegetables" were totally cremated. I felt as though I should spread them on the sea or something. *Requiem eternam . . .*

Father Tarcisius, Brother Paul, and another Brother brought up a truckload of the most beautiful fresh-cut cedar, from a large dead cedar tree. It burns warm now in the fireplace, and saturates the surrounding countryside—today calm, brilliantly sunlit—with the marvelous odor of piñon; and enough of it escapes to smell up the cabin's interior, too.

It is noon, and I have not even cleaned my glasses or brushed my teeth. Steady work all morning. Must stop and do those things now, and warm up the chicken since the pork is just a pile of black ashes in my garbage can.

JANUARY 21, 1971

Thursday. A dark and windy day—something rare in my experience here. It is usually so still in the forest. But last night I was awakened by the sound—like the wash of the surf—and got up to find a strong wind blowing high in the pines. This morning the sky is filled with rolling black clouds that move rapidly below a grey overcast. Slept deeply to the lulling wash of the wind in the trees, awaking occasionally to lie there in contentment, except for the growing need to go see my wife and children. Once during the night it got so acute I decided to see if I could not go on today. But that is foolish—I would be interrupting the work at an impossible stopping place.

Later, much later, 4:30. Very dark and threatening outside. I turned on the little transistor at 4:30 to see if I could get a weather forecast. Heard the final bars of what sounded like all of Shostakovich's Symphonies, and then a very cultivated lady's voice, or the cultivated voice of a lady, rather, saying this in the suavest tones: "Aren't you glad you live in an age where health problems can be discussed openly? Doctors have discovered a remarkable new medication for pain of hemorrhoidal tissues . . . ."

"No, lady, I'm not happy I live in an age where health problems can be discussed openly," I said, and switched off the radio.

JANUARY 22, 1971

Friday. Worked finally until 3:00 a.m., and then slept until 8:00, so I don't feel like skipping rope or dancing, but don't feel too bad either.

Good work. The weights and balances begin to form in the biography. Tom's need to make the total gift of himself to God and his painful inability to make a parallel total commitment of himself to any man, any institution, any country, etc. His struggles to open himself, his sense of unworthiness to be loved at any profound levels. He appears to have had such a dread of disillusioning people who got close to him that he acted in a way either to keep them at a distance or else to make sure to destroy any illusions they might hold about him (which was equally a means of putting them off). And yet the capacity was there. His compunction for the poor and the defenseless was clear, and without any shadow or defensiveness.

In any case, a second reading of the journals, now that I have the large picture of what they contain, gives me a great many new insights. I find that I have in a first reading latched onto things that really had no significance; and in the second I am finding very significant clues that I had overlooked. His deepest intimacy and his most unguarded friendship was almost never given, but those who came closest to eliciting it were Father John of the Cross and Cardenal [Ernesto Cardenal, Nicaraguan poet] here at the Abbey.

Now, need to go take my medicine and get myself cleaned up. Haven't shaved in three days, and am completely disreputable.

Tomorrow, Saturday, I am supposed to fly back home, and

I need to go. I am missing the family too much. But also I have not arrived at a good stopping place here. It has begun to rain. Snow due this evening and tonight, so I may have to stay on, and I could stay in good conscience if the weather made me—with delight, even, though I am being pulled now, very hard, to get back to my family.

Six p.m. And a great fog has developed in the forest this late dusk. A tremendous and exciting fog that turns the nearest tall pines into ghosts and completely obscures those further away in a grey blank. I don't know if I will be able to go or not tomorrow.

Now, at seven, a real storm, and a real intestinal storm, too. I have apparently caught the black plague, cholera, and a few other items. Father Tarcy came up to check on me and then went down to the infirmary and brought me up some medication for it. Have no fever. Had soup for supper, crackers and milk. I think I got it from the water. I used a glass that had been washed but not thoroughly dried; and this water does contain bugs (which is why we have to cart up the drinking water). Father has just gone back down, after building up a good fire with the large logs that I cannot lift.

Tom always wrote that no one on earth can work like a Trappist, and I believe it. I have never seen such willingness to fly in and do heavy work, rapidly. One of the farmers around here once remarked to Tom that one of the Brothers, when he chopped weeds in the garden, reminded him of a man killing snakes. Father Tarcy is a small, rather frail monk, but he grabs those heavy, thick logs and hauls them in with his eyes almost bugging out; and mops the floors and scrubs up the same way.

Fourteenth Visit

MARCH 20, 1971 . . .

MARCH 20, 1971

Only time for a note before I go to bed this first night of my return to the hermitage. I arrived, after some delay, only this afternoon; came directly out from the airport and got here around 5:30. It is cold, beautiful, clear. Father Tarcy and Brother Pat brought me immediately up here, where they had everything clean, the windows polished, and a good cedar log in the hearth. What wise men. They immediately left me to get myself accustomed to this always new, always fresh silence and solitude. I unpacked, got this typewriter out, and my work materials, and then just sat here a few moments and let the overwhelming joy and relief saturate me. But only a few moments, because Father Flavian (the Abbot) came to say Mass and have supper with Brother Pat and me. Wonderful hour. He is a marvelous man. And after all the "prudence" and caution with which other prelates usually speak, his openness, candor, and unguardedness are almost unbelievable. They left, after we discussed my talk in chapter in the morning (7:15 a.m.). It is 9:00 p.m. already and I must quickly get to bed to get up at 3:00 tomorrow and prepare my talk.

After they left I changed into pajamas, put on milk for hot chocolate, and got into the envelope of mail Brother Patrick brought up. I saved the Sussmans' [Cornelia and Irving Sussman, authors] letter until last, because it is always the greatest pleasure for me, and I save it to savor it. Three pages, and I wished there had been more. I sat in these woods before the dying fire in this tremendous silence and sipped at the hot chocolate and read those marvelous, glowing pages. It is all I can do to keep from answering it tonight. But if I start, then I will, in this mood of tremendous happiness, write until midnight or 3:00 a.m., and be shot tomorrow. So, with an iron exercise of the will, I put it off until tomorrow, finish up the chocolate, and get myself to bed.

MARCH 21, 1971

Sunday. 4:30 a.m. Been up an hour, have a good cedar fire going and hot coffee. The temperature is down to twenty with a clear and brilliant night sky and a quarter moon through black pines. I take my time. The marvel of having the illusion of endless time, at first deliberately, and then it becomes natural. I take the time to sit here and feel the warmth penetrate my back. I listen to the silence, typing by firelight that reflects in the window in front of my desk, to the sounds of silence: the water kettle simmering on the hot plate in the kitchen, the frozen stillness of forest in which no breeze moves—in which all nature seems to rest.

11:30. Spoke in chapter from 7:15 till 8:15, and then Brother Pat and Father Tarcy brought me up and we had a cup of coffee together. Very good chapter. They asked me questions, and I asked them questions. Warm, friendly, and helpful. After they left, I worked a while and then lay down to take a nap. The most terrible nightmares, unmasked evil, frightening me. I woke up desolate and cold. Went into the chapel and sat before the reserved Sacrament until some of the terror left me. Built up the fire. Clear, ravishing sunlight day outside. Feel emptied and uneasy without knowing why. It will pass soon, I am sure. Really look forward to Brother Pat's bringing me some lunch.

MARCH 22, 1971

Felt no rest last night. Prolonged and brilliantly detailed nightmares that woke me in an almost sickening fright. Foolish nightmares, all of them more or less lascivious and horror-filled. I was walking endlessly, blind, unable to find my way. Everybody I asked for help bawled me out. One lady in a rectory where I managed to seek help just raised hell with me because a year ago I told her it was good to make French bread and then eat it with butter and cheese. She ate it, and it was horrible, nasty, vile— how dare I have told her it was good! "And now before I help you one bit, I want to *know*: Are you going to give me any more lousy suggestions?" she screamed. I guess it was the fever that made the dreams so vivid and so sickening. Also dreams that Johnny had rebroken his foot, and Piedy was in terrible distress alone with all the children. This one so upset me that I telephoned her this morning, and was greatly eased to hear her cheerful voice, and to learn that nothing at all was wrong, and Johnny was doing fine. Well, now things are better. Brother Patrick is coming for lunch.

Later. Pretty good work. Did take a little nap after lunch, and had another of those leviathan nightmares, so got up and plunged into the work. The fever seems to be down now. It is almost time for Mass and supper. Dark, cold, very still. I have not connected with it yet. There is something wrong that I hope the Mass will cure in me . . . a distant, unfocused uneasiness. It does not worry me. I know it will pass. I long for sleep without the nightmares, for something to lift the heaviness. After supper, I will work until I am really exhausted, and then perhaps the sleep will be untroubled. My problem is that my nerves are still out there in Nashville and Philadelphia, while my body is here, and the nerves cannot come to a quiet. It makes for a grotesque inner contradiction, a lie in a sense, and I do not trust my ability to be truthful during such a time. Something keeps me from joining the silence, from giving myself to it all the way, and yet I throw myself into it as though I were giving myself, with the same sense of falsity as a faithless husband overdoing his illusion of fidelity to his wife.

Later. Oh, well, hell . . . the above does seem overserious in the light of this later evening. Father Tarcy came alone and just the two of us celebrated Mass—the Epistle, of all things, about the two harlots. I got tickled, and at the Mass intentions simply prayed for my problems of nerves and nightmares. It was a remarkably beautiful, simple Mass. Then we cooked supper and had a splendid hour, and I was frank about my difficulties, and he understood them, and now they seem to be pretty much gone because dinner was really relaxed and happy and splendid. I am going to try to go on to bed now, at 8:00 p.m., and see if I can't get a decent night's sleep and start all over again tomorrow. We tried to find a weather forecast on the little transistor. It is sleeting a little outside. But we heard only idiocies. The FBI had counted the sore places on the mules' rumps during the Poor People's March to see if they were mistreating the mules! Another agent was stationed in a tree above a group of protestors to listen for anything unusual "and be especially on the lookout for obscenity." Anything to blackmail the people, especially the poor and the black people. And this by an agency of the federal government financed by tax monies.

Hearing these news items, Father Tarcisius's eyes bugged in astonishment. I was glad he was here because I would have distrusted myself had I heard it alone—thought I was having another nightmare.

MARCH 23, 1971

Tuesday. 4:00 a.m. Bravo. It worked. Slept very deeply and woke up just before the alarm went off at 3:15. Awakened with a sense of energy and contentment, and got immediately out of bed, turned on the heat for coffee water, built up the fire in the fireplace, splashed some water on my face, checked the temperature outside—a windless twenty-five with some stars showing dimly in a black sky, probably overcast. No sign of the moon, though I didn't remain long enough to look. Put out the stale bread for the squirrels, and am back here now with the coffee getting some warmth into my back from a roaring blaze of cedar logs.

The cabin is dark except for the reflections from the fire and a desk lamp which I found. Much better than the overhead light I usually use before dawn. Enough light to cast a small circle on my desk top and typewriter without the brilliance of the other. It makes the room *seem* even quieter and does not block out the forest night so much as the big, brilliant overhead light.

Later. Now, just rising, is the great misty sliver of moon.

I think of yesterday briefly—the kind of distracting aberration that comes sometimes to show the short distance between a blurred view when self gets in the way and the other view when self is transparent and lets you get directly to reality. It is a deep aberration because it fools you into attaching more interest to self than to what is. You are experiencing reality through this film, focusing on the film rather than the dirt on your glasses. You fall into that so easily. It is in a place and time of solitude that you become aware that you have fallen into it. You know it because time is filled with the guilt of "wasting" it. This morning, time is abolished—or rather that preoccupation with time. There is time to go sit forever in front of the reserved Sacrament, time to watch forever as the moon rises through mists to sharp clarity for a moment and then back into haze. Every occupation, even the most piddling, is right—sweeping up the floor, washing yesterday's undershirt, brushing teeth, fixing an egg.

Well, it comes and it goes, and I judge that a good portion of mystical speculation revolves around techniques of keeping it as whole and intact as possible. I have only the dimmest grasp of it . . . dim, experiential. Reading others doesn't really help all that much—you can learn it as "learned knowledge" and never get more than a hint (if that) of the lived experience. You can, and men do, presume to teach it based on the experiences of others, but such teaching is full of holes because the teacher has too often not been transformed himself by his subject, has not experienced it, has only an intellectual grasp but no interior intimacy with it—that kind of intimacy that melts all the crusts within one.

The experience liberates. That is perhaps why those who write of it—from the point of view of lived experience—are always being analyzed and shredded by critics who have only the "acquired knowledge" of it, and who split hairs and other things, too; the difference between the saint and the theoretician of sanctity who will say of the saint: "Well, you know he had mystical gifts, some insights, but highly imperfect ones. There were all kinds of flaws. Why he scarcely *understood* the passive purifications, whereas Garrigou-Lagrange devotes 632 pages just in footnotes to them. And all that preoccupation with secular things like poverty and peace and . . ." Like the FBI men counting the sores on the rumps of mules or perching in trees to overhear the talk of protest groups and being especially "on the lookout for obscenity."

The contrasts: I stepped outside to put more stale bread (whole wheat bread) for the squirrels and birds. Chill pene-

181

trated as I crumbled the bread. The sky began to lighten. Unmoving black traceries of bare trees and masses of pine foliage detach from the clouded horizons, while the moon and one star shine above the cloud mass, in a brilliance that was almost dizzying to me. Then back in here, thoroughly chilled, and to the fire's warmth and fragrance, and the awareness of emptiness in my belly, and the prospect of cooking an egg. From the cold and the overwhelming grandeur of view, to the intimacy of this cabin and the action of cooking and consuming an egg (the one made tremendous by the other and making the other tremendous) . . . this counterpointing of contrasts that causes things to sharpen one another, that deepens the affections, that turns self into pure and glowing union with every pebble, every tree, every sight and sound and sensation, with that union pointed directly on the creator of all these things, and thus full of awe and silence, utterly unblemished. There are no blemishes at such a time, because what men would consider blemishes are taken up into this wholeness, and become a part of it, and thereby lose any quality of blemish. The father loves the cross-eyed daughter, not because she is cross-eyed, not in spite of her "imperfection." No, he simply loves the daughter, and in the ardor of that love there is no blemish. Blemishes are for people who do not know about love. We hide our blemishes or minimize them for people who do not know about love.

Odd . . . odd . . . in the dim light I glance up to see a giant, wolflike dog sniffing at the bread on the porch. And then a hooded monk comes into view, out for a walk in the earliest dawn, bundled into his robes and jacket, and the above paragraph is thrown into my face. I check to see if I have on my pajama pants! I have, but I might very well not have. And I think: "Good, he has seen me through these open windows, perhaps has seen me from some distance as he approached, saw me typing here and thought, 'That Griffin really works.'" What crockery lies there to shine in its falsity the moment the chance is presented! Ah, the blemishes and the nonblemishes.

The monk and his great dog wander on and disappear through the trees. He probably never even looked in this direction, if the truth were known. He was out in that cold dawn with his dog and God, probably lost in his meditation. I could have been standing out on that porch stark naked, scratching my belly and spitting at the trees, and it wouldn't really have mattered to him. He might even have been more edified by such "holy simplicity" than by seeing me dressed in clean pajamas, teeth brushed, hair combed, typing away like mad in a dawn of such magnificently communicative silence.

And I look over and see that it is already a few moments after 6:00 and hear the self-righteous murmur within me: "Why isn't he down there for conventual Mass? What's he doing out here in these woods communing with God when he ought to be in there celebrating Mass? What kind of dangerous singularity is this?" The really splendid comforts of pharisee-ism (God forgive the spelling). Yes, they are to the spirit of religiosity what don juanism is to the body . . . .

Well, finally to go cook that egg.

Now. Dear God, what a revoltingly healthful and virtuous meal: one soft-boiled egg, one piece of toast, and a small glass of tomato juice. If I eat more I get sleepy. It is nice to eat frugally—it is in *good taste*. I am going to be nice today, just for the hell of it, nice and fastidious and admirable.

No, hell, better not to waste the day.

MARCH 24, 1971

4:00 a.m. Down to twenty, and feels colder because of a little breeze this morning, but it is warming in here with a great fire and hot coffee. Am not very well awake yet.

Quiet morning, working on journals, on French and British versions of *The Seven Storey Mountain*, particularly Evelyn Waugh's introduction. Now the moon, sharp, thin, almost apricot-colored, rises behind the trees near a brilliant white star that emphasizes the color of the moon. No hint of dawn yet, though it is 5:45. Stopped for breakfast—soft-boiled egg, toast, milk. The fire no longer blazes—it just burns easily and steadily behind me. Although I had a good night's rest, I feel so peaceful I am sorely drawn back to the bed. I feel that I could sleep for a month. No, I will not go. But I know how much Tom enjoyed these very cold, clear nights, the warmth of that bed under blankets. He spoke of it often as one of his delights. It takes an authentic poverty of such basic material matters as heat to make you appreciate such a delight.

Yesterday it was not full night when I went to bed, something Tom also knew well, because he usually went around 7:00. When we have Mass in the evening, it is always after dark before I retire; but now, with Mass at noon, I can get to bed earlier. And that moment, when dusk comes in the windows and the forest is very still, and there is great fatigue, those few moments before sleep in the dim light of that small sleeping room are balm to all the senses and especially to the spirit. The growing warmth beneath the covers, the pervasion of rest . . . they are like gifts handed to you directly from God. You feel a kinship with all the creatures of the forest, with the chipmunks and the squirrels settling into their nests and into rest. You are a creature of the forest doing those unashamedly animal things—arranging the body for rest—that have such reverberance in the spirit, far deeper reverberance than deliberately spiritual things such as formal prayers, exercises, and "practice of virtue." Here is the deeper prayer, which is wordless and formless and unselfconscious love . . . a vague sense of loving and a vague gratitude for it.

Later. Beautiful Mass at noon, and it is almost 3:00 as I write this, preparing to go into New Haven with Father Tarcy to buy some supplies. We talked again about the growing problem of finding anything contemporary that the monks can see in the way of books, etc. Brother Pat remarked that some of the monks felt that the new Herder and Herder catalogue had some highly dubious (only for monks, of course) photos and book advertisements; and I remarked that I had brought two professional photo magazines for Brother Matt, but realized that they were full of nudes—something no one pays any attention to anymore, but capable of scandalizing Trappists. I told Father Tarcy that everything was this way now, probably all to the good, too; and that probably the best thing to do would be just to let down all the bars to monks and let them have one grand trauma, and soon they would come to view the human body, the nude, etc., with no more shock than anyone else, and no more temptation either.

MARCH 25, 1971

Hardly time to write, but I must jot down these notes. It is Thursday, the Annunciation, and I have worked since early, early morning on the book, on writing, stopping only for Mass at noon and lunch with Brother Pat and Father Tarcy. Then Brother Ambrose came at 3:00. He is the "Mexican from the slums of Fort Worth"—third-grade education, a Brother for thirty years now, a small man in his fifties probably, hard as a knot, but with the unguarded black eyes of a man long given to God. It was one of the most moving hours I have spent in a long time. He did not really come here to talk about monastic life or anything else, really, but to tell me how much he thought of the book *Black Like Me*, and of his profound identification with it. We talked with a great union of spirit about his life and his family. He has a mother and two sisters still living in Fort Worth. I will go see them. His older sister recently lost her husband, who had been paralyzed for three years. The whole family is very poor. He had heard me speak in chapter Sunday and had decided that if we needed help with the housework or cooking, he would ask his sister to come and help us. I suggested that there were times when we did desperately need help, and if she needed the work . . . .

Oh, no . . . he hadn't meant that. He had meant that it would be their way of repaying me for the stance I had taken. Dear God, I almost wept—the very poor contriving to help out someone in need. He assured me they were not in our social stratum. I asked him how he could even suggest such a thing, that surely social strata were the least of my preoccupations, the least of my family's also; but that if his sister could occasionally help, I would consider it a great favor, providing she would let me pay her for the work, even though I profoundly appreciated the offer simply to help. But there was nothing in my work or my "stance" that made me worthy to receive such help.

Well, it was a tremendous time. We discussed Oscar Lewis, and a lot about the monastery and the monastic life. I thanked him for cutting all this wood for me (he stayed up here nearly three weeks and polished and cleaned and cut an enormous supply of wood). As we talked, it began suddenly to snow quietly but heavily. Beautiful. Now at 5:00 the huge flakes fall straight down, unmoved by any breeze. What a glorious thing to experience in this hermitage, with plenty of wood. He insisted on building a fire before he left, and hauling in more wood from the porch to stack by the fireplace.

Father Tarcy just called to say they were having something good. One of the novices was "experimenting" with something he thought I might like—*quiche Lorraine*. I assured him I loved it; so he is bringing some for supper, and will come after vespers.

So I sit here in front of the window at dusk, watching the great silent snow, feeling the warmth of the fire behind me, filled with tiredness and contentment because the work goes well, because I am so edified by Brother Ambrose's visit—and his face, which I persuaded him to let me photograph. He was horrified that anyone should want to waste film on such ugliness. I assured him that photographically he had a very beautiful face, which caused him to break out laughing, and I got excellent shots because he kept getting amused every time I shot and with each shot said: "Beautiful . . . marvelous face . . . great." For certain, I will hit the bed as soon as I have had supper tonight. Monks, at my request, are sending up their recollections of Tom . . . splendid anecdotal material of the sort I really had hoped to get.

A snow now so thick it blurs the views in all directions. Must put out food for the squirrels.

Now, at 6:00 p.m., the snow is so thick and covering the ground, hiding the crocus blooms, I wonder if Father Tarcy can get up here. The food I put out for the squirrels did not bring them, but brought cardinals that are spectacularly brilliant against the white snow. When I went out to distribute the food, I saw a very small cottontail in the hedgerow.

Also today received a detailed note from Brother Thomas about his four encounters with Thomas Merton. What continues to impress me is that these men lived in physically close contact and yet in isolation from one another—they knew each other but did not speak, did not have "encounters" except by hazard.

Now—7:00 p.m. The night is white, with snow covering the ground completely. Father Tarcy brought the *quiche Lorraine*, made by Brother Damien, one of the best *quiches* I ever tasted. We had a slice of that with an *oeuf a la russe* with homemade mayonnaise and a big glass of V-8 juice. A great supper, - and Father washed the dishes and then put an enormous log on the fire and took off in the jeep through the snow to return to the monastery. He asked if I would be going to bed soon, and I assured him that I would the moment he left, and I intend to very soon, not because I really feel that tired, but because I am at the end of a long day. The idea of getting into that bed under the covers in this forest on a night of such splendid snow (which always seems to make the silence that much deeper), and to watch in the dark from my bed the play of reflected light from the fireplace and from the vigil lamp, is simply too good a thing not to do.

MARCH 26, 1971

Friday. Up at 4:00. Cannot really tell what it is doing outside, only that snow is all over the ground; it is too dark to determine anything else. No sign of stars or moon; I believe it is still snowing.

Now, then, just the beginnings of dawn, enough to give me a view of this snow-covered landscape and the movement of a single small bird eating crumbs from the porch. The snow gives an illusion of deeper silence. The fire gives light behind me, and I have only the small desk lamp for illumination. So I live now between the warm silence of this cabin and the frozen silence of the forest outside. Snow has begun to fall heavily again.

I wonder what there is about this place and this hermit life that gives such vivid dreams? Except for occasional (very rare) nightmares, I am never aware of having dreams and couldn't care less. But here, I suppose because everything is open and unguarded, the dreams are extraordinarily detailed and prolonged and clear. So far this week they have been tortuous, due probably to the fever, which is gone now. This morning's was different, utterly bizarre; I was late in waking because my alarm was simply incorporated in the dream.

MARCH 27, 1971

Saturday. Piedy just called. Johnny was beaten up last night by a gang of thugs. They had attacked one of his friends, and he had gone to the friend's aid. They broke his wrist and kicked him in the head. At emergency room until 3:00 this morning. He is in some shock but is home. Doctors want him watched closely for a few days, though there is no head fracture. What a horror. They had never seen any of their attackers, no provocation. The gang just approached and started in on one of them, and then beat up Johnny when he tried to intervene. Am going home.

Now, waiting for the time to leave. I have managed to bathe and shave and pack in a complete daze. Don't know what I am doing. I keep weeping and pray that I will not break down during the Mass we are to celebrate before I take off for the flight. I don't weep so much for Johnny, though his pain and suffering and shock horrify me. I weep for the young men who did this to him, for young men who would attack one helpless and on crutches, and then deliberately amuse themselves by kicking him in the head. Johnny was brave, and I feel that bravery in him—not only for going to the aid of his friend when he himself was helpless, but also for his crazy bravado act in shouting cheerfully to his mother that he was fine, okay, not hurt, and for her not to worry, even while his broken wrist was hanging to one side. Well, he was in shock, of course, all the more reason to admire his intuition.

It is maddening not to be there already, to have to wait until the next flight.

I am praying for him mostly that he will understand things, not allow his friends to seek vengeance and become as dehumanized as those who attacked him (and we will have to control our friends and relatives, too, so that they don't hate). We have to pray for God's mercy and healing on his attackers, those dehumanized ones.

In this I am haunted by Clyde Kennard's [black activist] dying words: "What happened to me is less terrible than what this system (racism, prejudice) did to the men who killed me. It turned them into beasts and it will surely turn their children into beasts." So we have to grieve for them and what has happened to them to make them this way, and we have to seek justice (others must be protected from them) without seeking vengeance. And we have to stand beside Johnny as he begins to sort these things out, and as he begins to recover from the physical wounds and the psychological shock. But we must also leave him the dignity of his privacy and not seek to "guide" him in sorting all this out: that will be part of his manhood and the continuation of his bravery. I would love him exactly the same amount if he were the greatest coward in the world, but I am edified by his bravery in this. It does not make me love him more (how can you love *more* when you love your children all the way already?), but it inspires me to see any brave action.

Brother Pat is on his way, so I must finish packing.

JULY 1, 1971

Dusk. 8:20 p.m., and the countryside is utterly still under the gentlest rain. I have been here since last Sunday (Thursday today), and this is the first moment I have written in this journal. Too much work and too little strength, so that when I was not actually working on the book, I was hitting the bed and sleeping. I don't like that. I should be keeping these journal notes because already now I have missed putting down many things of great interest to me. Well, I will try to keep it going now.

I am going to stay here another week, thank heavens. That knowledge makes me feel less pressured. Ordinarily I would be in bed and asleep by now, but I am waiting up for Father Tarcisius to return with my supply of water and milk. We have already had Mass and supper, and he decided that since he is going to his hermitage tomorrow, it would be easier to come back now with the milk and water supplies. So I sit here, feeling very well indeed, drowsy and contented, and watch this greenish countryside and smell the rain on dry woods, and feel it turn cooler. Talked to home this afternoon. All is well there, so a profound happiness fills me in these hours of isolation in the heart of the woods. I anticipate that I will sleep like an infant as soon as I crawl between those fresh white sheets Father Tarcy put on the bed. Strange to go to bed before nightfall . . . strange but also somehow pleasant . . . to look out and see a grey sky and deep green trees, and hear the rain dripping from the gutter and beyond that the call of the first whippoorwill, liquid and rich as a flute in the resonance of the forest.

Now I hear Father Tarcy chugging back up the hill. Must go out and help him carry in the supplies.

JULY 2, 1971

Friday. Stayed up and worked finally until 4:00 a.m., and have slept until 9:00. Now with coffee, I come out of the drowsiness—at least a little. Have taken the medication, used the bathroom and washed up, brushed teeth, got the basic needs of this body fixed for a while, and sat in the cool chapel long enough to make the Morning Offering, but no longer. If I attempted to sit still and meditate I would soon be sound asleep again.

The sun is out, but it is not too hot. Mid-seventies. The countryside peaceful and still; pale blue sky filled with thin white clouds.

Later—almost 6:00 p.m. No sleep, but good rest, lying on the bed marking and transcribing from the journals. Lost in that, absorbed in it, until finally I looked up and saw that it was 5:30. I got up and came into the main room to check the clock here. Could the afternoon have gone so quickly? Brother Patrick left around 1:15 today. How odd and strange. When I came in here, I saw my empty coffee glass on the desk, and more surprisingly my cigarettes and lighter. I had forgotten even the inclination to smoke. It is many years since I have spent an afternoon without smoking, except for times when I was unconscious in the recovery rooms of hospitals after surgery.

Enormous peace and happiness from having worked this afternoon.

Father Tarcy is due up soon to say Mass and have supper with me. Just the two of us tonight, since Brother Patrick is occupied elsewhere with one of the guests down at the Abbey. I went into the bathroom and shaved. It is warm, yes, but not so hot that sweat bothers me. Very still, quiet. Even the birds are silent right now.

Later. Beautiful, quiet Mass (Visitation), and then we heated up some leftovers for supper and ate together. I insisted Father Tarcy take some leftover cake for dessert. He did, but before eating the dessert, he put two brass candle holders in a steel saucer on the fire to melt out the wax of old candles so we could put fresh candles in them. And we forgot until sitting here

191

at the table we smelled the burning wax. He rushed into the kitchen and grabbed them off the stove with only a thin towel, got burning wax on his fingers and a pretty painful burn. He was admirable in holding back his oaths. When I burned my hands flaming *crepes* up here one night, I ripped out a whole string of oaths, quite unconsciously. Last night I told him: "I could see on your face that you were thinking the very things I said when I burned my hands." He almost bent double laughing, and said I couldn't be more correct. We put some medicine on his burn, and then he attempted to wash the dishes, but I would not let him. So I washed the few dishes while he stood in there and talked with me.

JULY 3, 1971

It cooled during the night. I had to pull a blanket over me, and it is almost uncomfortably cool this morning still, though the sun is nearly out and it seems clear and will heat up during the morning.

Late afternoon. Worked marvelously this morning, and then Pat called to remind me that Carolyn Hammer was due today to bring the first copy of her edition of the early Thomas Merton poems and bring lunch for me. I hurriedly bathed and shaved and cleaned up a bit. She and her nephew arrived late, around 1:30, and brought a great lunch (chicken, salad, etc.). But most movingly, it was simply good to see her again. She is a great lady, and I understand more and more how much Tom felt comfortable and edified by her presence. She brought the first copy of the poems—in a first *tirage* of only seven marked copies. It is breathtakingly beautiful, set in Victor Hammer's American Uncial typeface, the poem titles in red and the body text in rich black on handmade paper. I was quite overwhelmed to receive this first copy as a gift from her.

They left around 3:00, and the minute they were gone I got out of my clothes (it is hot), filled the mop bucket with soap and water and bleach, and dumped in my clothes—undershirts, a towel, my pajama pants, and put them on the stove to let the water boil. I had just finished washing and rinsing them and hanging them on an improvised line in the sunlight on the front porch, and was lying down to rest in nothing but a pair of very ragged shorts, when I heard a sound in front. I came back toward the front door, and there was Father Raymond with a professor from Lexington and two middle-aged ladies. I nearly croaked. I dashed back and slipped into a pair of slacks and an undershirt. I dashed backwards because the whole seat of my shorts was out, gone, kaput. In the meantime I wondered how much they had seen, if anything. He called out, and I said I would be right there. I came in blushing like anything, and he passed it off very nicely, introduced his friends, apologized for barging in, etc. Well, we showed his friends around the cabin, he joked a bit, promised me some prayers, and they went out. I noticed they were lining up for photographs with my laundry as background, so I went out and brought it in so they would have a good view of the cabin. And they insisted I be in the pictures, although my pants were falling off and I had to hold them up with one hand.

They left soon afterward, and I put my wash back out. By then I was in agony with my hip from having tried to run to get on some clothes when they first arrived, so I lay on the bed and groaned until it began to ease up a bit. Now it is nearly 5:30. Tarcy and Pat will soon be up for Mass and supper. I feel absolutely dead on my feet and hurting again, so better go lie back down again until they arrive. My pajamas are dry, and I have them on so I will not be caught so sleazily garbed again.

Today is the anniversary of my being struck by lightning here. In spite of all the interruptions, this has been one of the happiest and most peace-filled and prayer-filled days I have ever known. The prayer of the heart goes on, no matter what I do. It is a conscious unconscious kind of self-perpetuating thing. Even when I awaken fitfully in the night that is the one thing I am first aware of—that the heart is praying incessantly as a counterpoint to whatever else goes on in me.

JULY 6, 1971

Back in the hermitage this beautiful, dampish morning after spending yesterday and last night in the Bardstown Holiday Inn because the hermitage was needed for those days, and had long been reserved.

Just happened that Brother Pat mentioned a marvelous story I had not heard. He said that at the time of Tom's death, rather at the time of the funeral, one of the Brothers (Lawrence) went up to fetch Dom James in his hermitage to bring him down for the funeral Mass.

Dom James began to say what is almost a cliche in religious houses:

"Now dear Father Louis knows more theology than all the rest of us."

Brother Lawrence replied spontaneously: "He always did."

I must use that, perhaps at the very end of the book.

Note from a Brother who does not want his name used. "What a man does and how he acts when alone, and apparently unobserved, is more what he is than in the public presence. Often after a Sunday or holyday Mass I went to the chapel in the library room for meditation, 'just to sit,' one might say. More than just a few times I saw the very humble and devout manner of a person who sat or knelt before me. That was Father Louis, absolutely absorbed in veneration and very obliviously ignorant of the presence, the intruding presence, I might add, of anyone else, [except] that of His unseen but real presence.

"Really, the first time I ever walked in on the scene, I didn't know it was Father Louis. It was like happening upon a deeply loved and loving couple, the love that exists between a bride and groom, between a man and wife, at the realization that they have a share in the giving of a new life, in the shared joy silent but so alive of the elderly couple who wait together for the Other One. One withdraws quietly at such times.

"When he was finished just sitting faced to the altar, he would get up, genuflect, and leave. Sometimes he would come in when I was already there, genuflect, and be in another world. No histrionics, just simplicity, honesty, humility."

Later now, nearly 6:00. Very still and very hot, with the sun out bright, but large banks of clouds above the blue knobs across the valley. No leaf moves and even the birds are silent. It was this kind of stillness from which the bolt of lightning came a year ago.

194

JULY 7, 1971

Wednesday. Almost noon, and I have been working steadily since long before dawn, but interspersing the work on the book with other work—putting out my wash, again by boiling my clothes for a long time in the bucket with soap in it and then hanging them on the line on the porch to dry in the sun. They really do look good and white, and are a joy to see. Also, as the day has grown warmer (cold and foggy early this morning, a real delight), I have dictated more because I wanted to get as much of that done as I could before turning on the fan, which makes such a roar on the tapes. Morning of real solitude and deepest happiness. All chores, all work are bathed in this magnificent serenity so that no one activity is less good than any other, and all are sources of the most perfect joy. Now, it is noon and I await Brother Patrick's arrival with food. I have bathed, shaved, etc., and am in clean pajamas and tee shirt. Good profound sleep last night. Tonight we celebrate Brother Martin de Porres's birthday, also Father Thompson's, by saying Mass for them and having a dinner for Brother Martin. I am preparing to cook a big roast on the spit. Or rather I have prepared the roast to cook later.

Later—9:00 p.m. Good supper for Brother Marty, and a beautiful Mass. We had that roast, some potatoes, some corn on the cob which Father Tarcy found; in place of a cake, they had some apple pie and ice cream. A wonderful quiet evening. They just this minute left, and I am going to hit the bed right now.

JULY 8, 1971

Thursday. Did not get to sleep until after 3:00 this morning—got too involved in the 1967 journal, and read until I could hardly see anymore. Only four hours' sleep, and I feel it. Appalling the number of Tom's friends who told him insistently that he should leave here and "get involved" in this or that activity: Rosemary Reuther [radical Catholic theologian], Sy Freedgood, and John Slate [Merton's friends from Columbia]. He was constantly being told what to do by people who apparently had no understanding of his vocation or who showed little respect, and often just contempt, for the hermit vocation.

JULY 10, 1971

Saturday. Leave this afternoon.

Remarkable late afternoon yesterday. Around 5:00 it turned as dark as night, and the wind got up, and thunder and lightning were intense. Then, just after 6:00, a flooding downpour blessed this forest. Lightning struck close, knocking out the lights temporarily, though nothing actually struck the cabin. A good test for all those lightning rods and other safety measures.

Father Tarcy, who spent the day in another hermitage, walked over and got here just as the rain was beginning to fall. Then a bit later, Brother Pat and Brother Marty came to join us at Mass. Since it was my last night, we cooked up nearly everything in the box—a small chicken, potatoes, salad, etc. Today they will come at noon to say Mass again, and we will finish off the remains for lunch.

Later—dawn. It remains comfortably cool—a thick fog surrounds the cabin, but through it the sun begins to diffuse its rising light.

Sixteenth Visit

SEPTEMBER 21, 1971 . . .

SEPTEMBER 21, 1971

Tuesday. **Feast of St. Matthew.** Have been here since Sunday afternoon, but no time to make any notes, so now, late in the afternoon of this feast day, I try to catch up a little. Michael Dunn [a Texas friend] drove me here. We left Fort Worth early Saturday morning (I picked him up in Arlington at 8:00 p.m.), with the car packed with the photographs that go to the Abbey, the Legacy Trust, and Bellarmine. Made very good time, though Michael is a most cautious driver, far more so than I ever am, and yet I take longer to get places. We stopped the night at Jackson, Tennessee.

When we arrived, we came directly to the hermitage, unpacked, had some coffee, and let Michael absorb some of this atmosphere before I called down to tell Brother Pat we were here. Michael took the car down around 3:15, and Patrick got him settled into a room for the week; and then they came back with Father Tarcy for Mass and supper. Very beautiful Mass, utterly simple in the dusk light of the forest, the weather quite warm. Michael was so overwhelmed to come to Mass here in the hermitage that he got a nosebleed. He took communion, I think, though he has not been a practicing Catholic for reasons of his own. And then as soon as Mass was over, he revealed his bloody handkerchief, said it was the emotion of returning to the sacraments in this place, of "beginning again" after many years.

Sunday night it began to rain and turned quite chilly, so that yesterday morning I had to build a fire in the fireplace. Good day's work, and not too tired from the trip—got more done than I usually do a first day here.

We arranged it so Michael could come up at noon with Brother Patrick and have lunch with us, and then again in the evening for Mass. They keep him busy, and so do I—many errands to run. Last evening he said this was the greatest experience of his life, and I suppose it is certainly a high point. He helped the monks with a cow having a difficult delivery yesterday.

Today clear skies, gorgeous autumnal sunlight, and cool breezes.

Because of a function down at the Abbey, we had Mass at noon and then lunch. Only Michael will come to supper tonight, and should be here shortly. I have not cooked yet, though I have stuff in the box, but have given all energies to the work. I am hoping I can get to sleep tonight and get up early in the morning. Also put out my wash today—boiling everything in a bucket on the stove and then hanging it on the porch to dry. It is not drying very fast. Too much coolness and moisture in the forest, I suppose.

This afternoon Michael went into Elizabethtown to get some more cassette tapes. I have used more than I thought I would need, and even borrowed some from Father Tarcy. I have much more to dictate, so I am hoping he can find some.

Now it is almost 6:00, and the evening silence has settled deeper through the woods. Across the valley, sunlight still touches the very tops of the hills, but all is in dusk shadow here around the hermitage. It is too beautiful. I turn off this clattering typewriter to take full advantage of the moment.

Later—8:30. Good supper and good talk with Michael. I made some French cream of onion soup with a nice little onion I had here, and it was very good and rich, and then we had some salami and a little asparagus with mayonnaise and whole wheat toast. Now, with the dishes washed up, and Michael gone, I am going to try to get to bed and to sleep without any delay. Am really tired and sleepy, so maybe it will work tonight.

SEPTEMBER 23, 1971

Thursday. Night of great discomfort and misery, and I was still awake when the monastery bells awakened the community at 3:15. In fact, I thought they must be tolling someone's death until I got up and saw the time. Slept from about 4:00 until shortly before 8:00. Working ever since, dead tired, but incapable of going to sleep. Michael and Brother Pat came for lunch, and I ate well, thinking a full stomach would let me have a good nap, because Father Charles Dumont from Scourmont Abbey (Belgium) is coming to concelebrate Mass this evening and have supper here with us. I put on the supper (lamb with white beans) and made the batter for the *crepes*, and then in quietness and stillness I went to take that nap. But no . . . no sleep came, and so rather than lie there and sweat it out, I got up and am now back at work. At least I can type with fair accuracy, no matter how fatigued the brain. Hips and legs ache constantly, like a toothache. Lying down certainly does not seem to help one bit. Sitting in this wheelchair is the most comfortable.

It is now 3:30, and I have been typing on the manuscript, but must soon go and shave and clean myself up a bit. Supper is pretty well done. Since Father Dumont cannot take fat, I have cooked the salt pork in a side pan, will take his lamb out, and then add the salt pork and its liquids into the pan for the rest of us. It does taste "unrobust" without any fat.

Father Charles Dumont came to concelebrate and have supper with us. It all turned out all right, and his diet is not quite as rigid as I thought. He ate four large *crepes*, buttered and sugared. A delightful and very touching human individual. He told a couple of good anecdotes on his Abbot. He was reported for exceeding the speed limit in Belgium on his motorcycle. The Abbot asked his Prior, "Do we have insurance on Father Dumont?"

"Oh yes, about a million francs."

"Oh, well, then," the Abbot said, and never did call in Father Dumont to scold him for speeding.

SEPTEMBER 24, 1971

Friday. Beautiful clear and bright autumn morning, cold enough to have a fire in the fireplace. We have decided to stay on until next Wednesday, which will be a great help.

Later—3:00 p.m. The day has somewhat collapsed around me, and I am having a nervous fit. Call this morning from someone who needs to see me and wants to see me tomorrow. I tried to explain it was a bad time, but my hints got nowhere. In charity I cannot refuse. But the call came right in the middle of intense and happy work, and I found myself getting dizzy with rage and frustration. By noon I could not eat. When I went over after lunch and tried to look up on the top shelf of the bookcase for Eckhart, I got dizzy and fell down—a momentary fainting, though I was conscious again in a moment. Then I talked with Piedy to see if it was all right to remain on a few days, and of course it was, but she mentioned that Susan was planning on a house guest for a concert on October 8. I literally went sick, because I have asked the children not to have any more guests or intrusions whatsoever, until the book gets finished, and never will I be busier than that weekend. I also counted on Susan to help me with some of the typing of the manuscript.

Brother Pat and Michael came in while I was talking. I wrote a quick note to Susan asking her please to cancel those and all other plans for visits until after this book is finished, and they took it down and mailed it. And then it occurred to me that neither she nor her guest have the remotest idea of what this is all about, because when it happened before the guest just assured me he would stay out of my way, and not disturb my work. But that doesn't do it. It means that Piedy has a great extra burden, that they are constantly coming in to see if it is all right to do this or that. So, all in all, those two calls and the necessary letters (I wrote Susie another this afternoon to try to explain more fully) have cost me about four hours—probably much more—of work, and I am so torn up now that I have no feeling that the work will be any good this afternoon.

Damn all of this. Each person feels that I mean my restrictions for all other persons, but not for him. Each one laments when others interrupt the work, but does not hesitate, usually on some guise, to interrupt that same work.

The only way I know to do final draft work is to keep your mind and attention obsessively on the work, and to let nothing penetrate into that area of intense concentration. You are honed up like a concert pianist ready to give a recital. You can go like an angel if people will only understand and leave you be. But people do not understand, and it gets nerve-wracking.

On the other hand I constantly get letters from people telling me how important the book is, how much they are praying and hoping for it. A note from Sister Luke, that marvelous lady, this morning ends: "Every good wish for the book. Somehow I believe it will cast a radiant beam of hope across our poor land." And of course it will, if I can do it properly. If I am constantly called on for other things, or interrupted, then it will be a damned patchwork, and nothing to compare with what it ought to be, and what I have the responsibility to make it.

The worst part of it is that those who do the interrupting are people I love and admire and would welcome under any other conditions and circumstances. But I resent the intrusions now so frustratingly and bitterly that my instincts for preservation, for decent work, lead me to vicious response, and I have to fight back the inclination to tell them to get the hell gone and leave me to hell alone. I don't do it, and I would be paralyzed with guilt if I did, but I spiral closer and closer to the temptation to do it, and am completely shot as a result. And so almost every day I wake up full of happiness and enthusiasm for a long day's work, but now far too often I see interruptions that cause those happy dreams to crumble long before the day is done. Crumble in the middle of a sentence, crumble in the midst of a creative act that can never just be picked back up with the same vigor, and as a result, just turns sour and screaming.

Seventeenth Visit

JANUARY 21, 1972 . . .

JANUARY 21, 1972

At the hermitage, *9:00 a.m.* Win Hooper [a Texas friend]and I left Fort Worth yesterday afternoon and arrived in Louisville at 5:30, took a car and drove on to get here at 7:00 p.m. Much rain and fog slowed the driving. We came on up to the hermitage, where Brother Pat and Father Tarcy had everything cleaned up and a good fire going in the fireplace. The rain began to pour on the roof as we walked in the door. A sense of excitement and profound joy to be in these woods again after so long. And then to my utter astonishment, Brother Maurice walked in from the chapel. He is here to attend the retreat and have a conference with Father Eudes. And Brother Martin de Porres came up to celebrate Mass, so it was like old times—marvelous. After a beautiful Mass in the little chapel here, Father Tarcy fixed the supper—some little steaks, mashed potatoes, green peas. Again the rain poured outside in the forest, heightening our sense of celebration.

They cleaned up the dishes and left late—almost 10:00 p.m., since Father Tarcy had to make two trips down in the jeep. I unpacked a little, and then went to bed and slept well until 4:30 this morning, when hunger awakened me. I got up, put on coffee water, stirring up a good fire from the ashes in the fireplace, ate two hard-boiled eggs Father Eudes had left up here, some cheese and crackers and a glass of milk. Then slowly, in the deep silences before dawn, I finished unpacking and got my list of supplies made and cleaned up the place (it didn't need much).

Not much here in the way of supplies, so I put on some small white beans to simmer until they are mushy and will fix a good rich soup for tonight. Also found a half-pound piece of salt pork to cook with them. Then I got into the work, until now I am tired and ready to take a little nap this cold, grey, foggy, and very still morning.

Read two remarkably beautiful articles on the plane in the current issue of *Realities*. The first, an illustrated study of the places where Proust spent his childhood, marvelously photographed and written. The other, a piece, also with lovely photos, of winter in French villages in the Auvergne district, villages that resembled Solesmes: the description of how the villagers hole up for the winter against the cold, and think up marvelous ideas for cooking meals to delight themselves. A beautiful piece that took me back to many winters in France; all this brought back to mind by the odor of this wood fire, a fragrance that fills the cabin the way wood fires filled the rooms in which I spent my winters in France.

JANUARY 22, 1972

Up early this Saturday morning after a splendid sleep. Father Tarcy, Brother Maurice, Win, Brother Marty came up for Mass and supper last night (soup and cheeseburgers).

Piedy called yesterday afternoon, very distressed, to tell me Jean Casadesus and a young couple he was traveling with in Canada were killed in a car wreck after a concert. I wrote Robert and Gaby, and we said Mass for Jean and his family here last night. This knocked me, and I was just dead on my feet when the monks left at 8:30 last evening. Went promptly to bed and did not wake up once until I got up at 4:00 this morning. Feel completely rested, physically. It is still deep night, foggy and misty and cool.

Rev. Father John Eudes, the new Abbot of Genesee, is coming to spend an hour at noon, so I am preparing a little chicken in cream and tarragon which is easy, but takes a while. I have the onions, bay leaves, and butter simmering now.

Later. Have bathed and shaved and got the chicken on and the timer set, and it just begins to be dawn. Am warming up a hard-boiled egg for breakfast, and get ready for the insulin shot, which is always a display of my cowardice. I am going to ask Father Eudes to give me a brief course in how to become a masochist. I still have great hesitation and trouble sticking that needle in myself, although it does not bother me at all when someone else does it. It is the matter of decision just when to plunge, and where. Father Tarcy said he would call and yell into the phone: "Now!"

JANUARY 23, 1972

Sunday. Grey morning, with a fog that obscures the distant hills. In that light, the cardinals are luminous on bare branches in front of the cabin. Cool, in the low forties, and still, this Sunday morning.

The birds come out of the fog for their feeding: the cardinals, the small, trim titmice, a spectacular bluejay, and an even more spectacular redheaded woodpecker.

Feels strange not to have to cook today. The monks insist that I do too much, and they are going to bring up food from the monastery from now on for most of the meals. They also say I spoil them, and that it is too hard to go back to monastic fare after eating up here. And most of all, they feel it is too much of an expense for me. None of this is really true, but anyway, I go along with whatever they decide.

JANUARY 24, 1972

Monday. Strange how in the first moments of waking, particularly in the hermitage, all things defer to the needs of the body. The sleepiness lingers, wiping out those middle tones that give gradation to our lives later in wakefulness. The needs and the feelings are simple, direct, stark as an etching. I come out of bed, intent on taking care of the body's requests, and little more. I tremble with the sense of urgency. It is cold. Slap the thermostat and get some heat in the cabin, put coffee water on to boil, knock on the lights because it is dark as midnight outside in the forest. Light a cigarette. Prepare the insulin fast and stand in the middle of the brilliantly lighted kitchen with an alcohol swab. Drop the pajama pants to the concrete floor, half twist to rub the hip, relax the buttocks muscles, put the needle in, and slowly press the plunger, then pull it out quickly and rub the place with the swab until the little knot of medication under the skin disperses. Glance into the dimly lighted chapel with its vigil lamp and try to find the words of the Morning Offering through the fog of body-signals coming from the need to get strong coffee into the belly.

The words are uttered, intercut by the brief banner of thought that breakfast must not be too long delayed now that the insulin is doing its work. Some toast, maybe. But there is no more butter, no more milk. Hell. Anyway, the coffee water begins to groan in the pot. Put coffee, dried milk, saccharine into the big crockery cup and pour the coffee water, and then some cold water. A long slug of it. Simultaneous feeling of relief to get the hot liquid into the stomach and need to get into the bathroom. Light a cigarette and hurry into the tiny, cold concrete room. Turn on the lights and the whitewashed stone walls shock the eyes—brilliant, cold white like an operating room. The cold seat. The deep silence. The sound of wind like the wash of the surf in the tall pines outside the black hole of the bathroom window. Then washing up the hands and drying them and turning off that too-bright light after running a comb through the hair and promising the teeth a later brush. Return to this chair and this desk with the coffee to let the insides settle back into place. And a moment of no urgency when the mind slowly begins to function and the plans for the day begin to take shape— to work on this for a while, then take a shower and shave, then wash the tee shirt and pajama pants, or let them soak themselves halfway clean.

JANUARY 25, 1972

Tuesday. Good rest, and it is cold as hell this morning. The windows all frosted over, but warm in here with a roaring fire. The porch thermometer reads about twenty-two, a drop of forty-eight degrees from yesterday's seventy. Vague awareness of high winds in the woods last night, though I never really woke up—at least not fully—just enough to huddle deeper into the blankets. A certain exhilaration in all this. Dark night outside, but the air is still and the silence deep. The stars brilliant in what must be a cloudless early morning sky.

Later. The sun now rising with great brilliance in a clear sky. Have taken the insulin shot and had breakfast—an egg, a piece of whole wheat toast, a glass of pineapple juice.

The birds have congregated and there is no food for them, so I must go take care of that, though it is so cold on the porch I dread going out.

Later—midmorning. Brilliant, almost blinding sun on the winter landscape, but the cold continues and it has only risen to the upper twenties. Marvelous morning to work, and the work goes along serenely and well so that the morning passes with unbelievable rapidity.

JANUARY 27, 1972

Thursday. Anniversary of my parents—the fifty-fifth, I believe. We said Mass for them last night, a thanksgiving Mass. I will call them today.

Dark this morning, and sleeting, but the cabin is warm and it is good weather for working.

Later. A steady rain falls straight down and new birds come. The small tree at the edge of the porch is filled with cardinals, brilliant and luminous against the monochrome landscape; I am sure there are wrens, too, and other kinds that I cannot identify. I looked for Tom's book of birds to identify them, but someone has taken it.

The rain accelerates now, a real drumming on the roof of the cabin, a perpendicular veil between the porch and the dark pines. I have had my breakfast now (a little late), a piece of buttered toast and a glass of milk.

Merton would do everything for Truth except lie about it.

JANUARY 28, 1972

Friday. The sights from this window at dawn are magnificent. Stillness, greyness, with every tree branch covered with ice, and with the pines like great graceful masses of unmovable green ice.

Eight birds are now congregated on the porch, waiting for me to throw out some food.

Later. Strange morning. I had got very well into the work when the phone started ringing and things started happening. Tommie O'Callaghan called about coming out tomorrow to work with me. We were discussing that when the phone made a lot of racket and cut off. I tried to call down to the switchboard and got no answer, so I supposed my line was broken from the ice. Then I tried the intercom line and got Brother Pat. He said he would try to call Tommie. Then when I hung up, Tommie called and we resumed the conversation until the same racket occurred, and we got cut off again. I had hardly hung up when Brother Pat called back to say the line to Louisville was occupied (by my call), so there was no need for him to call Tommie. Then Brother Lawrence called to see if I was having any problems with the electricity.

Then I had just got back in here to the desk when I noted a huge pine tree had fallen in front—a gorgeous tree. The roots and dirt stand nearly eight feet tall. I put on shoes and went out to check that, and while I did I heard another pine crashing in the forest nearby. A light snow falling. I made some photos. Returning, I saw the great pine by the sleeping room window leaning at a dangerous angle. If it falls, it will certainly crash through that wall.

Then Piedy called, and I was never so glad to hear from anyone. How much I have missed them! We had a long and very pleasant and good talk. God love her. She knows how to make everything seem right and perfect, and spreads balm to my heart.

Now, my feet frozen, I am back in pajamas. A bluejay has just come to the porch and made a real hog of himself, picking up a piece of stale bread, and then another and another, crowding them into his beak. The cardinals, so striking in these iced trees, have taken off now that I have the camera loaded with color film.

MAY 16, 1972

I have waited until this morning to make notes about yesterday. I was too heartsick to write anything yesterday. Wallace was shot, and that is lamentable. But what was disheartening was to see how this unmasked a lot of people with whom I am acquainted. I was at Westcliff when the news was announced, and the immediate reaction of people who would never admit this to me otherwise was a wail that someone tried to kill the only public figure who could save us from the niggers and the liberal Commies. The great hope for white supremacy had been downed. This law-and-order demagogue who himself so contributed to the calluses on this nation's soul, who did not hesitate to set an example of violence (his statement that if any protester lay down in front of his car, it would be the last car that one ever lay in front of).

Lord, I see and hear about me everywhere the insane rationalizations that we heard and saw surrounding Hitler in the thirties. The Germans were willing to leave the door open to unspeakable abuses against Jews and many non-Jews in order to support a man who promised to get rid of far more superficial abuses. We are willing and eager to leave the door open to unspeakable abuses (including the continuing war in Southeast Asia, the perpetuation of overt racism, the destruction of help to the poor) in order to avoid busing. What else really does it amount to? They can deny it until they are blue, but the great undertide of Wallacism is a manifestation of racism and nothing else.

This nation mourns not an act of violence committed against a citizen, but an act of violence committed against a racist leader on whom they had pinned such hopes. The wail is a wail of racism. And how does it sound for Nixon to assure the Wallaces of his prayers? Are these words as empty as they sound? Did he in some quiet place utter a prayer? Perhaps so, wanting it to be "absolutely clear to God" what the President wanted. These are empty games men play for the consumption of a gullible and gulled public, games that are transparent in their cheapness and have very little to do with prayer—or at least one feels that. To whom do they pray? Thor? Zeus? A Christ with short hair and a submachine gun? The word "prayer" in their mouths sounds as cynical as the word "peace" or the word "justice."

Later. The anomalies continue to pour out. Apparently Wallace is going to be all right, though he may have to continue campaigning in his wheelchair. However, with all the coverage on TV, he will hardly need to campaign. A moment ago, they ran a portion of his recent speech where he was interrupted by hecklers. The police ushered out a long-haired young man and Wallace made political hay of it—saying that these young people want everyone to have freedom of speech except him, and that they come and use all those four-letter words, which indicates a lack of ethical-moral leadership in this country. For this he got an absolutely screaming ovation. How laughable that a man like that should strike out at language as being the sign of lack of ethical-moral leadership. He will, I suppose, clean up the language and keep the minorities in their place.

MAY 29, 1972

Monday. The Duke of Windsor died yesterday morning, and the announcement brought back extraordinary memories. I was in France in 1937 when he and Wallace W. Simpson were married. In fact, I was spending the summer at the Duthoos' Chateau de Belles Ruries, whose properties adjoined those of the Chateau de Cande, where the duke and duchess were married and honeymooned. It did not mean anything to me, except that on morning horseback rides I would find myself at the property line looking up to the Chateau de Cande and wondering what grand things were happening in that household, so rich and with so many celebrities coming there for visits.

Tours was flooded that later summer with English ladies who apparently came to horrify themselves, because we met many who wanted just a glimpse of Cande, "where our dear Edward is living with that awful American woman." We took at least several of them to a place on the property line where they could see the chateau, and watched them break into tears of grief—all of which they were so transparently enjoying that we felt we were helping them in a delicious therapy. Not a single one of those British ladies felt it was anything but a catastrophe. I suppose the ones who did not feel this way simply did not make the pilgrimage.

All of that was terribly minor and incidental to the life I was living in those halcyon days—a life of student discovery, filled with books and music and long walks or horseback rides in the beautiful forests around the chateau, and simple but marvelous foods and wines at noon and in the evening, and good tea every afternoon. Breakfast—a great bowl of *cafe-au-lait* and a plate of tartines with sweet butter—was brought to my room each morning, and I saw nothing of the household (except by accident) until noon when we gathered for dinner. The guests were left free to do what we wished—play music, read, study, walk, ride horses—all the hours before noon and after lunch until tea time; and then we stayed together from supper time until time to retire—talking, listening to new recordings, playing billiards, etc. In those days I was on my Wagner binge, and Jacques Duthoo was determined I should become convinced that Debussy and Ravel were just as great or greater, so he really introduced me not only to Debussy and Ravel, but also to such composers as Roussel, Dukas, Faure, Honneger, etc., and quite especially to the French art songs—and Italian also. It was there, I believe, that I came to love the recordings of Roland Hayes, and played them so much I almost wore them out; also those of Maggie Teyte, Bernac, Bernadette Delpratte, Germaine Cernay, Germaine Lubin. And it was also in those marvelous rooms that I came to know intimately the Schnabel recordings of the Beethoven Concertos and Sonatas, and the Schubert Sonatas; the Ravel and Debussy piano works played by Cortot or Gieseking.

It was also there, from the library, that each night I took books to my room and read as long as I could hold my eyes open—the complete works of Balzac, all of Gide, all of Rabelais

and Anatole France and many, many more, including the René
Bazin biography of Charles de Foucauld, which so fascinated
me, and Proust (also a work I savored deeply), and of course,
Flaubert and Alfonse Daudet—and dozens whose names have
not lived, but who were being published at the time.

JUNE 15, 1972

Gethsemani. I am back at the hermitage and have been here about an hour, getting settled in. It is a dark, overcast, very humid day here in the woods; beautiful. It is now 4:00 p.m., and I am unpacked and ready to begin work. So delighted to be here, but at the moment so uneasy about my nephew, David, who underwent radical surgery this morning. I suppose everything went well or I would have been notified by now.

Drove up with Michael Dunn—a perfect trip—overcast, cool drive. We stopped before getting to Memphis, in or near West Memphis, Arkansas, and photographed some shanties against a spectacular sky of thunderheads. Went into one abandoned shanty and found a small wooden bowl. The evocations of those poor, desolate rooms with cardboard box interiors. Outside, we found an abandoned hospital cot, and deduced that people had lived there with an invalid until he died or got well, and they had gone on elsewhere.

Abbot Flavian leaves Monday for a lengthy trip, so he is coming up to say Mass this evening and have supper with us. Today is Father Tarcisius's anniversary to the priesthood, and tomorrow is Brother Pat's silver jubilee as a monk, and of course my fifty-second birthday. I hope and pray that I start my fifty-third year with a great day's work.

Now, nearly 6:00, and I have had a short nap. The air is cooling. I await the arrival of the Fathers and others for Mass. They are bringing supper with them. I am having some difficulty getting accustomed to the keyboard of this typewriter, more than I can remember having in the past.

The air is still, the sky heavily overcast and threatening. The day lilies and tiger lilies that Tom planted up here are in luxurious blossom, and almost glow in this gray light. A hummingbird sucks at one of them, but only for a moment.

Later—10:30 p.m. Good visit with Father Flavian, and a good supper sent up from the monastery—sausages and pancakes with Tillie Lewis diabetic syrup.

They left around 8:30, and I went to bed immediately and slept for a couple of hours. Have just awakened, and unable to return to sleep, I thought would get up and read a little. Found a glass of milk and some cheese and crackers, so that is filling me up and making me sleepy again. I am glad. I would rather sleep now and get up early and work.

Marvelous fragrance of the cedarwood altar now that the air is damp. It has rained sporadically all evening, a hard rain during Mass.

JUNE 16, 1972

Grey dawn in this forest, with thick white mists in the valley before me. The air is cold and still to the feel, but a riot of the most jubilant bird songs—whippoorwills, bobwhites, mourning doves close by in the trees, and from the distance the great bells calling the monks to office.

Today is Brother Patrick Hart's silver jubilee and my fifty-second birthday. It is as though all nature, all sights and sounds (squirrels now scampering, playing like kittens at the edge of the line of hedgeroses out front) were celebrating with us. Trees are in luxuriant foliage. A titmouse emerges from that foliage and flies down to the edge of this cabin porch for bread crumbs. I must go feed them, not that they need it in this time of natural abundance, but they are accustomed to that when they hear the typewriter going—and it is good for both of us.

I had hardly gotten the bread on the porch before they came—the most magnificent redheaded woodpeckers and cardinals. They were congregated there before I resumed my seat. Now a mockingbird has joined them. I go to replenish the hot coffee and wonder about lighting a fire in the hearth. It is uncomfortably cold, but will warm rapidly. I'll pass up the fire and put on a robe.

213

Father Tarcy will be up soon. He told me that the knitted shoes my mother makes me were left here because great holes were worn in the bottom and I had meant them to be thrown away. Instead, Brother Giovanni, one of the older monks, retrieved them and put new bottoms in them for me, and Father Tarcy is to bring them up around 8:00. Things like this—this kind of concern and thoughtfulness—go straight to my heart. What clothes I left here, in a cardboard box in the one closet, have been washed and ironed and are back in their place. I never see the people who do these things, don't even know who does them really, but I live here in solitude and it seems that hundreds of eyes are on the watch to see that everything is done that needs doing to take care of me. I do not see them. Whenever I find out who did something like this, I send notes down to thank them.

Father Flavian last night remarked that the old Trappist usages, which they did so much to change, were not unlike Zen training and had much the same purpose, and that perhaps they would have done better to change their attitudes about these usages rather than change the usages themselves. A point worth much investigating. Their objection was to the tendency to make the usages an end in themselves rather than the means to the end: which was to condition a man to the most direct contact with God or Reality or Truth, by making him lose himself, become nothing so that the divine could be all.

Certainly this is a striking clarification.

Certainly the hermit life brings much of this out in its unadorned nakedness, whereas the community life can allow it to remain obscured because in a sense it forces a man to play a role. Any community life does, I should think. My experience is that the deepest health comes in this solitude where gradually the roles are abandoned, and with them the euphemisms that oblige a man to hide certain of his acts and his reality (even to give the impression that they do not exist for him, though they do for everyone else). Here, the realities are simply faced and not hidden. Here, there is a constant communion with God whose presence permeates all sights and sounds and feelings— and the euphemisms drop. You wash when you need to wash. You eat when you need to eat. You doctor your rash and wash your clothes and fix your food. And all of that is on one same level because all of it is squarely in that framework of love of

God and in the sense of companionship with God and adoration of God. You are freed of those cultural niceties where some of these things are necessarily private and some of them are public. In solitude, such needs vanish.

Later—night. Beautiful Mass and supper with Father Tarcy, Brothers Pat and Martin de Porres, and Michael. They went in together and gave me a set of seventeen knives—carving knives, bread knife, steak knives, etc. I was overwhelmed. And overwhelmed by the other kindnesses. Brother Robert cooked a special no-sugar cake and also sent up dietetic soft drinks for me. They said he baked two cakes, because the first one did not turn out as he thought it should. Father also brought up the shoes that Brother Giovanni had so beautifully resoled. Tomorrow morning, I am going to send down notes of thanks to them.

Our Mass was simply a Mass of thanksgiving. The light over the countryside and in that whitewashed chapel was ravishing—the light of a pearl . . . silvery, soft. At the very end of Mass a beautiful grey squirrel, full of the most delicate tones of rust and white, climbed up the huge cross that is made of two pieces of tree outside the chapel window. In that light, it was the most joyful sight. Indeed, we were all full of happiness, and the food turned out well. The steaks, cooked over hickory sawdust, were splendid, the green beans served with brown butter (and lemon) sauce, a good salad, and then Brother Robert's delicious and beautiful cake.

JUNE 18, 1972

Sunday: Father's Day. And this afternoon, I must put a call in to wish my dad a happy one. This great consort of birds seems to be wishing me one. A clear, cool morning, a marvelous morning for work. I think of my family with longing, but aside from that I am happier here than anywhere. Happy with these long, long hours of solitude and silence. Brother Patrick brought up a portable phonograph with some splendid recordings: Serkin group doing the Mozart Quartets; Casadesus doing French piano music; Monteverdi; the Beethoven violin and piano Sonatas with Szigeti and Arrau; the piano music of Poulenc, and many others—things I would grab and hear immediately. But here, and only here in the world, I do not play them: I cannot let go of this silence which is so full of natural sounds, the incessant and rich bird songs, the wash of a breeze at the tops of the pine trees.

Yesterday evening Brother Pat brought up the new *Christian Century*, which says on the cover that the issue is devoted to monasticism. Interesting. An astonishingly naive and enthusiastic article by W. Paul Jones, written as notes during his visit to the Trappists at Snowmass [St. Benedict's Abbey, Snowmass, Colorado]. Dr. Jones is associate professor of philosophical theology at St. Paul's School of Theology (Methodist) in Kansas City, Missouri. It is full of the newness and wonder that can so delight a man in Trappist silences. He quotes from Merton, and in fact, he seems to have absorbed Merton with such a flash of recognition and longing that his own best lines, really, are those he apparently memorized and then forgot, from Merton. This is easy to do. He makes a parallel between monasticism and the counterculture.

The best thing in the issue is a marvelous drawing by Joe Noonan. It shows an enormous black dog, quite innocent-looking, towering over a lady who lies on her back. The dog's forepaws are on her chest and he holds her down. A man kneels bending over her face and says: "Frankly, Wilma, I don't think the Hound of Heaven would be this overt." I must photograph that before I send the magazine back down to the Abbey.

How in the hell does Joe think of these things? They delight me in the same way Mozart delights me.

Now the squirrels come up to the spot just off the porch where I usually throw toasted bread. They find none, and I sit here feeling like a neglectful bastard—so I had better remedy the situation before they give up and go elsewhere.

Now, later, I have made the photocopies of Joe's drawings, including the one on my letter from him yesterday, showing two monks, one of whom says, "I thought it was one of the monks who carved all the trees with 'John loves Elizabeth.'"

Also, I put out the bread for the squirrels, who, this time at least, have not lost faith, because both of them are there in the grass eating. Put out bread for the birds, too, so they would not steal that destined for the squirrels. Also fixed some breakfast: a hard-boiled egg with buttered toast and a big mug of hot coffee.

At 4:00 this afternoon, they are to take me down to the Abbey for a private showing of the Dutch TV film made of Tom's last hours in life—his talk and the subsequent events at Bangkok. They say it is splendid.

Now, a sudden hush in the forest. The birds, except for an occasional twitter, have fallen silent. A breeze has come. It rapidly becomes overcast, and the breeze through this cabin, full of the fragrance of pines, is a balm to the senses. I interrupt the work with activity. I stop to make up the bed and to make more coffee. Later I will shave. Later still, bathe; later and last, get myself into some clothes (I am still in pajamas). I am reluctant to leave this place in the forest even to go down to view the film for an hour.

Later—at midmorning now. The forest is as dark as late dusk because of the heavy overcast, and the breeze that blows in has the smell of rain on fields somewhere beyond.

Because the birds are silent, waiting, and nothing moves, I do put on some music, music for the moment . . . Lili Kraus's recording of the Schubert Impromptus. From a pine tree in front of me, a mockingbird begins to sing, and from the woods behind the cabin, a crow shouts its hot midsummer sound here on this cool spring morning.

Now I must cut this journal page off and get back to work. The temptation, at such a time, is just to go on writing because these are hours of such rare perfection, but work is promised—that is the hell of it—work promised. It must be done, and now, without any further delay.

Later—5:30 p.m. Went to see the Dutch TV film, and am very glad I did. It was beautifully done. Brother Paul is going to bring the film up here one night so I can shoot some stills from it. My own feelings surprised me. I saw all of these shots with profound joy and pathos, as though I were watching my own son. He looked beautiful, in good health and in good spirits. Someone had remarked that he looked awfully tired. I did not find it so at all. The statement by a Sister (which one, I must find out) at the very end, after his death, must be copied. I would like to end the book with that.

JUNE 20, 1972

Tuesday. Last night while I slept, a drama took place on the porch. When I went out this morning, I saw a blood spot, with some residue of intestines near the door, and leading from it, small, clear, blood-dyed animal tracks. Perhaps one of the squirrels was caught there by a fox and consumed except for these remains—though there is no fur or hide.

Put in a good hard day's work yesterday, typing from the moment I got up until 6:00, when the Fathers and Brother Pat and Michael, and Tom Barnes and Jamie Knorr (friends who just arrived from Lexington) came up for Mass and supper. They left by 8:30, and I was in bed shortly after. I pulled my same stunt—slept an hour and then lay awake for what seemed to me like many hours. I was exhausted, desperate for sleep, but no sleep would come. When it did, I slept on until 7:00, which means I am getting a later start this morning. But I feel good, and wasted no time getting right back into the work. I have stopped now to take the insulin and to make these notes about the footprints on the porch.

Apparently it was not a squirrel, because just now the two are playing in the grass in front, gamboling like kittens. I am glad it was not one of them. Perhaps it was a chipmunk? In any event, I am going to have to clean up the mess because flies and ants are being attracted to it.

The morning is so incredibly fresh and beautiful—the silence, except for bird calls, so profound; I would love to sit here all day and do nothing but watch and listen. In such an atmosphere, even the simplest and lowliest (if there are such values; I don't believe in them) of man's activities become a part of the miracle: to mop the porch; to shoot insulin into my hip; to sit here with a piece of toast, a hard-boiled egg, and a glass of milk for breakfast, and then wash the dishes afterward; to put a shirt and an undershirt in a bucket of soapy water to soak—all of these doldrum things become a part of the felicity of this healing forest.

Later. Sitting here, after doing my wash, I reflected on the love I have for this place, and the repugnance I have, not for the world, but for the awful noise and heat and pollution of the senses, and the pollution of values, and the unquenchable thirst of society for possessions—human possessions, material possessions, simply the desire to possess—and how this has afflicted even our capacity for lovemaking.

I feel about this what Merton felt when he said that his only regret about dying was the years of this solitude he would not have. I feel myself praying that I live long enough to get my children cared for in the lives they choose, and that perhaps at the end of our lives, Piedy and I can return to this kind of simplicity of minimal needs, time to live without pressure, the solitude that first heals and then magnificently nourishes.

Later—5:45 p.m. As I was working, the phone rang. It was Piedy, with the desolating news that our sons' close friend, and really ours too, David Edgar, was in the hospital very near death. He had been ill, had gone into the hospital again on Sunday, but we didn't know. Father George called to tell Piedy that she should call me and ask for the prayers of the community. David is apparently dying either of a brain tumor or an aneurism, and Piedy said Father George does not think there is much chance that he will live very long. The doctors seem not to know what to do. Father said he attempted to give David communion in his room this morning, but he could not manage his mouth enough to take the host. He apparently is semiconscious. I think of his parents and weep for what they must be going through. Piedy broke down on the phone telling me about it. He is sixteen.

I called down and asked Brother Norbert to put a notice on the bulletin board, begging the prayers of the monks for David and his parents. And of course we will offer Mass for them up here in a few moments.

The boys were not home yet, so they did not know when Piedy called. It will hit them both very hard indeed; Johnny was the "special favorite" of Mrs. Edgar. I will pray for my sons, too, that they will be filled with the grace to bear this without that deep, forlorn pain which they do not need at this time in their lives. I mean just to live as young people these days is painful enough. Of course, their grief will be great, and that is as it should be, but I do hope it will not hurt them too much.

And of course, with Piedy and me, there is that unspoken

empathy—our sons are the same age. How could we bear what the parents of David are being called on to bear? The very idea fills us with a grief that is added to our grief over David's suffering and over his parents'. David was a large, loud, good, affectionate youngster who often spent the night at our house. I always had to be firm with him to make him go to bed, because he liked to sit up all night and play records and keep my sons awake. But he always took it as it was meant, and he was a lad who knew how to capture our affection and for whom we had a deep affection. We must pray that God's will be done, and that if it is God's will that this good youngster be restored to life, be saved from the death that stalks him now.

JUNE 21, 1972

Wednesday. Slept very little last night, and fitfully, waking again and again in the chill darkness to pray for David Edgar and his family. How many times—perhaps a dozen, or so it seemed. I did not get up all night, but I did put more covers on me, pulling up first the cover sheet, then a blanket, then another. I thought I would be useless today from no sleep, but finally at 5:05 I did awaken, got up and went to the bathroom, turned on the heat under the coffee water, trembling from the cold. I decided I should go back to bed and sleep it out, since there was still no sign of dawn. But perhaps stay awake. No, I turned off the coffee water and went to the bed. Strange, I felt rested, just sleepy and chilled through. I put on my robe, returned to the kitchen, turned the coffee water on again (at night I leave the pot with very little water so it won't take so long to boil in the mornings). I then definitely awakened and decided to go into the chapel and pray for David before the reserved Sacrament. That flickering vigil lamp, the damp predawn fragrance of the cedarwood altar. I prayed with words first and then with no words, to the incredibly rich accompaniment of whippoorwills and bobwhites. I heard the water boil and came out. The sky had lightened. I fixed the coffee and brought it to this desk without turning on the light. Outside, in the dim light, the baby cottontail played in the grass by the hedgerose and one of the squirrels flicked its tail nearby. I brought stale bread from the kitchen for the squirrel and the birds, putting large chunks in the grass for the squirrel and smaller crumbs on the porch for the birds. I fixed my insulin shot, which I took without hitting a vein or a nerve. Now, at dawn, I am ready to work, have my files out in proper order here on the desk, my paper and carbons. I have boiled a full pot of water and have a second mug here on the table.

Meditating much on Merton's theology of prayer. What is really different about it? The unlearning and unknowing, the being before doing, the transformation of conscience . . . are not all these in the great line of mystical theology stemming from St. John the Baptist's desire to diminish within himself so that God could increase within him? And the Tao and Zen masters cast a new light on the old principle by suggesting that it was not something you do, but something you undo (or allow to be done to you); that it is already there (you have what you seek), and you have to dispose yourself, let the layers fall away, and it will reveal itself, it will be, function . . . this when you get rid of self, of desires that are learned, of ambition to possess, or any organized plan for attaining God, since such plans and ambitions are self-defeating in their very nature. A man can attain a kind of virtue that is usually full of holes and believe that he has arrived, so that even deliberate virtue can be a delusion and ultimately self-defeating, making a man appear holy. When virtue is the natural overflow of love, then it is authentic and spontaneous. Otherwise, "this kind of thing eventually ends with people eating each other raw" (Chuang Tzu, *Flight from Benevolence*, 147).

Though fame was a burden, Merton did not despise it that much, and made statements on any and all subjects. He became famous, and certainly all of this inspired other men. But at the end, he refused to make public statements without great care, and would have been happier to make none at all, and promised himself not to do so.

Midmorning. Perfect morning. I am chilled. The sky is overcast, and the breeze circulates through the cabin. A good moment to go lie under the covers for half an hour.

Later. Slept for an hour, rather than the thirty minutes I planned. Deep and heavy sleep. Woke up to find a great puddle

221

of water on the kitchen floor, where my drinking water can is apparently leaking. Have put the mop in there to absorb it as much as possible. Have put one of the big metal cups under it to catch the drip until someone comes up to find out what is wrong with it. It remains almost cold and overcast and very beautiful. I will need a fire in the morning if it gets as cold as they anticipate—in the upper forties or low fifties.

Must get back to work. Damned devilish to feel this pressure, right on top of reading Chuang Tzu. Well, he does not say you should not do your duty; he just says you should not try to win, which is also right there in the Precautions of St. John of the Cross. Just as he also says that the most authentic way to happiness is to abandon all seeking of it, all pursuit of it. A stronger breeze now, and all the birds have fallen silent. Utter lack of sound except for the wind in pines. Now the distant lowing of the monastery cattle, so faint it can hardly be heard.

Hunger makes itself felt in my belly. Now, the penetrating rich call of the bobwhite resounds from the forest, as though amplified with an almost cathedral-like resonance. And now here within me, my belly audibly rumbles its hunger. Well, it will only have to wait an hour before they bring lunch.

Night, 8:20. And I make these notes fast, because it is time for me to go to bed. Tonight Father Tarcy came up and said Mass, and, without my requesting it, he said the Mass for David Edgar and his parents, as we did last night. I was deeply moved. The whole community has taken this situation to heart. Father said there was another notice on the bulletin board, requesting prayers for David and telling a little more about him. Piedy said his parents, who are broken over this, were just overwhelmed when she told them the monks were storming heaven for David. He was able to live through the night. They will do a craniotomy tomorrow. He apparently understands things, though he cannot respond to anything, but his mother feels that he is almost terrified to death; and, of course, if he is conscious, that is probably true, and it breaks your heart. Johnny and Greg were at the hospital all afternoon, but I do not know if they spent much time actually with him, or if they elicited any response. They were terribly hit by this.

222

JUNE 22, 1972

Thursday. Cool, almost cold, but not really cold enough for a fire—at least I am not lighting one.

Monastic humor here. Last night Father Chrysogonus, one of the best scholars here, was to give a conference to the community on St. Alice, who, I believe, is one of the obscure Cistercian saints, a person who suffered leprosy heroically.

Under the announcement on the bulletin board, some joker put this notice:

Everything You've Always Wanted to Know
About Saint Alice But Were Afraid to Ask

The notice was quickly taken down.

Piedy called. David has a rapidly growing brain tumor. It doubles in size every forty-eight hours. They will attempt to remove it in the morning. A plane is standing by to fly him to the brain center in Houston if that becomes necessary. Piedy will be there all during the surgery. They anticipate it will take from five to seven hours. My heart is full of fear for him. Piedy said he knew who she was when she went in last night. It is most difficult to work well with this constant concern and with my feelings that I should be with Piedy, who takes on everyone's burdens and could certainly stand the help that would come from my just being there. How can I put all of that out of my mind as I must in order to do the sort of concentrated work I have to do here?

I cannot; it is that simple.

JUNE 23, 1972

Friday. A record cold for this time of the year—down to forty-three, but it is not really all that cold. I got up at dawn and lighted the fire in the fireplace. So it is good and warm here—and the skies are bright and cloudless.

This morning is David's surgery. I decided the best thing I could do was get up and work, and offer all that to God as my form of prayer, and leave it all in God's hands. A thing like this shows the shallowness of faith. I told Father Tarcy last night that I had been unable to stop "helping" with my nervousness and my incessant prayers, which had really meant that the work I did yesterday was not good. Today, at this very hour when they are beginning the surgery in the operating room at St. Joseph's, this scene from my window has never been more ravishing and heart-filling.

I had a lot of dried-out bread, so I put small pieces on the porch for the birds and larger pieces in the grass for the squirrels. For some reason, the squirrels do not venture onto the porch (though they come right up to it), except in winter when wood is stacked out there.

I decided to put on a little music. Brother Pat had brought up the Mozart Concerto for three pianos played by Jean, Gaby, and Robert Casadesus, an enchanting work. Bless my soul, in a few moments, I looked up to see the squirrel right here on the porch eating the bread along with four birds. When I moved he did not seem a bit afraid. So I got my camera and photographed him with a companion cardinal or woodpecker, side by side. Got several excellent shots before the music went off, the bread ran out, and he ambled off the end of the porch. Now, I have put the music back on and here he comes back. It must be the music that reassures him. He is back on the porch now, cleaning up the smaller crumbs.

Now I have put new bread out, and put the music on again, and taken the screen from the window so I can get a better shot, this time in color, if the guests return.

JUNE 24, 1972

Saturday. **Feast of St. John the Baptist.** My feast day, and my last day here for this trip. Never was a day more glorious—absolutely still, sunlit, cool. The air as clear and fresh as can be imagined. Every leaf is seen cleanly. Birds, which sound more like canaries than anything else, fill the air with their roulades and trills.

Chuang Tzu says, "When the shoe fits, the foot is forgotten; when the belt fits, the belly is forgotten." It is like that here this early morning with everything—everything fits, and self is forgotten. Everything in sight has been taken care of before and at dawn. Food was put out for the birds and the squirrels, who have eaten and gone off into the woods. They had plenty. They even left a little. This old body has been taken care of—insulined, breakfasted, washed, and freed from all pressing needs so it can be forgotten for a while.

It is not a time for music. I played the music for the animals early this morning; the Mozart Concerto for three pianos and the Mozart Quartet in G Minor (piano and strings). Now it is the time for this silence . . . this silence that is not heavy and burdensome, but light and transparent as the view.

I am split two ways: the excitement at deep levels, unseen, almost unfelt but there . . . the excitement that runs ahead as I think of going home to my wife and children. The need for that; and at the same time the wish that this morning could last forever, that this stay here in the hermitage did not have to end. Regret to leave this cabin with its whitewashed chapel where I have lived for ten days with the reserved Sacrament, where, whenever I awakened at night, my eye was immediately drawn to the flickering light of the doorway into the chapel.

Not a soul has wished me a happy feast day. Some Catholics I've got for friends. I will send them all accusing postcards, self-righteous ones. "You didn't really pay any attention to the church calendar, did you? You don't follow the office, do you? You're a Christmas and Easter type, aren't you?"

David, thank God, survived that terrible surgery yesterday. The doctors will not be sure for about twelve days whether he has any chance to live, but at least he got through the surgery.

A beautiful wood thrush is on the porch now, looking for crumbs that are no longer there. I put some out for him, but he or she does not come back.

SEPTEMBER 19, 1972

This afternoon while we were having company, sitting in the living room talking with Margaret and Melanie Hooper (both of them my goddaughters), I got a call containing only the news that Robert Casadesus had died. I have seldom been so immediately and deeply afflicted. Odd, too, that he had been in my thoughts earlier this day when I was spotting the portraits of Lili Kraus and decided the time had come to write Robert and ask him about setting up a time when we could be together and I could do a complete photographic archive on him. I stood there with the phone in my hand full of the most terrible anguish over the loss, and even more so over the desolation Gaby must be feeling to have lost a son and a husband within less than a year.

I sat there, and all that was vivid. The countless concerts, getting ready in the hotel rooms, staying backstage while he played so that after each segment of his program, when he would come offstage, I could grab his hands and tell him how great it was. And then afterward, when he had signed all the autographs and was sweated through, and he would remove his shirt and undershirt and I would towel his back, rubbing as hard as I could (but never hard enough), and then he would put on dry clothes and we would go looking for food.

Well, no sense going on with that flood of recollections. I thought of his death, and there was in it a terrible sense of my own weakness and vulnerability; and I thought of the pictures just printed of a terribly weak Jacques Maritain, and the letter today that he had survived the summer and was returning to the Little Brothers at Toulouse, who had really not expected to have him back; and of the deaths of that whole group who were so profoundly involved in my life: Merton, Reverdy, Casadesus, Jacques, Dominique Pire; and how only Jacques and I remain, and Jacques just barely in life; and I felt the greatest confrontation with the death of my existence as though the grave were stalking me in the deaths of these friends. No real somberness in this, for except for that cackling counterpoint of conversation at a time of profound grief, there was peace in me—and now that it is over, and I have had time to be alone and have written Gaby Casadesus, there is only the deep peace of a deep void.

I wonder if he died at home. I am haunted by his remark to me, made again and again, and indeed every time I visited 54 rue Vaneau in Paris, that this was the apartment in which he was married, in which he had lived ever since, and in which he hoped to die. He was seventy-three last April. We had thirty-three years of friendship. I stay back here as the night grows late, listening to Gregorian chants for a moment before going to rejoin my family. Blessed Susan who knows the depth of this loss to me has said nothing at all, but she has baked a marvelous loaf of carrot and coconut and walnut bread, one of the great breads, and has served it hot with butter and a glass of milk. She knows the secrets—she knows that in a time of death you bring consolation not with words, but with something so redolent of life that it gives the message. Nothing is more full of health (in spirit as well as to the senses) than this bread made from stone-ground whole wheat, which smells of fields on a summer's day. Bless them. They are all wise.

Now Piedy and Mandy come with the pet gerbil which stands up in Piedy's hands like a tiny squirrel and washes its face with its paws. They make the wound heal.

Later—midnight. Impossible to sleep. I came back to the studio to see that everything was turned off. The FM was playing to the empty room—marvelous works of Thomas Tallis, and now a glorious harpsichord suite by Couperin. How everything ties in. I will stay up a while and make these notes. Earlier, to my surprise, Susan and Johnny, knowing how afflicted my mother was by the news of Robert's death, simply took off in the car and brought her over here, ostensibly so she could practice the Schubert with Susan (one of the works for four hands). Well, they played together for a while, and then we talked for quite a long while in the family about Casadesus. Mother recalled the day one winter when he was in the area on a concert tour. It was when I had been wounded in the Pacific, and she had had no news from me in a while and was very worried. Casadesus sat down and played the Beethoven opus 111 Sonata for her, and then told her it was for me, to give her hope, to allay her fears—or, more exactly, to share them with her and give the strength that such an immense act of charity could give. I don't believe that anything anyone has ever done has meant quite so much to her. And again, some years later when I was so ill, and he sent me a note to meet him in Dallas and stay with him for the time he was there, telling me that the beautiful music I heard would heal me.

Well, the house was peaceful, full of love and consideration; and finally I put on the finale of the Beethoven First Piano Concerto, with Robert and the Amsterdam Concertgebouw Orchestra, and we listened to that rollicking strength, and then played the finale of the Mozart Concerto no. 23 (Casadesus and Szell). One by one the children and then Piedy drifted away to bed. I felt that if I lay down I would lie there awake for hours and relive every moment of my friendship with the Casadesus family. I said I would take some hot milk, work a little longer, and perhaps get drowsy enough to sleep when I did go to bed.

My mother fixed the milk and then went on to bed. I am here making these notes, surrounded by manuscript, manuscript everywhere in the room, on all the tables, in boxes on the floor, on both sides of this typewriter—manuscript and photographs stacked everywhere, as the writing and the darkroom each day give up their pages and photographs, the one relaxing me from the strain of the other. It seemed for a moment that I was left all alone with the manuscript, but that sense of forlornness has passed now. What I have really meant by all this is that I was very young when I attached myself to the heroes of my youth—these great people of genius and dedication who knew how to sacrifice everything for their ideals, and so those were friendships etched forever in my first affections, and now I have outlived them all except Jacques. But the peace is there first because I cannot feel anything but gratitude that we had those lifetimes together, and second because those areas of the affections have not been left bare by the deaths, but rather have been filled not only by the friendships in this family but by others who are so deeply united to me: the Sussmans, Brother Patrick and Father Tarcisius, the Noonans, Brother Kurt, Father Stan, the Geismars, Brad Daniel, and a few others; people with whom I am as free as ever I was with Casadesus, which means totally free, which means incomparably blessed, because I really think there are people in this world who are never free with anyone.

SEPTEMBER 20, 1972

Up at 7:00. A little more news this morning. Casadesus played in Prades, his last concert. He was operated on in Paris two weeks ago, and died as a result of complications from the surgery yesterday.

Later. I guess I have to give it time to work out of my system. Now there is an almost hallucinatory obsession with it. Just had breakfast, an egg on a piece of whole wheat toast—a meal that he particularly liked. And suddenly it lost all taste when I was assaulted with the thought that he would not know this taste again, but that I go on knowing it. The same with everything. The sensation of brushing my teeth, the odor of soap when I washed my hands. Every sound, taste, sensation is brought into sharpest clarity by the death of someone very dear. Perhaps that clarity is what we ought to have all the time. I remember a striking phrase from Raissa Maritain: *"Notre deuil est si grand que le soleil m'étonne."* ("Our grief is so profound that the sunlight astonishes me.")

So, I scratch an itch on my arm. I feel the stubble of my unshaved face. I listen to music. And it astonishes me that all of these things exist, and that I can know them.

Two letters from Paris today, one from Odile and Claude Sebenne announcing the overwhelming good news that they have finally had a child, a daughter, after all these years of marriage. They have so wanted a child, and had about given up hope that they could have one. Now this. I thought of it in connection with Casadesus's death. The dolorous death of a friend one day, the news of the joyful birth of a child in that same city the next day. I am so happy for them.

Coming through the den a moment ago—a cool, overcast,

rainy afternoon. Mandy was sitting in a chair, her feet propped up on her small rocker, a blanket pulled close about her, watching "Mister Rogers" on the TV. A soprano was singing "Un Bel Di" from *Madame Butterfly*. Mandy, after a long day at school, looked so comfortable, so contented. I bent down over her and said, "You're really living, aren't you?" And she replied, "I sure am!" without ever taking her attention from the program.

Later, 8:00 p.m. Fr. George bought an AP release about Casadesus. The last work he played (at Prades) was Mozart's final Concerto (No. 27 in B flat), which was also the last work Jean played before he died. In looking at the headline on this clipping, PIANIST CASADESUS DIES—AFTER 3,000 CONCERTS, I realize that it is one I have long dreaded reading.

I feel a profound sense of void when I think that my research in the hermitage at Gethsemani is now finished. Certainly that experience over the past few years has been one of the high points of my life. I am sad it is over, but forever grateful to have had it.